D0850706

Multinationals from Small Countries

Multinationals from Small Countries

Edited by
Tamir Agmon
and
Charles P. Kindleberger

The MIT Press
Cambridge, Massachusetts, and London, England

Printed and bound in the United States of America.

Second printing, 1978

Library of Congress Cataloging in Publication Data

Main entry under title:

Multinationals from small countries.

    Consists chiefly of papers presented at a conference held at M.I.T. on January 8 and 9, 1976.
    Includes bibliographical references and index.
    1. International business enterprises—Congresses.
I. Agmon, Tamir. II. Kindleberger, Charles Poor, 1910–
HD2755.5.M845 338.8′8 77–1369
ISBN 0-262-01050-X

Contents

Contributors

Michael Adler, Columbia University

Tamir Agmon, Tel-Aviv University

Gilles Y. Bertin, Centre Nationale de Recherche Scientifique, Rennes, France

Sune Carlson, University of Uppsala, Sweden

Carlos F. Diaz-Alejandro, Yale University

Jose D. Epstein, Inter-American Development Bank

Helen Hughes, Australian National University

Charles P. Kindleberger, Massachusetts Institute of Technology

Stephen J. Kobrin, Massachusetts Institute of Technology

Donald R. Lessard, Massachusetts Institute of Technology

David MacClain, Data Resources, Incorporated

C. J. Maule, Carleton University, Ottawa

Jürg Niehans, Johns Hopkins University

Louis T. Wells, Jr., Harvard University

Introduction

Tamir Agmon
and
C. P. Kindleberger

Politics and economics are inextricably bound up, or so it seems, in the multinational corporation. There are some, indeed, who identify the multinational corporation with American imperialism.[1] Others suggest that the multinational corporation will serve in the future as the main vehicle for international trade and that every participant in international trade will either set up a multinational corporation or will join one. In an effort to abstract from considerations of international politics, we thought it might be useful to analyze the economics of multinational corporations with home bases in what may be called small countries. The idea originally came from Tamir Agmon, who was asked to give advice to multinational corporations with parent headquarters in the miniscule state of Israel. In conversation, we decided to tackle the economics of the operations of firms headquartered in small countries more generally. With the support of the Center for International Studies and the Sloan School of Management, both at M.I.T., we held a conference on January 8 and 9, 1976, at M.I.T. The result is this book.

The conference was organized with seven papers and originally sixteen discussants, at least two discussants per paper, and three or even four for some. Unfortunately, we were unable to induce any of the leading political scientists working on the issue to contribute so that we lack a paper directly bearing on the political issue, although Stephen Kobrin's comment on the Wells paper explores political dimensions. Moreover, as in the 1971 M.I.T. symposium on *The International Corporation,*[2] we lack a paper on Canada, a "small country" only in strictly limited senses, and accordingly we asked for a comment by C. J. Maule, apropos of the Swedish experience, to make good a portion of the deficiency. In any event, only a limited number of the commentators submitted written texts, so that the bulk of the book consists of the seven original papers.

What is a small country? The organizers of the conference

gave no clear instructions on this point to the participants, who were frequently bemused by the issue. It quickly became clear, however, that we meant both rich, highly industrialized, not-populous countries such as Switzerland, Sweden, the Netherlands, Belgium, Canada, and Australia—some of which are massive in the extent of their territory—and poor, undeveloped, less-developed, or developing countries—depending on how you look at them—some of which like India, Brazil, Mexico, and Argentina also bulk large in square miles. There was no under- or overtone of the rather trendy notion that small is beautiful, or cozy, or accommodating. What was meant particularly was that small was politically lacking in power, except insofar as it could gain adherents or shine by example-setting. The idea was to abstract from the identification of large firms with large governments, who are interested in pushing other countries around—or are perceived that way—so as to isolate the economic dimensions. It was impossible, as should have been clear in advance to sophisticates. We learned during the course of the discussion that when Central Americans refer to the "colossus of the North" they mean Mexico, that Uruguay and Paraguay are fearful of both Argentina and Brazil, and Finland of the imperialist designs of Sweden. Big and small are relative terms.

The conference itself was organized to accommodate the transport schedules of the participants. The present volume follows a more logical order, starting with the papers by Niehans on Swiss companies and Carlson on Swedish, which deal with the long-established firms of small, highly developed and rich European countries all over the world, including the other rich and large industrialized countries in Europe and North America.

Professor Niehans opened his oral presentation with the remark that his conversion from theorist to economic historian could be dated from January 8, 1976. A striking methodological point was that he found neoclassical equilibrium theory and econometrics of little help in attacking the problem. Starting out with five case studies, he then searched for the common factors and found them in (1) vertical specialization between countries, which leads to (2) vertical integration between countries. Specialization by countries in ordinary international trade theory takes place in final product. With complex processes going through several stages, it is possible to specialize by activities and to conduct trade in intermediate goods and even services, like financial management. A question then arises: When are these stages conducted by separate firms and when within a firm that crosses national boundaries? The Niehans answer lies in three areas: integration within the firm will occur because of fear of bilateral monopoly with the risk and uncertainty that it offers; economies of scale, when, for example, management can be furnished in an industry to more than one productive unit; and protection, which makes it difficult to sell intermediate products in normal trade. Adopting a counterfactual approach at the end, he concluded that Switzerland would have many fewer multinational corporations (MNCs) if protection was much reduced, but would be much poorer, given present protection, if MNCs were forbidden. The technique used by Niehans—developing his theory on the basis of five case histories—does not enable him to determine how much small-country direct investment is really large-country investment in disguise. This question arises in later papers and comments, specifically in Professor Maule's references to Canada as a conduit for large-country investment in third countries and in Bertin's identification of a considerable but declining volume of small-country investment in France as large-country in ultimate origin.

Professor Sune Carlson of Uppsala University approached the small-country multinational corporation more from the viewpoint of business than of the economy as a whole but made a telling argument favoring vertical integration between nations. Increasingly, he suggested, firms sell goods that need instruction in their use. Software must be provided with the hardware, to instruct the buyer. SKF, or Svenska Kugellager Fabrik, sells fewer bearings than antifriction services, complete with advice as to whether a particular friction problem is best met with ball, roller, or taper bearing. Swedish foreign subsidiaries have typically started as service units and have gradually been upgraded—if we have the direction right—into production subsidiaries. The longer a firm has been in business, the higher the proportion of foreign production to export sales after normalization for differences in the industry concerned. The essence is service. Professor Carlson suggests that virtually every long-distance airplane in the world has at least one Swedish sales-engineer aboard.

Dr. Gilles Y. Bertin was asked to look at the question from the other end of the telescope; he considered whether France, which has been highly sensitive to American firms operating in France, was equally sensitive to subsidiaries established by multinational corporations domiciled in small countries and in the European Economic Community. His conclusion was that it was difficult to tell, so many changes having occurred in French policy toward foreign firms established within her midst, but that on the whole, and despite some unflattering remarks by the late President de Gaulle and J. J. Servan-Schreiber about American companies, French decisions seemed to be based on considerations other than the nationality of the home country.

Helen Hughes writing on Australian policy provided the appropriate bridge between the developed and the developing "small country." Her assigned task was to contemplate the intermediary role of the small country, which serves as both host and home country for multinational corporations, especially in the field of technology. The theme arises again in the paper by Louis Wells. Dr. Hughes stated that Australia receives advanced technology from multinational corporations based in the rich countries and passes on, through very different and largely local firms, an indigenous technology that is more suitable for the surrounding developing countries than the technology that emerges from North America or Europe. She commented on Australia as host to foreign investors and home of Australian investors abroad, emphasizing that the multinational corporation is not a unique phenomenon of United States origin.

The paper by Louis Wells is more about direct investment than multinational firms, especially in the Far East. His material relates to foreign subsidiaries of relatively small firms in India, Singapore, and the Philippines, which are likely to be highly competitive, ethnically owned, and technologically fairly primitive. The technology is often an adaptation of a more advanced

Western technique that has been changed to meet the requirements of the tiny scale of developing-country markets and that
finds an opening in a foreign country's market. In some senses
such firms are better described as new enterprises established
abroad by members of families—frequently expatriate Chinese—than as subsidiaries, since the flow of dividends and interests to the home country may never materialize. The profits
are consumed locally. In French economic history there is the
phenomenon of setting up a separate textile mill of 40,000
spindles (an uneconomic size in most economies by 1900) for
an uncle, a brother-in-law, or a relative of some sort just to get
him out of the way of the parent company. Much of the investment examined by Professor Wells is more of this nature than
multinational enterprise, as it is known in the United States.

The last geographical investigation, by Carlos Diaz-Alejandro,
deals with Latin America and with the attempt of many groups
in those countries to establish multinational corporations in order to benefit from scale economies in working toward economic development, to counter the MNCs of the United States,
and to tackle projects that are too large for a single country or
that lie athwart national boundaries. He made a number of
points about these enterprises, many of which are between
governmental bodies in contrast to the usual MNC in the developed world. Many MNCs are the products of immigrant entrepreneurs on the periphery of the dominant Spanish-American
culture. Like customs unions, they are sought by the larger
countries in the area and feared by the smaller.

The final paper by Donald Lessard and Tamir Agmon deals
with the capital-market aspects of the problem and asks whether the MNCs of small countries are at a disadvantage in dealing
in world capital markets, which are largely located in and dominated by large countries. Moreover, the existence of MNCs with
home bases in small countries raises the question posed by
Robert Aliber's theory of direct investment and set forth in the
1970 M.I.T. symposium: Does the advantage of MNCs lie largely
in the preference shown by investors for securities denominated in leading currencies? A further issue is posed by the extent
to which foreign investment by small countries is a means of

escaping the jurisdiction of local authorities or, in other words, is a vehicle for capital flight.

These summaries fail to convey the breadth of ideas that were set out in the papers or arose in the discussion or that surfaced in several papers. For one thing, the MNCs from small countries were thought to be readier to enter into joint ventures than those of developed, large countries such as the United States, but that theory may apply primarily to the firms from developing countries and not so much to Sweden and Switzerland. Neighborhood effects were considered important. The MNC from small countries is less global and more regional in its outreach. Since it excites less political sensitivity, it may be less vulnerable to expropriation, although this is not certain.

One significant economic point turned on economies of scale. In his thesis David MacClain found a distinct tendency for small countries to invest in the United States proportionately more than larger countries.[3] MacClain attributed that tendency to the need to achieve economies of scale in production and distribution, something difficult to do within small countries. Some years earlier, Jacques Drèze had suggested that small countries needed to concentrate on exports of standardized products to gain economies of scale in production, and he cited Belgian experience because their domestic markets were so small.[4] He noted, however, that where a country like Switzerland or Sweden sets the standard, it can export or produce abroad products initially developed at home.[5] Where protection abroad, fear of bilateral monopoly, or software effects combined with market orientation obtain, small countries may be drawn into multinational corporations. In the discussion Y. Aharoni observed that small countries like Israel produce an exportable surplus of educated, middle-class members of the work force who cannot be absorbed at home. One means of allowing them to keep their national identity and to work abroad is to use them in multinational corporations based in the small country. But a Belgium or New Zealand lacking the capacity to produce idiosyncratic manufactures of high demand abroad will fail to achieve this outlet.

The conference was designed to avoid recounting the sins of

American multinationals. In the event, it proved impossible. In the discussion of French attitudes the old errors or blunders of firms allegedly closing down without providing new jobs for the discharged workers were rehearsed, and the discussion of the Hughes paper digressed from technologies in general when it tackled the restrictions placed on foreign subsidiaries and foreign licensees alike in the use of advanced technologies from developed countries. On the whole, however, eliminating political judgments about ITT and the United Fruit Company helped to clarify the economic implications of firms coordinating economic activity in more than one country.

Professor Niehans's point that vertical specialization between countries led more or less inexorably to vertical integration between countries yielded an interesting corollary. Trade may involve dependence, just as direct investment and the multinational corporation do. American dependence on Swiss makers of baby food and condensed milk or Swedish producers of telephones and ball bearings is perhaps different in degree but hardly in kind from a smaller country's dependence on imports, on the one hand, or on IBM and Exxon, on the other.

Notes

1. "The term 'multinational corporation' is still largely a euphemism for the outward expansion of America's giant oligopolistic corporations." Robert Gilpin, *U.S. Power and the Multinational Corporation: The Political Economy of Foreign Direct Investment* (New York: Basic Books, Inc., 1975).

2. C. P. Kindleberger, ed., *The International Corporation, A Symposium* (Cambridge, Mass.: The M.I.T. Press, 1970).

3. David MacClain, "Foreign Investment in the United States Manufacturing and the Theory of Direct Investment," unpublished dissertation, M.I.T., September 1974.

4. Jacques Drèze, "Quelques réflexions sereines sur l'adaptation de l'industrie belge au Marché Commun," *Comptes-rendus des travaux de la Société royale d'économie politique de Belgique* no. 275 (December 1960). Jan A. Van Houtte, also a Belgian, notes that the Netherlands has developed at least three major international companies—Lever Brothers, Royal Dutch Shell, and Philips—and wonders why no Belgian firm has reached their dimensions. He asks whether this may not be because of Belgian businessman-individuality (see, "Economic Development of Belgium and the Netherlands from the Beginning of the Modern Era," *Journal of European Economic History* vol. 1, no. 1 (Spring 1972): 116–18.

5. See G. C. Hufbauer, "The Impact of National Characteristics and Technology on the Commodity Composition of Trade in Manufactured Goods," in R. Vernon, ed., *The Technology Factor in International Trade* (New York: Columbia University Press for the National Bureau of Economic Research, 1970), and C. P. Kindleberger, "Comment," ibid., p. 285.

1. Benefits of Multinational Firms for a Small Parent Economy: The Case of Switzerland

Jürg Niehans

Introduction

To determine the benefits to an economy from its multinational firms, one should, in principle, compare the state of the economy in the presence of multinational firms with its state in their absence. The pure theorist might try to build a model of an open economy in which the association between the degree of multinationalism and other variables like output or capital intensity could be studied by varying suitably chosen parameters. The econometrician might propose time-series or cross-section studies relating some measure of multinationalism to other variables. I believe at the present time those approaches would not be promising. Just as a fever is one aspect of a large number of highly diverse syndromes, so the multinational character of firms can emerge from many different sets of circumstances that may have little else in common. I have thus chosen a more qualitative and historical approach by studying in some detail the case of the one small country I know best. However, since Switzerland, like Sweden and Holland, is one of the prototypes of a small mother country to large multinational firms, the conclusions should be of some general interest.

In the first part I shall describe the present role of multinational firms in the Swiss economy. In order to form an opinion as to what the Swiss economy would look like in the absence of some or all of those firms, we should understand the forces that determine their international structure. These forces are identified in part 3 by case studies of five large multinational corporations on the basis of a taxonomy of determinants provided by part 2. Part 4 draws the conclusions about the probable effect for the domestic operations of these firms and the structure of the Swiss economy if circumstances had been adverse to multinationalism.

The Actual Situation: Multinationals in the Swiss Economy

It is difficult to give a quantitative picture of the role of multinational corporations in the Swiss economy. In part such difficulty is due to the fragmentary nature of official statistics. Even the official national income series were discontinued in 1970 because they were believed to have become too unreliable to be useful. In part the difficulty is also due to the lack of detailed information on some of the firms. Furthermore, there are, as far as I know, no previous studies on which one can build. We shall thus have to be content with broad outlines.

We first note that per capita income in the Swiss economy has grown at a relatively high rate during recent decades. Comparing 1974 with 1959, we find that Swiss per capita income, converted into dollars at the current exchange rate, grew by 359 percent, while the corresponding rate for the United States was 143 percent. While in 1959 per capita income in Switzerland was roughly 60 percent of that in the United States, it was 112 percent in 1974 (see Table 1.1).[1]

A second observation concerns the expansion of the foreign sector relative to the economy as a whole (see Table 1.2). During the last twenty years, commodity exports and imports grew from very roughly one-fourth of national income to roughly one-third. International markets have become even more impor-

Table 1.1. National Income

	Switzerland		United States	
	1959	1974	1959	1974
National income (bill. nat. curr.)	29.9	115.8[a]	357	1,142
Exchange rate (SwF/$)	4.32	2.97		
National income (bill. $)	6.9	39.0		
Population (mill.)	5.26	6.46	179.3	211.9
National income ($ per capita)	1,316	6,036	2,214	5,389

Sources: 1954–1969 Statistisches Jahrbuch der Schweiz 1974 Ertragsbilanz der Schweiz im Jahre 1974, Volkswirtschaft, July 1975.

[a] Est., Union Bank of Switzerland.

tant for the national economy than they were in the earlier postwar period. Imports traditionally exceed exports, but the size of the import surplus, while fluctuating widely, shows no clear trend.

The goods-and-services account as a whole expanded even more than commodity trade, indicating that invisibles are of growing importance. The current account is more nearly balanced than the merchandise account alone, reflecting the fact that receipts for invisibles exceed payments more than two to one. In fact, receipts for invisibles are just about half the receipts for commodity exports. To an increasing extent the Swiss economy is a services economy.

Within the invisibles, the most dynamic item is the returns on Swiss capital investments abroad. While returns paid on foreign capital investments in Switzerland have barely held their own relative to national income, returns received on Swiss assets abroad have increased their share, and net receipts have more than doubled relative to national income. In 1974 the net return on capital assets abroad amounted to no less than SwF 851 (roughly $300) per head of population or 5 percent of national income. These figures, while impressive, actually underestimate the true significance of foreign capital earnings since they omit reinvestments abroad. The net Swiss holdings of foreign assets were estimated at SwF 140.3 billion in 1974, equivalent to SwF 21.712 per capita.

We thus obtain the picture of a growing economy with progressive international integration, with a growing share of services in the current account, and with a rapid increase in earnings on foreign assets. It is difficult to determine how this twenty-year development compares with the long-term trend since the turn of the century. It is fairly certain that international integration and returns on foreign capital were actually higher around the turn of the century than they would have been if recent developments had just extended the long-term trend. Just as developments in the 1920s helped to restore the pre-World War I asset position, so post-World War II developments helped to correct the abnormal situation created by the Great Depression and World War II.

Table 1.2. Current Account

Year	National Income (Mill. SwF)	Goods and Services				Merchandise (Percent of National Income)		Capital Returns	
		Exports		Imports		Exports	Imports	Receipts	Payments
		Mill. SwF	Percent of NI	Mill. SwF	Percent of NI				
1954	22,250	8,143	36.6	7,080	31.8	23.7	25.1	3.3	1.0
1959	29,030	11,305	38.9	10,547	36.3	25.1	28.5	2.9	0.8
1964	46,570	18,129	38.9	19,904	42.7	24.6	33.4	2.5	0.5
1969	67,130	30,900	46.0	28,630	42.4	29.8	33.9	3.8	0.5
1974	115,800[a]	55,250	47.7	54,740	47.3	30.5	37.1	5.8	0.7

Sources: 1954–69 Statistisches Jahrbuch der Schweiz 1974 Ertragsbilanz der Schweiz im Jahre 1974, Volkswirtschaft, July 1975.

[a] Est., Union Bank of Switzerland.

The question is what multinational firms may have had to do with this development. One clue is provided by the breakdown of net foreign assets by type. We may assume that foreign assets of Swiss multinationals are largely represented by direct investments and insurance assets. Out of the estimated net foreign assets of SwF 140.3 billion, these two items accounted for SwF 46.6 billion or one-third, while the remainder consisted largely of monetary reserves, securities, bank and government loans, and bank deposits—hardly an overwhelming proportion (see Table 1.3).

More information can be obtained from the list of the largest Swiss firms compiled by Union Bank of Switzerland. In Table 1.4, the thirty-five largest manufacturing firms are grouped by sales in 1974. Subsidiaries of foreign multinationals and six firms with 33,837 workers, for which no breakdown of the labor force was available, were omitted. The largest five include Nestlé, Ciba-Geigy, Brown, Boveri & Cie., Alusuisse, and Hoffmann-LaRoche. For each group Table 1.4 shows the total labor force and its breakdown between domestic and foreign operations. The total number of workers of the thirty-five firms turns out to be more than half the labor force in all manufacturing. However, more than two-thirds of these workers were

Table 1.3. Foreign Assets and Liabilities, 1974 (Mill. SwF)

	Swiss Assets Abroad	Foreign Assets in Switzerland
Monetary reserves	20,783	
Banks, short-term	66,678	50,700
Loans, government and banks	16,012	
Securities	78,869	31,911
Direct investments	50,750	8,500
Insurance funds	13,180	9,000
Real estate	1,400	7,260
Net assets		140,301
	247,672	247,672

Source: Union Bank of Switzerland, July 7, 1975.

employed in foreign subsidiaries and less than one-third was actually in the Swiss labor force. Foreign employment in large Swiss manufacturing firms thus amounted to about one-half of domestic employment. Large Swiss firms are typically multinational. In fact, among the top fifteen, only two—Allgemeine Schweizerische Uhrenindustrie AG (ASUAG) and Von Roll Iron Works—had a domestic component of more than 60 percent. It is also interesting to note that the multinational character is less pronounced with diminishing firm size. While the top five employ five-sixths of their workers abroad, the firms in the seventh group employ only one-tenth abroad.

We can try to translate these employment figures into national income terms. In 1970, value added per worker in manufacturing was just about SwF 30,000. If it increased from 1970 to 1974 at the same rate as GNP, it was about SwF 48,000 in 1974. Value added in foreign subsidiaries is unknown, but in most cases it is probably lower. Taking SwF 40,000 as a rough guess, the top five may be estimated to have produced a foreign income of SwF 12.8 billion, while their domestic income was only SwF 3.1 billion. Their total value amounted to more than 13 percent of national income. For the top thirty-five the foreign value added was of the order of SwF 18.4 billion, their domestic income about SwF 10.3 billion, and their total value

Table 1.4. Employment in 35 Largest Manufacturing Firms, 1974

	Total	Domestic		Foreign	
	No.	No.	Percent	No.	Percent
Largest 5	386,111	64,756	16.8	321,355	83.2
Second 5	128,155	61,005	47.6	67,150	52.4
Third 5	69,449	31,888	45.6	37,561	54.4
Fourth 5	37,961	21,320	56.2	16,641	43.8
Fifth 5	23,654	12,200	51.8	11,454	48.2
Sixth 5	14,498	9,859	68.0	4,639	32.0
Seventh 5	14,822	13,282	89.2	1,600	10.8
Largest 35	674,710	214,310	31.8	460,400	68.2

Source: Union Bank of Switzerland, Die grössten Unternehmungen der Schweiz im Jahre 1974.

added may thus have amounted to about one-quarter of national income.

It is difficult to estimate the export contribution of the top thirty-five, but based on the available figures the order of magnitude seems to be about one-third. The interesting point is that it is not larger. If total exports are 30 percent of national income and the top thirty-five account for one-third of exports, their exports are about 10 percent of national income. This is just about the same proportion as their domestic value added in relation to national income. It seems that the top thirty-five, including most of the larger multinationals, are not clearly more export-oriented than the rest of the economy. This fact is consistent with the observation that multinationals, while internationally oriented, are characterized by the substitution of foreign production for international trade. Nestlé, as the prototype of an international firm, has no significant exports from Switzerland at all.

The growth performance of Swiss multinationals is even more difficult to assess. Most of them are old firms, and the larger ones were multinational half a century ago. Multinationalism is not a new phenomenon in the Swiss economy. Over the decades multinationals have probably turned in some of the most consistent long-term growth performances. However, in recent years they have shown neither more rapid growth nor a better stock market performance than the rest of the economy. Nominal GNP grew by 60 percent from 1970 to 1974, and very few Swiss multinationals exceeded this rate in their sales growth. Figures are available for thirteen out of the twenty largest firms. Of these only Nestlé (63 percent), Landis & Gyr. (81.2 percent), and Alusuisse (122 percent) exceeded the GNP growth rate, and in the case of Alusuisse the Lonza merger was the main factor. In the stock market the good performers tended to be in service industries like banking, insurance, and retailing, in construction, energy, and food products, while metals, machinery, engineering, pharmaceuticals, and chemicals with their large multinational firms were lackluster.

It is likely that the multinational firms, by shifting an increasing part of their manufacturing operations to foreign subsidiaries, made a significant contribution to the general shift of the economy from manufacturing to services, both in production and in exports. In the progressive concentration of their domestic operations on service-intensive intermediate products like marketing, technology, management, and finance, their individual development parallels the analogous development in the economy as a whole. By holding internationally diversified portfolios, they helped to reduce the risk of Swiss capital investments, and by holding these portfolios in fields in which they had specific expertise, they provided asset diversification of a type not available to the individual stock holder. With the floating of exchange rates reinforcing the pressures for asset diversification, this role of the multinationals has further increased in importance.

These observations suggest, in summary, that the Swiss multinationals, while not the most aggressive or dynamic sector of the economy, are its solid, durable, and resilient backbone and that they have contributed significantly to the shift toward services, to the yield on foreign assets, and to the reduction of risk in the economy.

Determinants of Multinationalism

In order to determine the actual forces shaping the structure of Swiss multinationals, we need to know what potential forces we should look for. What is needed is a taxonomy of determinants as provided by economic theory. There are two general requirements for the emergence of multinational firms:

1. Successive stages of production (represented in Figure 1.1 by I and F) must be separated by national borders (represented by the broken line), resulting in international trade in intermediate products.
2. Successive stages of production must be integrated in the same firm across national borders (represented by the box).

The conditions under which these requirements may be satisfied will now be discussed. While this discussion is general in nature, points that promise to be of particular relevance for the Swiss economy are noted in passing.

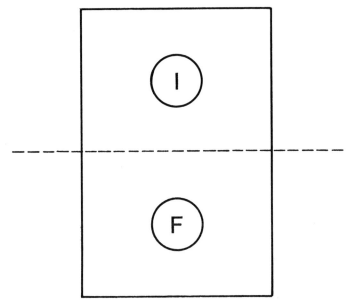

Figure 1.1

International Trade: Vertical Specialization of Nations
In order to explain the emergence of multinational firms, we
have to explain, first, why there is a vertical division of labor
with intermediate goods crossing national borders. These intermediate goods may range from highly conspicuous raw materials like alumina to invisibles like managerial services, technical
knowledge, or marketing expertise. In order for a firm to be
truly multinational (instead of only binational or trinational) one
of the stages of production must be scattered over numerous
countries. In the case of a small, headquarter country like Switzerland with its narrow domestic market, it is likely to be the
final-product stage that is internationally dispersed, while the
intermediate product is supplied by the headquarter country.
To identify the determinants of the specialization of nations we
have to consult international trade theory.[2]
Comparative Cost   A first set of determinants is the relative
factor endowments and technologies of different countries as
analyzed by the theory of comparative cost. Suppose there are
no transactions costs or trade barriers, no joint products or
scale economies, and the world is in competitive equilibrium.
International specialization is then such that the world is on its
production-possibility frontier. At each point of this frontier the
assignment of products to countries is governed by comparative advantage as generalized to the case of many countries
and many commodities.

The relevant question is under what conditions this specialization becomes such that there is trade in intermediate products. The question has no simple answer.[3] The efficiency of
intermediate product flows depends on the whole array of input coefficients in all countries, and there is no simple criterion
for national specialization. It may be a change in American agriculture that makes it efficient for a Swiss watch manufacturer
to assemble his watches in Hongkong. Generally, the artificial
prevention of vertical specialization would certainly reduce the
world production possibilities and thus be inefficient. However,
there is nothing to suggest that vertical specialization will usually be a one-way street. It may also happen that country A will
supply B with one intermediate product, while B will supply A
with another. Since multinationals often (though not necessar-

ily) have their headquarters at the intermediary stage, each country may be a host country for some firms, but a headquarters country for others. Nevertheless, to the extent that management itself is an intermediate product, there may be countries with a comparative advantage at this particular stage of production and thus they will have a relatively large number of corporate headquarters. Switzerland seems to be one of those cases.

In some situations the decisive influence of comparative cost is obvious. Thus the production of bauxite and aluminum, since production demands on resources are different, will often be assigned to different countries. Similarly, research and development, requiring highly skilled labor, will often be assigned to technologically advanced countries rather than assembling and packaging, which require lower skills. In other cases, the relevance of comparative cost is less clear. In fact, it is a frequent comment in the executive offices of Swiss multinationals that from the point of view of production costs it would be more efficient to concentrate all stages, except perhaps the final packaging, in Switzerland. In many cases, vertical specialization across national borders seems to be a relatively inefficient, second-best solution imposed on the firm by other forces.

Scale Economies   The preceding argument assumed constant costs at all levels of production and is, therefore, more directly applicable to industries than to firms, where each industry consists of a variable number of identical firms, each producing at minimum cost. To bring the analysis down to the level of individual firms, it is necessary to introduce economies of scale in an explicit way. It is frequent in multinational firms that the successive stages of production are characterized by different scale effects. For example, numerous national or regional markets may each be large enough to support efficient plants at the final stage, while only the world is large enough to support efficient operations at the stage of research or financial management. In other cases, local sources of raw materials like minerals or agricultural products may be subject to diminishing returns and thus internationally scattered, while the efficiency of processing plants requires concentration. Scale factors may thus become decisive determinants of vertical specialization.

Transport Costs   In addition to production costs, traditionally analyzed in the theory of comparative cost, vertical specialization is affected by transport costs as analyzed in location theory. It is clear that two successive stages of production are more likely to be geographically—and thus perhaps internationally—separated the higher the transportation costs for the raw material and the final product are relative to those for the intermediate product. On the other hand, transportation costs that are sufficiently high for intermediary products can always force two successive stages to the same location.

State of Demand   Once cost considerations have established the international production-possibility frontier, demand conditions have to determine the point chosen. Demand can again influence the degree of vertical specialization. Thus it may be that at a low level of demand for a certain processed food it is efficient to produce in a single country, but at a high level of demand it is efficient to produce in many. While this situation is true, in principle, even in the absence of scale economies, it may become of decisive importance with increasing returns to scale. If the state of demand is interpreted to refer to the individual product, we obtain the product-cycle model of multinationalism. While this model helps to explain the development of some Swiss multinationals, it does not appear to be relevant for others. If the state of demand is taken to relate to aggregate economic growth, we obtain the proposition that economic growth could be expected to be associated, as a normal feature, with increasing vertical specialization. Vertical specialization seems indeed to have been a normal concomitant of economic growth in the case of the Swiss economy.

Trade Barriers   Tariff protection for the finished good at a higher level than for the intermediate good may be a powerful reason for vertical specialization, even though such specialization is socially inefficient. Customs unions, by discriminating against nonmembers, will tend to have the same effect. In an extreme case, the intermediary goods may be reduced to duty-free technical knowledge and management services, while all manufacturing activity has been shifted to the market area. Some Swiss multinationals come close to this extreme.

Similar considerations apply to nontariff protection. In particular, tax laws, national food and drug laws, insurance and bank regulation, rules and practices on the bidding for public contracts, patent legislation, safety standards, and the like may put the foreign competitor at a disadvantage compared with national firms. Such considerations will turn out to be the single most powerful force behind the development of Swiss multinationals.

Trade barriers may also affect multinational firms (MNFs) in another way. As Mundell has shown, protection of a capital-intensive industry may induce capital inflows.[4] In some MNFs the final stage of production, requiring large-scale manufacturing plants with comparatively unskilled labor, seems to be relatively capital-intensive, while the intermediary stage, requiring large research inputs, is comparatively labor-intensive. Pharmaceuticals are a case in point. In such cases, protection of the final stage would not only result in vertical specialization but would also facilitate the capital flows necessary to finance local production of the final product. It is tempting to argue that in a world with imperfect capital mobility Swiss interest rates are relatively low, in part because of the relative decline in domestic capital requirements due to the emigration of capital-intensive stages of production.

Exchange Risk   If exchange rates are subject to fluctuations relative to the purchasing-power parities, the efforts of firms to minimize their exchange risks tend, in the long run, to reduce the volume of trade flows.[5] If a company exports final products, the full value of its sales is exposed to the exchange risk. If it moves its manufacturing operations to the market areas, exporting only its technical and management services, it is only the profits and the payments for these services that are exposed to exchange risk. As a consequence, the larger the exchange risk, the larger—other things being equal—will be the tendency to national decentralization of production.[6] Indeed, in the annual reports of Swiss firms during the last few years, one of the recurring themes has been the pressure to reduce exchange risks by going multinational.

Industrial Organization: Vertical Integration of Firms
Once we have explained the vertical decentralization of pro-

duction across national borders, we have to explain why
production is still carried out in the same firm. Once we have
explained why the production process is international, we have
to explain why it is intrafirm. The general, and somewhat emp-
ty, explanation must be that the international whole is worth
more than the national parts. To understand the specific reasons for this outcome, we have to consult the theory of industrial organization. Most—but not all—of the reasons are the
same as those for the vertical integration of geographically
scattered multiplant firms in a national economy. If the United
States were broken up into fifty independent states, a large
number of firms would become multinational without any
change in the underlying economic conditions. Ceteris paribus,
the importance of multinational firms should thus be inversely
related to the size of an economy.*FN;7*M; While an American
may still regard them as a somewhat special and slightly myste-
rious phenomenon, for a Swiss they are the everyday case.

In one way or another the reasons for the vertical integration
of firms all have to do with imperfect markets. Suppose there
are no increasing returns to scale, no externalities, and no
fixed setup costs at any stage of the production process. Suppose, furthermore, there are large, competitive markets for
each intermediate product. In this case there would be no reason for the vertical integration of firms. Vertical integration
tends to occur only if some of the conditions are not satisfied.

It should be noted that the argument runs in terms of imperfections in the intermediary markets. It has often, and correctly,
been emphasized that multinational firms owe their existence
to imperfect competition.[8] It has not always been clear that the
relevant imperfections are not those of monopoly at the final-
product stage. It should also be noted that imperfect markets—
the enduring myth of monopoly profits notwithstanding—have
no necessary relationship to profits. First, monopoly in the
sense of a falling demand curve for the product has no necessary association with profits, freedom of entry pushing profits
to the same level as in pure competition—namely zero—and
not necessarily more slowly. Second, many of the relevant market imperfections arise not from the monopolistic power of the
multinational firm but rather from the threat of its being ex-

posed to monopolistic power by its counterparts in the market. After these general remarks, some specific sources of market imperfection of particular relevance for multinational firms will be reviewed.

The Horrors of Bilateral Monopoly Imagine a research-oriented drug manufacturer introducing a new tranquilizer. He has the option of selling licenses to local manufacturers in foreign countries. Ideally, the royalties would capture all of the profits expected from vertical integration. However, the market for such licenses is highly imperfect. First, the research firm will often have more certain information on the market potential of the new drug and thus a lower risk premium than a potential licensee. The licensee would then not be willing to pay what the research firm hopes to earn, even if there is no discrepancy in the expected values of future profits. Second, a licensing agreement is not like stock that can be daily traded at the going price in a large market. Once made, it is difficult to renegotiate, cancel, or transfer. As a consequence, the research firm either has to accept the risk that the licensee's business policy may run counter to its own interest or it will have to impose contractual limits on the licensee's freedom, possibly reducing him to a mere satellite, of course at the price of a lower license fee.[9]

A similar situation arises if chemical manufacturer A buys some intermediate product with high transport costs from competitor B, while B buys another heavy raw material from A. Other examples are alumina and energy, the market for alumina being highly imperfect and that for electric energy, almost non-existent. The problem is particularly acute if the intermediate product is management, including such things as marketing techniques, financial management, administrative experience, and the like. Of course, theoretically these services could be hired out across national borders for a fee, but their market is extremely imperfect.

In all these cases, market imperfection in the absence of vertical integration would result in strong elements of bilateral monopoly with its inherent risk. Firms abhor such situations. The means to avoid them is vertical integration. Since vertical integration can, in principle, reduce risk without reducing the expected value of income for anybody, it will often produce a net social gain.

Economics of Firm Scale   Suppose there is a large number of producers both for the intermediate and the final product and thus a competitive market for the intermediate good. It may still be that the integration of a group of producers into one firm is profitable. A possible reason is economics of firm scale. In an insurance company the pooling of risks will often be advantageous, particularly for large risks. In a manufacturing firm, integration may create a more diversified and, therefore, more efficient asset portfolio. Financial management for large firms may be more efficient than for small units. The production process may involve fixed setup costs or externalities at various stages that would make decentralized operations inefficient. Market transactions also involve transactions costs, and these will often be higher than the corresponding administrative costs in an integrated firm. One of the potential economies of firm scale is, of course, the restraint of competition. However, such restraint is basically a question of horizontal integration in a given market and not of vertical integration across national borders.

Fluctuating Exchange Rates   Even if all commodity markets come close to the ideal of perfect competition, fluctuating exchange rates may still give rise to vertical integration of firms. There are two reasons for this. The first reason is the expectation of exchange-rate changes.[10] If the expected future depreciation of the dollar relative to the Swiss franc is larger than the interest differential, the dollar thus enjoying a "currency premium," there is an incentive for capital to flow from the United States to Switzerland. This incentive tends to stimulate, together with flows of portfolio investment and bank deposits, direct investments by U.S. firms in Switzerland or the liquidation of Swiss investments in the United States. When the currency premium is the other way around (as it was recently), Swiss firms will find U.S. plants a bargain, while U.S. firms may find their Swiss subsidiaries a burden. While such an analysis helps to explain waves of multinationalization in alternate directions, it does little to explain the long-run trend.

The second reason is uncertainty about future exchange

rates relative to the purchasing-power parity. In the face of such uncertainty, firms will tend to diversify their assets among currency areas. In principle, diversification will occur irrespective of whether a firm is engaged in international trade. In the particular case of firms engaged in the import or export of intermediate products, the result will tend to be an increase in the degree of international integration. Just like international specialization, intrafirm integration is encouraged by fluctuating exchange rates.[11]

This taxonomy does not claim to include all conceivable determinants of multinationalism, but it should at least be comprehensive enough for the Swiss case. Most theoretical analyses of multinational firms have concentrated on one of the determinants to the exclusion of the others. It is important to realize that for different firms and countries determinants subsumed under vertical specialization of nations can be combined with determinants subsumed under vertical integration of firms in innumerable combinations. This diversity is what makes it so difficult to find general propositions about multinational firms, and it makes one doubt whether such propositions can realistically exist at all.

Five Swiss Multinationals

The next task is to evaluate the relative contribution of the various determinants to the development of Swiss multinational firms. In view of the just mentioned difficulty with generalization in this field, I propose to conduct the evaluation by examining the growth and present structure of a sample of important firms in some detail. The sample includes the four largest Swiss manufacturing firms, Nestlé, Ciba-Geigy, Brown, Boveri & Cie., and Alusuisse, representing, respectively, food processing, pharmaceuticals and chemicals, machinery, and metals. The sample also includes Swiss Reinsurance as a representative of financial services. In addition to published material, the case studies are based (except for Nestlé) on interviews and correspondence with executives. I gratefully acknowledge the assistance I received, but the sole responsibility for errors is with me.

Nestlé

Nestlé Alimentana SA, with consolidated sales of SwF 16.6 billion, is the largest firm in Switzerland and one of the world's largest food processors. Its basic activity is the processing of agricultural commodities like milk, cocoa, and coffee into manufactured food products, protected by trademarks and often by patents, and the marketing of these products to the retail trade.[12] Following a long-established corporate strategy, Nestlé does not engage in either agricultural production or retailing. As a consequence, the degree of its vertical integration is low. On the other hand, Nestlé has followed a strategy of extending its operations over an increasing variety of foods, thus reaching a relatively high degree of horizontal integration.

The multinational character of the company is extreme. Production takes place in more than three hundred plants scattered over more than fifty countries. The role of the home market is negligible, domestic sales amounting to less than 4 percent of total output. In this respect Nestlé resembles other Swiss multinationals. However, while other firms maintain a considerable domestic production for export, Nestlé's exports from Switzerland are virtually zero. The firm thinks and plans in global terms.

When the Henry Nestlé Company and the Anglo-Swiss Condensed Milk Company merged in 1905 to form Nestlé and Anglo-Swiss, both firms had long been multinational. Nestlé, with baby food as its main product, followed the product-cycle pattern. First it captured the home market. Then it built up a growing export business. Finally, as domestic milk supplies could not keep up with demand and a number of foreign markets became large enough to support their own production facilities, the company moved into foreign production. The development of Anglo-Swiss followed a different pattern. The firm was multinational almost from the beginning, having factories in England and Germany within a few years after it was founded and expanding foreign production rapidly. This foreign production was necessary because the condensed milk of Anglo-Swiss, unlike Nestlé's baby food, had a high sugar content and was thus subject to high import duties in an increasing number of countries.

In Nestlé's early decades, multinational diversification of production was due to three main factors. The first was a U-shaped cost curve with increasing plant size. Later, the optimal plant would have not more than a few hundred workers and would process the milk from about 10,000 cows, owned by, say, 1,100 farmers within a radius of about fifty miles. The initial cost decline was provided by the indivisibility of efficient equipment, and the eventual increase was caused by the rising cost of milk supplies to a given locality. The second factor was tariff protection. The third factor was the difficulty of guaranteeing a steady supply at the retail level if finished products had to be shipped over long distances. Aside from this difficulty, the actual cost of transportation seems to have played a secondary, though not insignificant role. In later decades it became increasingly important to adapt the products to local tastes, adding a fourth reason for diversification. The risk of exchange fluctuations and exchange controls became a fifth factor, which assumed increasing importance during the interwar period and has recently been given added significance by the collapse of the gold-exchange standard.

On the other hand, there were economies of firm size that made it efficient to combine a number of nationally separate units into a single corporate entity. First, research and development had to be centrally provided to keep the product competitive. Second, since trademarks were essential for marketing, central control had to guarantee uniform quality for the product. Third, since the product was a part of the daily diet of consumers, central coordination of production and shipping schedules and control of inventories was necessary to assure continuous availability at the retail level. Fourth, to the extent that Nestlé manufactured its own machinery and equipment, which it no longer does, it had to do it in a centralized way. One can generalize by saying that the firm was held together by the fact that firm size reached its optimum level at a much higher point than plant size. These basic principles, well understood by 1905, describe corporate strategy to the present day.

The later development of Nestlé proceeded in two directions. One direction was geographic. Again in the spirit of the product-cycle model, the supply organization was extended to more and more countries, progressing from importing agents to branch offices to producing subsidiaries as local markets expanded. At the same time the share of aggregate exports in the firm's total sales declined.

The other component of corporate growth was in the direction of horizontal diversification. Once a central management and marketing system was available, it was efficient to use it for a larger range of products. Such efficiency was the driving force already behind the 1905 merger, as Anglo-Swiss had expanded into milk foods, while Nestlé had attacked it in the field of condensed milk. Up to World War I, milk remained the basis of the company. The 1920s saw the diversification into the neighboring field of chocolate, again achieved by merger. Instant coffee was added in the thirties, providing a third pillar to the company. In the course of the postwar years a vigorous program of mergers and acquisitions extended the product range to a large variety of products sold through retail food stores, including soups, frozen foods, canned goods, bakery products, mineral water, and, most recently, cosmetics.

Today, Nestlé is the prototype of the international firm. Its headquarters in Vevey supply the subsidiaries with management, research and development, and marketing techniques. Arrangements have been made to keep the corporate structure intact in just about any sort of international emergency. Wherever the firm has to protect its own trademarks, it tries to have complete control over the subsidiary. Production schedules and inventories are centrally monitored, and while the subsidiaries are in charge of operating decisions, their corporate policies are closely coordinated by headquarters. Cash and financial management is also centralized. The buying of raw materials and production, however, are decentralized, with the subsidiaries playing an important role in the development of local agriculture, particularly in underdeveloped countries.

Ciba-Geigy
Ciba-Geigy Ltd. is one of the world's two largest producers of dyestuffs, one of the leading manufacturers of pharmaceuticals and agro-chemicals, and an important producer of plastics.

With consolidated sales of SwF 9.3 billion it is the second largest Swiss firm, and with a share of 8 percent of total exports,
the largest Swiss exporter. It is also an excellent example of an
international firm in the sense that only about 2 percent of its
output is sold in the home market.

Ciba-Geigy's corporate structure is marked by a high degree
of forward integration down to the final product. This is inherent in the character of its basic output, namely the results of
product-oriented chemical research. This research is very costly, but once the results are in, their utilization has virtually zero
marginal cost.[13] As a consequence, with free access to results
no research would be undertaken by private firms. While the
imitators would cover their costs, the innovator could never
break even and would thus disappear. To provide for continued
stimulus to research, it has always been found necessary in
such cases to impede the entry of imitators either by secrecy
or, preferably, by patent. While such control introduces an element of monopoly into the competitive process, it does not
necessarily raise profits above the competitive level. Although
entry is impeded for individual products, it is free for the industry as a whole. As a consequence, whenever the industry is
more profitable than other industries for a long time, research
activity—both by old and new firms—will increase, the rate at
which new products are introduced will accelerate, and profits
will again be reduced to the competitive level. The problem,
therefore, is not a monopolistic profit margin between prices
and average costs, but the proper balance between the dynamic benefits from more rapid product innovation and the cost in
terms of static efficiency resulting from a difference between
price and marginal cost.

Under these conditions there can be no perfect, or even approximately perfect, markets for intermediate products. If the
research results were sold to the manufacturer under a license,
the relationship between the partners would most likely include
strong elements of bilateral monopoly. The same would be true
if a manufacturer of the basic substance sold it to distributors
with their own packaging plants in various countries. As I have
suggested, private enterprise tends to abhor the risks of bilater-

al monopoly. The result in the pharmaceutical industry is a
high degree of forward integration from the basic research
down to the final product. The same motive has sometimes
caused Ciba-Geigy to integrate backwards. For example, an important intermediate product for dyestuffs used to be bought
from Bayer, its most important competitor in the product market. To eliminate the inherent risk, Ciba-Geigy started its own
production.

Both Ciba and Geigy, who merged in 1970, began to develop
their multinational structure around the turn of the century. At
the beginning of World War II both companies had their own
production facilities in all the countries that now form the
European Economic Community (EEC) and also in the United
States. After further progress in the postwar period, the process of decentralization slowed down in the last few years.
Since 1969 the share of the parent firm of the total labor force
has remained at 28 to 29 percent. Its share of fixed investments
is no lower today than it was in 1969, and its share of total
sales has actually increased. However, this stability may be just
an interlude, perhaps related to the merger, and one hears the
opinion that as a matter of corporate strategy future growth
will be concentrated in foreign subsidiaries.

To some extent the multinational character of Ciba-Geigy is
motivated by marketing considerations. Packaging and advertising have to be differentiated according to local needs and
languages. In countries like the United States a domestic drug
would tend to be more highly regarded than an import (though
in other markets a Swiss product might be preferred to a
domestic one). Decentralization thus started with the market-
related stages of production. Another motive was probably the
reduction of risk. By far the most important motive, however,
was protection. For the most part it is national protectionism
that gave the firm its present structure.

Some of this protection is in the form of tariffs. In the U.S.
market, for example, the American Selling Price rule gave an
added impulse to local production of final goods. In Europe,
import duties on dyestuffs imposed national decentralization of
plants, while the Common Market, in turn, opened the way to a

process of concentration and specialization on the basis of comparative advantage and economies of scale.

For pharmaceuticals and agro-chemicals, however, the main problem was nontariff protection through widely different national food and drug laws. While tariffs were gradually reduced, drug laws remained a national prerogative, and with the stiffening of admission requirements for new drugs, the protective effect actually became stronger. As a consequence, foreign firms tended to be at an increasing disadvantage relative to the domestic producer. Some countries, like France, do not allow the importation of finished products at all, a practice that obviously stimulates foreign direct investment. In addition, an increasing proportion of research had to be allocated to market-oriented development and testing, which can only be done on a national basis.

Research for new products still remains largely concentrated in the parent firm, which apparently enjoys strong economies of scale and advantages of location compared to the subsidiaries. Even in the United States, research for new products still has to justify the effort. This difficulty raises the question of how the parent company can reimburse itself for the research burden. Transfers of profits from subsidiaries cannot be relied upon to escape double taxation. License fees and royalties avoid the problem, but for that very reason they are regarded by the tax authorities with suspicion. Complete vertical specialization between a parent concentrating on research and subsidiaries engaged in development, production, and marketing would thus produce a precarious and vulnerable corporate structure. As a consequence, the parent in Basle still maintains a very considerable level of exports, about two-thirds of it going to the subsidiaries. The fact that the sales/labor ratio of the parent increasingly exceeds that of the firm as a whole reflects the progressive concentration of these exports in research-intensive products of relatively high value per unit of labor.

Today the corporate outlook of Ciba-Geigy seems to be in a process of transition. Up to their merger, both Ciba and Geigy, despite their multinational structure, were still thinking in terms of highly export-oriented Swiss firms. The merger could not change this outlook overnight. However, under the added pressure from floating exchange rates such an orientation is increasingly seen to be inadequate, and the firm is groping toward a system of corporate control that will finally transform it into a truly international firm.

Brown, Boveri & Cie.

Brown, Boveri & Cie. (BBC) is one of the major manufacturers of electrical equipment. While traditionally the emphasis has been on heavy equipment for power plants, transportation, and heavy industry, BBC's production program is highly varied, reaching from turbines to liquid crystals. With consolidated sales of SwF 7.5 billion, the firm is the third largest in Switzerland. However, only about 6 percent of its output is sold domestically, and the rest of Europe accounts for about 75 percent.

BBC, having established its German subsidiary within two years of its foundation, was multinational from the beginning. Today, little more than one-fifth of total output is produced in Switzerland, while almost four-fifths is produced by subsidiaries in more than one hundred countries. By volume of sales, the German subsidiary is actually twice the size of the parent.

The principal reason for this diversification turns out to be trade barriers. Historically, the main barriers have been the national buying practices of major customer groups. A significant part of the firm's products are large pieces of equipment individually built for public authorities, utility companies, and large private firms. These buyers will often give preference to domestic suppliers, sometimes being compelled to do so by national regulations. Compared to these nontariff barriers, tariff protection has played a secondary and declining role. As a consequence, the lowering of tariffs in the postwar period and the European Common Market affected BBC less than others, except for mass-produced items. In developing countries import restrictions and industrialization programs increasingly require local production. In such cases BBC can compete only by selling its services under licenses and consulting agreements to local subsidiaries or foreign firms.

Other motives for diversification are the high transportation

costs for heavy equipment, the regional or national differences
in technical standards in certain fields, and, recently, the wide
fluctuations in foreign-exchange rates. Another important factor is the necessity of maintaining a sales and service
organization in each market area. This necessity requires local
engineering staffs of high competence and also adequate
installation and servicing facilities. In many instances the facilities are complemented by local production, particularly of
relatively standardized items. Overall, about one-third of the
sales of subsidiaries is from local production.

As in every multinational firm, the centrifugal forces must be
balanced by integrative forces. In the case of BBC, the main integrative force is technological progress. About 6 to 7 percent
of sales are spent on research and development, but this figure
probably underestimates the importance of technological progress as a large part of it is tied to individual projects and thus
cannot be separately accounted for. While the subsidiaries are
less research-intensive than the parent company, it is by no
means generally true that new technology is generated only by
the parent. The firm is more appropriately regarded as a multinational system for the pooling of technology, where the subsidiaries contribute to the group's research and development
efforts on a cost/benefit-compensation basis so as to make
optimal use of available expertise and familiarity with specific
market requirements. As a consequence, the multinational firm
is significantly more efficient than a group of independent
national firms could be.

A second integrative force, and a force of growing importance, is the worldwide sales organization. Until a few years
ago, each subsidiary was essentially restricted to its own market, while exports were left to the parent. Today a growing proportion of exports is contributed by subsidiaries, which now
sell an average of about one-fourth of their output abroad.
Offers are centrally pooled and distributed among the manufacturing subsidiaries on the basis of an annual budget, taking
into consideration capacity utilization and specific advantages.
In return, each subsidiary shares the benefits of the scale
economies of a global sales and service organization.

So far the discussion has been in terms of production and

marketing economies. Another forceful determinant of BBC's multinational structure is risk. On one hand, as a multinational producer it is less exposed to risk than if it were an export-oriented Swiss firm feeling the full force of any shift in comparative advantages between Switzerland and the rest of the world. Thus the growing export share of the subsidiaries during the past fifteen years was, in part, an adjustment to the shortage of labor in Switzerland and to the appreciation of the Swiss franc. On the other hand, since it can consolidate divergent national and product markets, the multinational firm is less exposed to risk than each of a number of independent firms producing for their respective home markets. In particular, BBC's multinational diversification has often helped it to adjust to cyclical fluctuations. From the point of view of risk, BBC has certain features of an internationally diversified portfolio in the electrical industry.

These considerations seem to suggest a relatively high degree of central planning and coordination. While corporative strategy has indeed developed in this direction during the last few years, BBC traditionally had little central management. The subsidiaries were largely free to act like independent firms, making use of the parent's technology and financial resources against the payment of royalties and dividends. This relationship is still reflected in the financial structure of the firm. In many subsidiaries there are substantial minority holdings, and in some cases BBC does not even have a majority. There is little central cash, portfolio, or debt management. Under these circumstances, central coordination is handicapped by the necessity of avoiding conflict-of-interest charges by minority shareholders in subsidiaries. It seems to be present corporate strategy to realize the optimum of central coordination consistent with the inherited financial structure and the strong national ties of the foreign subsidiaries.

Alusuisse
Alusuisse, active in twenty-seven countries, ranks sixth in the Western world, and fourth in the United States, as a producer of primary aluminum. It is the second largest producer of aluminum foil in the Western world and, by volume of sales, the

fourth largest manufacturing firm in Switzerland. For the purpose of this study, Alusuisse appears as the prototype of a resource-oriented multinational firm. Its products are relatively undifferentiated, sold in highly competitive and cyclical markets, and its technology is process- and cost-oriented rather than product-oriented. At the same time the firm, having five major competitors for primary metal, seems aware that its own output decisions have a certain, if perhaps marginal, influence on market prices. It is worth noting that both the resources of raw materials and the product markets are mostly located in highly developed Western countries.

The international structure of Alusuisse may be said to be determined by four major location factors: (1) bauxite as the primary raw material, (2) electric power for the reduction of alumina to aluminum, (3) markets for products, and (4) management for the planning and scheduling of complex international production and transportation operations. The company is a multinational firm, in part, because the comparative advantages favor different countries for different factors. Another part of the explanation is that the markets for the intermediary inputs at the various stages of production are small and far from perfect compared with the needs of a large firm. At each stage a nonintegrated firm would thus be exposed to the risk of pressure from monopolistic suppliers or customers and of disruption in the flow of raw materials and products.

Before World War II, Alusuisse was a European firm. Directed from headquarters in Switzerland, bauxite from France, Hungary, Rumania, and Yugoslavia was shipped to the sites of cheap coal in Germany for the extraction of alumina, which was in turn reduced to aluminum by hydroelectric power in Switzerland, Germany, and Italy, and the products were sold mainly in the European market. It is worth noting that the firm was, by necessity, multinational from the beginning; the product-cycle model does not apply.

The war and its aftermath deprived Alusuisse of its bauxite base in Eastern Europe. The efforts to build a new resource base made the company a worldwide enterprise. After the development of bauxite mines in Sierra Leone and Guinea, the decisive step was the acquisition and development of extensive bauxite leases in Gove, Australia. This move brought four secondary factors into play. First, under the terms of the lease, the Australian government required Alusuisse to convert a substantial part of its ore into alumina on the site. This requirement imposed an increase in vertical integration in the early stages of production, irrespective of economic efficiency. If the trend continues, it may well result in integrated plants down to primary aluminum, though possibly at the expense of higher production cost, mainly for energy and labor.

Second, the Gove complex produced important scale economies. In order to be efficient the complex had to be planned on a large scale from the start. While plant capacities at subsequent stages were determined by factors largely independent of the size of the alumina plant, the overall smelting capacity had, of course, to be brought into line with the Gove output. This, in turn, required an expansion of capacity in subsequent stages of production where scale economies were somewhat less pronounced. This process is still continuing.

Third, Alusuisse became highly dependent on one source of bauxite. Its dependence created a strong incentive to add another alumina production line, based on Central American ore, through acquisitions in the United States. These acquisitions were, in part, also motivated by exchange-rate considerations. With the Swiss franc thought to be overvalued relative to the dollar, direct investments in the United States seemed a good bargain, and in some lines the U.S. market had to be protected by local production.

Fourth, the extensive prospecting, planning, and engineering operations for these expansions caused the company to assemble a large and varied engineering staff that could not be fully utilized at all times for internal needs. To exploit the resulting scale economies, Alusuisse, besides moving into other mining ventures, began to offer its advisory services commercially. For this purpose it established close cooperation with Motor Columbus, a large consulting firm operating in thirty-four countries. The provision of services thus began to take the place of what otherwise might have become direct investments.

While the rebuilding of the bauxite base with all its ramifications was phase one of postwar developments, phase two was product diversification to reduce market risk. The decisive step was the recent acquisition of the Swiss firm of Lonza Ltd., which made Alusuisse an important producer of organic and inorganic chemicals, plastics, and agro-chemicals.

Taken together, these developments, under an imaginative and audacious management, resulted in a dramatic expansion of Alusuisse. They also seem to have produced a progressive shift of activities away from Switzerland to foreign subsidiaries, though it is difficult to measure numerically. In terms of the value of fixed assets (at cost) such a shift has indeed occurred, the share of Swiss assets declining from 34.5 percent in 1954 to 14.1 percent in 1974. In terms of the labor force, however, no corresponding shift is found, the domestic share being roughly constant at 21 to 23 percent from 1954 to 1973 and actually increasing to 25 percent in 1974 as a consequence of the Lonza merger. The significant trend seems to be that the capital-intensive stages, which are also resource- and energy-intensive, are increasingly located abroad, while the headquarter country tends to retain and develop the more labor- and service-intensive activities.

Swiss Reinsurance
With gross annual premiums of SwF 2.5 billion, Swiss Reinsurance Company is one of the world's largest professional reinsurers. Its market is highly international, with only 7 percent of premium income originating in Switzerland. The international character is essential for reinsurance for two reasons. On the underwriting side, efficient risk management requires diversification across different insurance lines and geographic areas. On the investment side, efficient portfolio management does not require that assets and liabilities be matched in every national market separately but does require that the firm be able to shift assets freely to meet claims in the various national markets.

Of the foreign premium income, about two-thirds are earned by the parent company in Zürich. This income is from receipts for the export of services. The remaining third of foreign premiums is received by foreign subsidiaries, making Swiss Reinsurance a multinational firm. The parent company can be

visualized as supplying its foreign subsidiaries with "intermediary products," consisting of technical and financial management services, while the subsidiaries produce the final product.
The subsidiaries pay for these services in part by routinely
reassigning a fraction of their policies to the parent company,
while another part is reflected in profits.

Swiss Reinsurance established its first branch office in New
York in 1910. The prompt settlement of large claims from the
earthquake of San Francisco, although it cost the company half
of its equity capital, permitted a rapid penetration into the U.S.
market, which had thus far been serviced from Switzerland. By
giving itself a multinational dimension, Swiss Reinsurance pre-
pared to cash in on this marketing success. Today there are
also subsidiaries in the United Kingdom, Canada, Australia, and
South Africa. The multinational dimension thus extends to the
United States and the highly developed members of the British
Commonwealth, while the rest of the world, including Europe,
is mainly serviced from Zürich and partly from the Munich
subsidiary.

From the point of view of the present paper, one of the two
main questions raised by this firm is why Swiss Reinsurance
does not handle all of its foreign business through subsidiaries.
The question is easily answered. In fact, one gets the distinct
impression that the multinational structure is the result of special circumstances rather than of basic economic efficiency.
There are several reasons for such a view. Parent-company
business tends to be more profitable than affiliate business at
the present time. It avoids the problem of double taxation of
profits and can be advantageous from the point of view of exchange and investment restrictions. There are economies of
scale for foreign subsidiaries, a staff of 100 to 200 being necessary to provide the required level of administrative and technical competence. Foreign-investment supervision is more
restrictive for subsidiaries than for the parent company. In
the European Economic Community, subsidiaries also have to
maintain technical reserves. Finally, the direction and control
of large subsidiaries that depend on the parent for virtually
nothing but management may become a rather difficult task. As
a matter of fact, the importance of the foreign subsidiaries,

as measured by their share of premium income, has rather
declined than expanded during the last decade.

The reverse question now arises: Why does Swiss Reinsurance not handle all foreign business from Zürich? The general
answer is that there are indeed special circumstances that justify and even require the multinational dimension. In the United
States, "admitted" companies have a marketing advantage over
foreign companies that is largely, but not entirely, due to
government regulation. In particular, claims of an insurance
company against an admitted reinsurer can be activated on the
balance sheet, while those against a nonadmitted reinsurer
cannot. With the British subsidiary Swiss Reinsurance recog-
nizes London's traditional position as an insurance center. The
South African subsidiary was originally planned as a potential
emergency headquarters in case of war. While this motive has
lost its persuasiveness, the subsidiary has turned out to be a
commercial success in its own right. The Australian subsidiary
owes its existence mainly to fiscal considerations. In the case
of foreign insurers the tax authorities assume that 10 percent
of premium income is profit, while domestic companies are
taxed on the actual profits, which are much lower. Tax considerations also played a role in the establishment of the Canadian subsidiaries, though marketing was more important in this
case. With slight exaggeration it can be said that Swiss Reinsurance is multinational despite itself.

Foreign-exchange fluctuations and restrictions on capital
inflows and outflows have recently added another dimension to
the problem. Under the Bretton Woods system it used to be
fairly evident that certain currencies were "strong" in the sense
that devaluation and restrictions on outflows were unlikely,
while others were "weak" in the sense that revaluation and
restrictions on inflows were not to be expected. Without
incurring significant risks, the portfolio managers of Swiss Reinsurance could thus follow a strategy of going short on weak
currencies while being long on strong currencies. This strategy, to the extent it was feasible under the regulations, proved
to be highly successful, providing a substantial part of the
company's profits. With the transition to floating rates the situation has changed. Open positions are now a two-way street,

and government interventions into foreign payments and investments have become more unpredictable. The floating of exchange rates thus makes increased demands on the central currency and portfolio management and its instantaneous command over relevant market information. At the same time, Swiss Reinsurance sees itself under some pressure to maintain a more balanced position in each currency, which of course reduces the efficiency of risk consolidation. While assets could formerly be concentrated in strong currencies, they now tend to be more diversified. Such a movement illustrates the general proposition that floating rates tend to produce a higher degree of international diversification of assets. If, in the course of time, this diversification should result in an increased emphasis on the multinational structure of Swiss Reinsurance, it would create a counterpart in a service industry of the reduction in the international division of labor that we would expect from floating rates in the exchange of commodities.

Conclusions from Two Counterfactual Hypotheses

Part 1 of this paper presented a brief description of the present role of multinational firms in the Swiss economy. In order to determine the benefits (or costs) to the Swiss economy from these firms one should find out, in principle, what the Swiss economy would look like in the absence of multinational firms. If there were few such firms and if their foreign operations were small compared to their domestic output, this would be relatively easy to determine. One would not err much by simply subtracting the income from foreign operations, leaving everything else unchanged. With multinational firms being in many respects the very basis of the Swiss economy, the problem becomes difficult because in their absence the whole economy would look quite different from what it is today. I shall now use material assembled in the preceding parts to obtain a tentative answer. I proceed by (1) constructing sets of counterfactual conditions that would have been adverse to multinational firms, (2) evaluating the probable effect of these conditions on the development of the sample firms, and (3) drawing conclusions about the repercussions on the Swiss economy. It is clear that the results, relating to the long-term development of the multinational firms and the Swiss economy under hypothetical circumstances, cannot be more than persuasive conjectures.

The discussion will be limited to two situations. In each case the underlying difference between the actual and the counterfactual conditions will be in economic policies, while resources, technologies, scale economies, and the like will be the same. These policy variations are assumed to relate to the world as a whole and not to Switzerland alone. In the first case, the single most important motive for the emergence of Swiss multinational firms is assumed away by postulating a world free from protection. In the second case, multinational firms are assumed to be suppressed by legal prohibition, taxes, or transfer restrictions. In the first case, multinationals have less reason to emerge because the motives for the international separation of successive stages of production are weakened. In the second case they cannot emerge because the successive stages of production, while internationally separated, are in the hands of different firms.

Absence of Protection
In the present section it will be assumed that international trade is free of protectionist impediments to trade. Such freedom means, in particular, that we imagine a world without tariffs, without discrimination against foreign firms in the awarding of contracts, with uniform admission requirements for food, drugs, fertilizers, herbicides, and insecticides, with equal access for domestic and foreign firms to the national insurance market, with nondiscriminatory tax treatment, with fixed exchange rates and free transfer of capital and income across national borders. In economic terms the world would be like one economy.

Some multinational firms would still grow up and prosper in such a world, just as there are multiregional firms in the national economies. However, as the preceding sections have shown, protection is one of the most important determinants of multinationalism. In the absence of protection, therefore, the

number and size of multinationals would be much smaller than
in the world we live in. The question is what the difference
would be for the Swiss economy.

At the present time, the question can only be answered in
qualitative and somewhat speculative terms. I begin with the
five-firm sample. It is my impression that Nestlé would retain
roughly its actual structure. It is true that, in the early history of
Anglo-Swiss, sugar tariffs were an important motive for decentralization. It is also true that the currency and transfer problems of the interwar period were an important factor. However,
the present worldwide structure of the firm seems to be mainly
governed by transportation costs for raw materials and products, by the relatively small size of efficient plants, and by
marketing factors. While the location pattern in our counterfactual world would probably be somewhat different, Switzerland
would still be the headquarters country without being a major
producer or exporter of Nestlé products.

The same argument can be made for the Swiss activities of
Alusuisse, though for different reasons and with some qualifi-
cations. The basic determinant of the firm's international structure, namely raw-material supplies, would not be affected by
the absence of protection. However, in the absence of government requirements the vertical integration of bauxite mining
and alumina production would be reduced; the absence of tariffs would result in a higher concentration at the stage of the
finished product; and the locational pattern of Lonza's chemical output would be more concentrated. Nevertheless, Alusuisse would still be a multinational firm with relatively low,
though somewhat increased, exports from Switzerland.

For Ciba-Geigy, Brown, Boveri & Cie., and Swiss Reinsurance
the hypothetical picture would be radically different. In the absence of national protection they would probably have found it
advantageous to supply their world market largely from Switzerland, maintaining only branch offices in the main markets.
Much of the labor force and capital now employed abroad
would be used in Switzerland. The same would be true for
most other multinational firms in the Swiss manufacturing
sector.

What would be the consequences for the Swiss economy?

They can be listed, though highly tentatively, as follows:

1. The primary effect would be an increased foreign demand for Swiss exports. Multinationalism, conversely, is associated with a decline in the demand for exports.
2. The improvement in the terms of trade would raise Swiss real income.
3. Imports would also be higher, partly because of the increased demand for raw materials and partly because of higher real income.
4. Foreign investment and the receipts from the returns on foreign capital would be lower. As a consequence, the import surplus would also be reduced.
5. Swiss interest rates would be higher relative to foreign rates.
6. Swiss real wages would be higher relative to foreign wages.
7. Since foreign employees of Swiss multinationals, on the average, are now at a somewhat lower level of skills than Swiss workers, the main beneficiaries would be the lower-income groups.
8. The increase in wage and capital costs would weaken the competitive position of present Swiss export industries relative to foreign substitutes.

By and large, the consequences associated with the relative contraction of multinational firms would be clearly beneficial for the Swiss economy in this case. Such a result is evidence of the fact, noted earlier, that for many Swiss firms multinationalism is a second-best solution. It is an effective defense in a protectionist world, but in a world without national protection multinational firms could play a smaller role and still accrue economic benefits. The socially most constructive policy toward multinational firms would be the reduction of those protectionist impediments, discriminatory policies, and national differences in legislation that are the single most powerful force behind their growth.

Suppression of Multinationalism
I shall conclude this study by comparing the actual situation with another counterfactual hypothesis, diametrically opposed to the first. It will now be assumed that all the conditions that

result in vertical specialization of nations (including cost of production, protection, and exchange risk) are in force. On the other hand, it will be assumed that the emergence of multinational firms is effectively prevented by taxation, legal prohibition, or transfer restrictions. There will thus be international trade in intermediate goods, but it cannot be intrafirm trade. By comparing this hypothetical case with the actual situation we obtain an answer to the question of what the suppression of multinationalism would mean for a small economy.

I again begin with a brief review of the sample firms. With the suppression of multinationalism, Nestlé would most likely just disappear in its present form. In its place there might be a medium-sized food-processing firm exporting specialty products like high-quality chocolate from Switzerland. Ciba-Geigy would be forced to concentrate its production in Switzerland. At the same time, however, the firm would be much smaller, thus losing most of the economies of firm scale. In particular, it could not maintain its research effort at anything like its present scale. As a consequence, the firm would probably not be competitive in world markets and might disappear. It was the pressure of competition that forced Ciba and Geigy to seek larger scale economies by merger. At a much reduced scale the firm would hardly be able to withstand that pressure. For its principal products, Brown, Boveri & Cie. would be restricted to the Swiss market for which it could not maintain its present research capacity. The firm might try to remain viable as a secondary supplier of heavy equipment to Swiss utilities through cooperative and licensing arrangements with American or German firms. Alusuisse, as a Swiss firm, would most likely be reduced to the role of a medium-sized producer of finished aluminum products, including foil. Swiss Reinsurance would be the only firm in the sample that would still be recognizable. It would, of course, be much reduced in size, and many of its foreign markets would be lost. However, the business that is now transacted from Zürich would still be essentially intact and would probably permit it to remain viable.

These observations can be generalized. With the suppression of multinationalism, the overwhelming majority of the larger Swiss firms would probably be reduced to a relatively small size or disappear. The fact that there is, at present, not a single export-oriented large firm without foreign operations suggests that such a firm would not be viable in the struggle for survival. The machinery, chemical, and pharmaceutical industries might have a structure more like the watch and textile industries, which lagged behind in the development of large firms and thus saw their competitive position weaken. In the Swiss balance of payments, the share of license and consulting fees would be higher, portfolio investment would take the place of direct investment, and the return on foreign capital would generally be lower. Output and employment would show stronger fluctuations, and exchange risks would be higher. The shift to high-skill technical, financial, and managerial services would be reduced, and the share of manufacturing would be higher. Multinational firms would, to some extent, be replaced by holding companies without control over their foreign investments. Overall, real incomes would be much lower.

The effects of a general suppression of multinationalism would, of course, not be restricted to Switzerland. The basic worldwide effect would be the disappearance of intrafirm trade in intermediate goods and services, while the total volume of trade in goods and services might increase. Direct investments would disappear, while portfolio investment would expand. The international transmission of technology would be slowed down, and the inequality in technology would increase. The volume of market transactions would increase, but a large part would be in highly imperfect markets, disturbed by elements of bilateral monopoly. The main effect, however, would be the loss of economies of firm scale. The loss would be unequally distributed. In the absence of multinationalism there would be a much higher correlation between country size and firm size. Large countries could still have large firms, while small countries would, by and large, be reduced to medium and small firms. The loss of scale economies would thus be concentrated in the small countries, while large-country firms would often gain in competitive strength. Multinationalism helps to equalize the economic opportunities between firms of small and large countries. It is not, as is sometimes argued, a new offensive weapon of large, developed countries to gain economic domi-

nance. It is the traditional defense of small, developed countries to preserve economic equality.

Notes

1. It should be noted that these comparisons are for nominal incomes. If exchange rates in 1959 and 1974 had about the same relationship to purchasing-power parity, they correctly indicate the relative shift in real income
between Switzerland and the United States, but, of course, they do not indicate the improvement in living standards, 1954–1974.

2. While multinationals have often been interpreted as conduits for direct investment, the theory of international capital flows has little to contribute in
this context. The reasons are that (1) the association between multinational
firms and capital flows is unclear, these flows going from headquarters to
subsidiaries in some cases, but in the opposite direction in others and (2) the
theory relates to net flows, while an understanding of multinational firms
requires an analysis of gross flows in both directions.

3. See L. W. McKenzie, "Specialization in Production and the Production
Possibility Locus," Rev. Econ. Stud., vol. 23 (1), no. 60 (1955/56): 56–64;
"Specialization and Efficiency in World Production," Rev. Econ. Stud., vol. 21
(3), no. 56 (1953/54): 165–80; R. W. Jones, "Comparative Advantage and the
Theory of Tariffs—A Multi-Country, Multi-Commodity Model," Rev. Econ.
Stud., vol. 28 (3), no. 77 (1961): 161–75; R. N. Batra and F. R. Casas, "Interme-
diate Products and the Pure Theory of International Trade: A Neo-Heckscher-
Ohlin Frame-work," Amer. Econ. Rev., vol. 63 (June 1973): 297–311; A. G.
Schweinberger, "Pure Traded Intermediate Poducts and the Heckscher-Ohlin
Theorem," Amer. Econ. Rev., vol. 65 (Sept. 1975): 634–43.

4. R. A. Mundell, "International Trade and Factor Mobility," Amer. Econ. Rev.
vol. 47 (June 1957): 321–35.

5. It should be noted that the relevant time horizon in this context is the one
for long-term investment for which no hedging is available.

6. In their demonstration that exchange risk does not matter for conglomerate acquisition and financing decisions, M. Adler and B. Dumas ("Optimal
International Acquisitions," Journal of Finance, vol. 20 [March 1973]) assumed that a merger had no effect on the profits of the component firms. For
the present argument this effect is essential. Thus there is no conflict between the two arguments.

7. This relationship is illustrated by the fact that U.S. direct investments
abroad in 1974, on the basis of Department of Commerce data, were 8.5 percent of GNP, while in Switzerland, on the basis of estimates of the Union
Bank of Switzerland, they amounted to 34.4 percent of GNP.

8. C. P. Kindleberger has credited this view to S. H. Hymer, The International
Operations of National Firms: A Study of Direct Investment (Cambridge,
Mass.: The M.I.T. Press, 1976).

9. It is interesting to note that in the Swiss balance of payments the share of

royalties and license fees in total receipts for goods and services does not exhibit a strongly rising trend.

10. This expectation was emphasized by R. Z. Aliber, "A Theory of Direct Foreign Investment," in C. P. Kindleberger, ed., *The International Corporation* (Cambridge, Mass.: The M.I.T. Press, 1970).

11. Adler and Dumas ("Optimal International Acquisitions") have shown that in a perfect capital market this diversification can be provided by the individual investor, making exchange risk irrelevant for the international integration of firms. In reality, individual investors and firms tend to possess very different access to information, making the market imperfect. Multinational firms, similar to international mutual funds, may thus provide the investor with a more attractive portfolio than he could buy himself.

12. For a history of the firm, see Jean Heer, *World Events, 1866–1966—The First Hundred Years of Nestlé* (Lausanne: Imprimeries Réunies, 1966).

13. On the following argument see H. G. Johnson, "The Efficiency and Welfare Implications of the International Corporation," in C. P. Kindleberger, ed., *The International Corporation*, pp. 35–36.

Comment

Michael Adler

This paper fascinated me. Its interest stems from its synthetic attempt—backed up by cases and based on the theories of trade, imperfect competition, and, partly, international finance—to assess the welfare effects of private foreign investment (PFI). These effects are elusive. PFI is therefore typically analyzed in relation to such partial objectives as restriction. To paraphrase H. G. Johnson, regulations are generally promoted and formulated by fourth-best economists and administered by third-best economists in search of a second-best welfare optimum. It is an honor to be called upon to comment on the first-best analysis that Niehans's paper provides.

The main conclusions of the paper are to my mind appealing. They are twofold and raise interesting questions.

First, assume a classical world with free trade and capital movements, fixed exchange rates, no taxes or equal taxes everywhere, and no discrimination. In the absence of protection in such a one-world economy, multinational firms (MNFs) would not exist in their present number. Transportation costs and scale economies would render viable some large multifacility firms that would be multinational because of the accidental disposition of international borders. Other firms would disappear. Their demise, due to the removal of protection, would, however, be expected to be accompanied by welfare gains everywhere, including Switzerland as the home country.

If, alternatively, the world were ridden by imperfections in the factor, product, and capital markets, any attempt to suppress and eliminate MNFs would be likely to bring about welfare losses especially in the home country and probably elsewhere as well. Niehans gives several reasons for this second conclusion. One that is left unspecific is that MNFs, by virtue of their ability to overcome impediments to trade and to bridge segmented and imperfect markets, probably bring about an allocation of resources that is superior to the one that would exist in their absence.

The trouble with these conclusions is that they are hard to quantify and therefore are likely to leave opponents of the MNF unconvinced. The analysis on which they are based is consistent with Kindleberger's dictum that direct investment belongs more to the theory of industrial organization than to the theory of capital movements. Certainly, PFI is the result, and the MNF is the creature of η imperfections in the international markets for traded goods and, I would add, financial capital. If these imperfections persist, the world indeed may well be better off with MNFs than without them, provided their monopolistic power to discriminate can be curbed. The rub is that it is generally possible to show that each imperfection will affect MNF decisions and their welfare effects in some specific and often complex way that is hard to measure *ex post,* much less *ex ante.* The effects of several imperfections together are even harder to assess and necessarily remain largely unpredictable. In short, my belief is that empirical verification of Niehans's conclusions lies, perhaps hopelessly, far ahead.

Finally, before I discuss specifics, let me say that Niehans's theory does not seem to apply specifically to small investing countries, though he argues that such nations would suffer relatively more from the suppression of MNFs in an imperfect world. If so, one can reverse his proposition and ask the following questions that are germane to the subject of this conference.

If PFI is beneficial to small, advanced countries in a distortion-laden world, how can policy be directed toward generating more such investment? How can every small country create a Nestlé? Is this in fact optimal? Direct investment seems to follow the trade flag around the world. Indeed, Niehans's point of departure is that PFI is a problem in trade. If so, what are the specific ways in which small countries' exports should grow for their firms to gain the scale economies and other market advantages so as to survive as MNCs?

The Analytical Framework
Because of the complexity and intractability of his subject, Niehans's approach is largely taxonomic. PFI is an imperfect-market phenomenon, the explanation for which emerges from

two distinct strands of theory: the theory of trade and international specialization and the industrial organization theory. A third strand, which I personally think is important—the imperfections in the capital markets—is omitted. Before dealing with this last area in more detail, a brief review of Niehans's analytical structure may be useful.

The first question is: What makes a firm multinational? Niehans defines the MNF as an internationally, vertically integrated firm, and a precondition for the emergence of such a firm is a world economy in which international specialization proceeds along vertical lines. A potential problem with this definition is that it seems to rule out international, horizontal integration that would produce international conglomerates. After considerable discussion with Professor Niehans, however, I am persuaded that the definition is sufficiently general, provided that one admits management skills and the knowledge produced by R & D as intermediate products or factors that provide productive services. All PFI can then be viewed as vertical integration. This definition of the MNC is well suited to Niehans's bifurcated taxonomy. Each strand of theory has several parts.

A. The Theory of International Trade and Specialization
i. Comparative costs and differential returns
ii. Scale economies (industry)
iii. Transportation costs
iv. Demand conditions (product life cycles)
v. Trade barriers
vi. Exchange risk

I take very few exceptions to Niehans's discussion of these components. In a multicountry, multicommodity world, comparative-cost theories do not seem to explain trade flows very well, much less PFI, except perhaps in natural-resource-based industries. Correspondingly, PFI does not appear to follow simple differences in rates of return (U.S. PFI in Europe continued after European yields on investment fell below those in the United States). Nor do MNCs tend to specialize in capital-intensive goods, and, therefore, they do not seem to have access to relatively cheap capital. Consequently the imperfections discussed under items two through five are needed to account for the requisite international specialization. In addition the absence of MNC specialization in capital-intensive products weakens the Mundellian case for PFI being the result of countries attracting capital by protecting their capital intensive sectors.[1] However, exchange risk may not account for PFI at all, as I argue below. Something more is needed. What Niehans adds is:

B. Industrial Organization Theory
i. Bilateral-monopoly avoidance
ii. Economies of firm scale
iii. Fluctuating exchange rates

Once again, I find little to disagree with in Niehans's exposition. Except for the third on the list, these additional imperfections will be sufficient to motivate PFI. The difficulty is to determine unambiguously the effect and severity of each and empirically to measure their influence, alone and together.

Capital Market Imperfections and Exchange Risk
If the paper has a flaw, it is that it seems to accept the argument, largely due to Aliber, that exchange risk alone can account in some measure for PFI. I do not think it can in the absence of other imperfections in the capital markets. But these last constitute a third and, I think, necessary addition to the taxonomy.

Niehans seems first to accept the conventional point that exchange risk will reduce the long-run volume of trade. PFI will then substitute for the reduced trade because PFI is less "exposed" than exporting to exchange risk. The latter is exposed to the extent of sales revenues, while PFI exposes only the annual remissions. This argument, it seems to me, might be true were there no forward-exchange markets or if the forward market were imperfect in the sense that traders could not obtain access to forward cover.

The bulk of trade transactions are, however, normally completed within six months and can usually be hedged forward. The volume of such short-term trade transactions will be reduced in the presence of exchange risk by imperfections that make forward cover unavailable to some firms. This effect is likely to be minor in normal times. The point takes on greater substance and the trade reduction will be bigger as the fraction of transactions that take eighteen months or more to clear grows larger. Forward contracts with such long maturities typically do not exist—an imperfection. The exchange-risk exposure, due to the absence of cover for long-term trade transactions, may in fact constitute an incentive for PFI, if, by virtue of being multinational, direct-investing firms can generally undertake balance-sheet hedging decisions on their own that render the existence of a long forward market unnecessary. It is generally believed that MNFs can do this by matching the maturity structures of the cash-flow streams generated by their assets and liabilities. This is the substance of Professor Niehans's point.

Indeed, it is possible for MNFs by appropriate balance-sheet hedging to reduce reported foreign-exchange losses where losses are typically computed as exposed net assets times the exchange-rate change. But to rely on such accounting rules governing exposure may not be optimal or even responsive to the need for the firm to reduce exchange risks on behalf of its stockholders. Note that these rules, inter alia, define as exposed any asset that is denominated in a currency other than the firm's home currency.[2]

The fundamental issue is this: in order for the stockholders of firms in one country to consider their entire foreign-exchange assets on a given date as exposed to exchange risk and in order for them to desire to convert all their foreign claims into home currency, it is necessary to assume that they desire to consume their home goods exclusively. But this desire in and of itself would altogether rule out the need for international trade and for international investment, since individuals' real wealth could never be improved by buying foreign money, financial assets, or goods. In such a setting there is no call for a firm to become multinational to reduce exchange risk.

At the other extreme, assume a world of free trade, capital flows, and exchange rate movements. Purchasing-power parity (PPP) would prevail. Assume that individual investors desire to maximize over time the expected utility of their consumption of a wide mix of traded goods. They will be averse to the risks of

changes in the relative prices of these goods. With PPP, exchange risk ceases to be a separate risk-dimension. If PPP is
breached exogenously, investors will seek to diversify into foreign assets so as to reduce their real purchasing-power risks.
There is still, in this case, no reason for hedging behavior by
firms. Value-maximizing firms will, optimally, diversify internationally only in the presence of imperfections that prevent the
investors from diversifying for themselves. Each imperfection
will bring about a specific, optimal corporate diversification-
decision, which may, however, call for the purchase of financial
rather than real assets.

In short, exchange risk need not, in the absence of additional
capital-market imperfections, motivate the international diversification of production by firms. Niehans seems to agree with
this point. In addition, however, it is highly improbable—even
could one identify relevant imperfections—that exchange risk
could account in any measurable or predictive fashion for the
international spread of PFI. As Niehans points out, it may be
one factor among many, though to my mind it is less important
than to his. The anticipated reduction in exchange risk that his
Swiss managers hoped to obtain via direct foreign investment
may therefore be partly illusory.

A relevant question is then: What kind of imperfections in the
financial markets, in addition to the risk of deviations of exchange rates from PPP, are required to bring about PFI? Some
confusion has arisen over this matter. It is important to realize
that one can reach any desired result by choosing the right imperfection. The Aliber theory, alluded to by Niehans, is a case
in point.[3]

The Aliber argument is that the market for stocks and bonds
is imperfect in such a fashion that differentials between interest
rates and yields on equities exceed expected exchange-rate
changes. If yields are sufficiently low in the strong currency
(SC) area, there is an incentive for financial investment in the
weak currency (WC) area.[4] But no convincing reason is given
for the existence or direction of the imperfection that might alternatively cause the currency premium to run the other way.
Indeed, if in fact the WC-area government is willing to absorb
reserve losses by intervening in the exchange market so as to

avoid high domestic interest rates, the interest differential
could well fall below the expected exchange-rate change.
There will then be an incentive for financial investment in the
reverse direction. Funds will be borrowed in the WC and invested in the SC. This incentive will be perfectly general; initially it
should affect portfolio investment by individuals. Firms' decisions will be affected only if individuals' portfolio investments
are restricted. But even if this last is the case, the result may
only be corporate portfolio investment, not necessarily direct
investment.

Firms always have optimal real investment decisions to make
because investors cannot invest directly for themselves—the result of an imperfection in the market for projects. In otherwise
perfect markets, however, it is reasonably easy to show that the
MNFs' risk-adjusted, required yields on investment, either portfolio or direct, will be independent of geographical variables
and of the selection of currency numeraires. Restrictions that
prohibit individuals from diversifying for themselves will create
an optimal portfolio-investment decision for the firm to make
on their behalf. This acquisition of foreign stock need not become direct investment unless some additional imperfection
necessitates the purchase of something akin to control. Thus,
for example, say not only that U.S. individual investment
abroad is restricted while corporate investment is not, but that
the information available to all U.S. portfolio investors in foreign securities is limited. Say the MNF, by buying control of
foreign firms, can acquire sufficient access to equate the
amounts of information available to its stockholders in all capital markets. Its ability to bridge the double imperfection, that is,
both the constraint on individual foreign diversification and the
information gap, will create the incentive for the MNF to undertake direct rather than merely portfolio investment. And while
portfolio investment alone need not follow vertical lines, the
fact that, when making acquisitions, corporate managements
tend to specialize in information and knowledge is likely to
support Niehans's vertical integration scenario.

Summary

Professor Niehans may well be right that his two-pronged tax-onomy of imperfections in the traded-goods markets and com-petition among firms is sufficiently comprehensive to cover the growth of Swiss MNFs. He himself suggests that the taxonomy may not be exhaustive. If my comment has had an objective, it has been to add capital-market considerations to Professor Niehans's list of determinants of multinationalism. There are two parts to this addition. First, exchange risk is not an imper-fection in the traded-goods market, and it does not bring about imperfect competition. It is probably best viewed as a financial-market phenomenon and is, therefore, improperly classified with the others. Second, exchange risk that can exist in perfect markets, though not independently of purchasing power risk, will not in and of itself cause direct investment. It can do so only in the presence of additional capital-market imperfections, which give rise to optimal MNF decisions.

In conclusion, one must naturally wonder what steps are re-quired or even whether it is possible to transform a taxonomic description of the determinants of PFI into a solid, empirically based explanation. The longer the list, the harder the task. It lies ahead.

Notes

1. This point can partly be rescued if one views management and knowledge as capital-intensive, intermediate goods that serve also as factors. Then, fol-lowing Johnson, firms with a monopoly on specialized factors will behave like discriminating monopolists in the product markets. They will extend produc-tion to any protected foreign market that offers a positive profit.

2. Clearly, the accounting rules also assume that purchasing-power parity governs the prices of real assets in various countries. They therefore do not allow either for the possibility of long-run misalignments of exchange rates—as was the case under Bretton Woods—or for the real effects of exchange-rate changes. If these last make more profitable firms producing traded goods, losses on exposed assets may be offset by gains in future profitability.

3. The issue to be discussed is quite separate from a persistent misalignment of exchange-rate levels that can cause production costs in one area to be lower than in another and in itself motivate PFI. The overvaluation of the U.S. dollar during the late fifties and sixties was presumably an important factor contributing to "excessive" U.S. investment overseas.

4. Even in perfect markets the interest differential will not be equal to the expected percentage of exchange-rate change unless the exchange rate is independent of the world market index.

2. Company Policies for International Expansion: The Swedish Experience

Sune Carlson

Introduction

According to a recent study made by the Industrial Institute for Economic and Social Research (IUI), 236 Swedish industrial firms had in 1970 altogether 1,424 sales and manufacturing subsidiaries abroad (Swedenborg 1973, p. 35). The study covered all Swedish industrial firms with 50 or more employees in Sweden. Not included were firms in building and construction industry, trade and transport, banking and insurance, and other services. Compared with industrial firms, these latter firms were much more national in character. The 236 firms mentioned made up a considerable part of Swedish industry, with regard to both employment and exports. Those which had manufacturing units abroad, 107 in number, employed around 380,000 people in their home plants in 1970, which was more than 40 percent of the national industrial work force. Their foreign employees exceeded 180,000. The contribution of these firms to Swedish industrial exports was even greater. It is estimated at 55 percent; if we add the exports of the 129 firms that had sales subsidiaries but did no manufacturing abroad, the figure increases to 73 percent (Ibid., p. 30).

The influence of the Swedish international firms on the foreign-trade transactions can best be illustrated by some figures from a special customs inquiry that has been carried out by the Statistical Office. In 1973, of the total value of the country's exports, 69.3 percent was contributed by Swedish firms with subsidiaries in at least one foreign country, and 33.3 percent by firms with subsidiaries in more than ten countries. The corresponding figures for imports were 35.5 and 14.8 percent (Lundgren 1975, p. 62).

The impact of the international firms on the Swedish economy is mainly felt through their influence on exports and thereby on the balance of payments. Of course, their activities also affect the service and capital transactions of the balance of payments, but these accounts are much smaller than the trade accounts. The international firms are also important for industrial employment, but their share of the total labor force is relatively small.

Since the creation of the European Free Trade Area (EFTA), there has been a certain amount of "textile imperialism." Some Swedish textile firms have established production units in Finland and Portugal to supply the Swedish home market, but the investments have been small and their employment effects of little significance. Unlike many American and British international firms, Swedish firms have rarely invested in foreign raw-material explorations, and when they have done so, it has mainly been in order to serve foreign markets or production units in foreign countries. Swedish industry has been built up on local mining, forestry, and water-power resources, and its international firms have primarily been market-oriented. Its international expansion has been determined by the struggle for foreign markets.

The Internationalization Process

It was during the decades before the First World War that the major export industries of modern Sweden, pulp and paper and mechanical engineering, started to penetrate the international markets (see Table 2.1). Several of the international firms—AGA Aktilbolag (AGA), Alfa-Laval, Allmäna Svenska Elektriska Aktilbolaget (ASEA), L. M. Ericsson, Sandvik, and AB Svenska Kullagerfabriken (SKF)—names that will appear later on in this essay—established their first foreign subsidiaries at that time. The internationalization process was more or less parallel to the industrialization process itself. Industrialization came late in Sweden, but its progress was rapid. In 1870 the contribution to national income from manufacturing, mining, and handicrafts was less than 15 percent (Lindahl, Dahlgren, & Koch 1937, Table 48). Ten years later, it was still below 20 percent, but in 1910 it had increased to over 30 percent.

As can be seen from Table 2.1, the predominant products in Swedish industrial exports at the end of the century were wood products and steel. These exports were handled primarily by

Table 2.1. The Distribution of Swedish Exports in Certain Branches of Industry, 1871–1971, as Percentages of Total Exports

	Agriculture and Forestry	Mining	Iron and Steel Industry	Forestry Industry		Mechanical-Engineering Industry, Incl. Electrical Engineering	Other Exports
				Wood Industry, Incl. Furniture	Pulp and Paper Industry		
1871	33.9	0.1	25.2	29.4	1.4	0.3	9.7
1891	16.6	1.3	13.6	33.4	6.0	1.5	27.6
1911	8.5	7.8	11.4	23.1	19.0	7.2	23.0
1931	1.9	5.7	6.4[a]	14.8	30.9	21.2[a]	19.1
1951	2.9	6.7	5.3	11.8	42.5	21.4	9.4
1971[b]	3.1	3.8	7.5	6.0	15.7	43.2	20.7

Sources: For the years 1881–1951, Lennart Ohlsson, *Utrikeshandeln och den ekonomiska tillväxten i Sverige 1871–1966*, Uppsala 1969, Table B:6. For the year 1971, *Statistisk Årsbok 1972*, Table 128.

[a] In 1930, certain product groups were reclassified; the percentage figure for the iron and steel industry was lowered and that for the mechanical-engineering industry was increased by a little more than 3 percent.

[b] Since the 1971 figures have been taken from another source, they may not be fully comparable to the earlier figures.

merchant houses in Gothenburg and Stockholm, which were also important suppliers of working capital to the exporting firms (Gårdlund 1947, chap. 5). There were few direct contacts between the Swedish sawmills and steel mills and the users of their products abroad, and the knowledge in these mills of foreign markets and of how to do business with foreigners must have been very limited. This isolation was natural. For their supplies of timber or charcoal the mills were dependent on the forests in their immediate surroundings. They were small and scattered, far from the trading and financial centers. To be able to rely on an internationally known merchant house in one of the big ports, both for sales and for credit advances, was most convenient. Also the larger sawmills along the coast in the north, which sometimes had their own sales agents abroad, used Swedish merchant houses as sources of finance. Thus, while Sweden's industrial exports were growing at this time, the country had no international industrial firms of the type that it later developed.

This kind of indirect export worked satisfactorily, as long as the firms produced standardized goods that could be sold in an expanding market. Such goods contained little or no software, and they needed little or no transfer of technical information between the producers and the users. For a long time this was the case with wood products, and for some time also with pulp and paper, which were gradually to become the leading export products of the forestry industry.

The situation was different with steel. By the middle of the last century, Sweden's old position as steel supplier to the international market had been shaken. New steel-making methods made it possible to use coke instead of charcoal, and the fact that the ores were free from phosphorus was no longer so important as far as ordinary steel was concerned. If Swedish mills using charcoal and expensive, phosphorus-free ores were to survive, they had to go over to making special steel of such technical superiority that it would fetch much higher prices than ordinary steel. Such a conversion required increased product differentiation, intimate knowledge of market developments, and an adaptation of the products to the customers' particular needs. For these purposes the old practice of selling through merchant houses was inadequate. That the Swedish steel industry actually succeeded in this painful adaptation process was to be important not only for the steel firms themselves but also for the mechanical-engineering industry that later developed. The international reputation of Swedish high-quality steel proved a great help in the export of engineering products.

The first firm to break with the old export traditions was Sandvik, which had established its first agency abroad as early as 1865. By 1870 the company had a network of agents covering not only the neighboring countries, Denmark and Norway, but also Germany, the United Kingdom, France, and Switzerland (Carlson 1937). These agents were regularly invited to technical briefings at the mill, and people from the mill visited the agents and their major customers for technical and commercial consultations. As Johanson found in his study of steel exports, the purchasing situation of industrial buyers of high-quality steel is characterized by stable and intimate contacts between the buyers and the sellers (Johanson 1966). The cost of change in getting a new supplier may be considerable when one does not know how he will behave with regard to quality control, delivery dates, and the handling of complaints. But direct contacts with the buyers meant that the steel mill representatives needed to know foreign languages and foreign ways of doing business. These changes required investments in human resources. They also meant increased investments in working capital. Trade credits had now to be financed by the steel company itself.

Later on, Sandvik's export policy was to be followed by the other high-quality steel mills, and in due time also by most of the exporters in the forestry industry.

For the mechanical-engineering industry, the need for direct contacts with the customers was even greater than for the steel mills. Around the turn of the century, a series of important inventions had led to the establishment of L. M. Ericsson, 1876, telephones; Alfa Laval, 1883, separators; ASEA, 1891, three-phase generators and motors; AGA, 1904, lighthouses and acetylene batteries; and SKF, 1907, spherical ball and roller bearings (Söderlund 1967). All were manufacturers of producer goods that had an important software content and that in many cases had to be adapted to the needs of individual users. Thus, from the very beginning these companies became heavily marketing-oriented, and for their exports they became dependent on a network of agents abroad. Seven years after its establishment, SKF already had its own representatives in twenty-seven different countries (Lundgren 1975, p. 86).

Once the contacts with the customers had been established, and the prospective sales seemed large enough to cover the cost, a sales subsidiary became a more favorable alternative than an independent agent. The selling and servicing of software-intensive products required technical specialists, and for the agents, with their uncertain future position, investment in such specialists was not always possible. Since the customers' requirements could vary greatly between different countries, the sending out of traveling sales engineers from the export companies in Sweden was not always enough. Often the companies had to place their own people in the agencies and to support the agents with equipment and spare parts. Later on when the agency was transferred to a wholly owned sales subsidiary, this transfer represented merely the final legal step in a gradual organizational process that had been going on for some time. The process was similar for Sandvik and the other companies in the specialized steel industry.

In the forestry industry, the establishment of sales subsidiaries came much later and had a different background. Pulp and paper are mostly homogeneous products, and the market position in Europe of the Scandinavian forestry industry had been that of a homogeneous oligopoly. The exporting mills had protected themselves against market uncertainty by gentlemen's agreements of various kinds, and the traditional agency system seems to have worked quite well. But at the end of the 1950s market stability was upset by the entry of the North American pulp and paper industry, and this new competition required more aggressive marketing efforts than before. In 1955, there were only seven sales subsidiaries of the Swedish forestry companies in Western Europe and seven in the United States and Latin America (Forsgren & Kinch 1970, p. 186), but during

the following fifteen years the number in Western Europe
increased by twenty-two.

The uncertainty that the forestry firms felt in the new situation led gradually to vertical integration between some of the
Swedish mills and their major customers, particularly in the
fields of corrugated cardboard and paper bags. These were
products for which the demand could be stabilized by product
differentiation, which meant that pulp and paper deliveries
from the parent companies could also be stabilized. Some customers were bought up entirely; in other cases Swedish companies acquired majority or minority interests. In a few cases,
entirely new conversion plants were built. Thus, during the period 1964–71, eight forestry companies established altogether
twenty-four wholly or partially owned production subsidiaries in
Europe, of which six and five respectively were located in the
two most important markets, the United Kingdom and West
Germany (Kinch 1974, p. 74). To two of the companies, Biller-
uds and SCA, these new subsidiary companies meant a great
deal with respect to their total Swedish exports. According to
Kinch, however, the main advantage of this forward integration
for the forestry industry was better market knowledge and increased possibilities for influencing product development in
the pulp- and paper-consuming industries.

As mentioned at the beginning of this paper, Swedish industry had been built up on local raw-material resources. Thus far,
the forestry industry has also relied on local resources. But if
the international market expansion is to continue as it has
done until now, Sweden's forestry resources will be inadequate. In order to safeguard their future expansion, some of
the largest forestry companies have begun to invest, mainly
through joint ventures, in pulp mills in countries with a more
favorable raw-material situation. But this development is so
recent that it is difficult, as yet, to judge its significance and
future prospects.

Let us return to the mechanical-engineering industry, which
is the fastest-developing international sector of the economy.
Once the engineering firms had got their own sales subsidiaries abroad for the marketing and servicing of their software-

intensive products, their extended operations frequently required local alterations and repairs of the goods exported from Sweden. Thus, some kind of engineering workshop had to be set up, and the establishment of such facilities led, quite naturally, to the next step, local assembly and production of spare parts. Bulky components with high transport costs were often cheaper to produce in the country of sale than to import, and tariff and nontariff barriers were often less for semifinished than for finished products. Later on, when the market had expanded and economies of scale were obtainable, these local workshops could be extended to form fully developed manufacturing plants. In some cases, it was more advantageous to take over an already existing manufacturing company. Thus, in the same way that the changeover from an agent to a fully owned sales subsidiary was a gradual process, the change of a sales subsidiary into a manufacturing subsidiary often happened step by step, and it was frequently difficult to state exactly when it actually took place.

In their study of the internationalization of Sandvik, Atlas Copco, Facit, and Volvo, Johanson and Wiedersheim-Paul introduce the concept "establishment chain" for this gradual change from no regular export to agents, sales subsidiaries, and production subsidiaries. They find that this chain is characteristic of the firms' penetration in individual countries (Johanson & Wiedersheim-Paul 1975). Of the four firms, Sandvik and Atlas Copco sell exclusively to industrial buyers, and their products have a relatively high software content. This is not so for Facit and Volvo, a substantial part of whose sales is consumer durables. Altogether, the four firms have sixty-three sales subsidiaries and thirty-seven production subsidiaries abroad. Of the sixty-three sales subsidiaries, fifty-six were preceded by agents, and the pattern was the same for all the firms. Of the thirty-seven production subsidiaries, twenty-eight were preceded by sales subsidiaries, and in no case did a firm start production in a country without first having had either a sales subsidiary or an agent there before. But there was a difference between the firms that sold software-intensive products to industrial buyers and the two others. For Sandvik and Atlas Copco twenty-two out of twenty-seven production subsidiaries were preceded by sales subsidiaries; for Facit and Volvo the corresponding figures were six out of ten.

The International Firms

The weekly magazine *Veckans Affärer* annually publishes statistics about the two hundred largest Swedish firms in industry and trade with data on their total sales turnovers, their total sales abroad (defined as "exports from Sweden plus sales by foreign plants, less any inter-company deliveries between the Swedish divisions and the foreign entities"), and their total exports from Sweden. Similar statistics, but only on total sales, are published by the international magazine *Vision* for the five hundred largest European firms. Since this latter publication started in 1971, I have selected that year in the following study (*Veckans Affärer,* no. 27, 3 August 1972 and *Vision,* October 1972, Edition en français no. 23). It would have been of value to use the year 1970, since that was the year used in the IUI study mentioned above, but the situation probably did not change much in one year, and it seemed to me more important for the readers to get some idea of the sizes of the various firms mentioned. Now they can see, for example, from Figure 2.2 that, while Volvo is the second largest Swedish firm, it comes only in the 71st place in the *Vision* list, and Svenska Fläktfabriken, which is number 51 in Sweden, is only number 418 in Europe. Volvo's total sales were $1,268 million, while the sales of the second largest in Europe, Unilever, were $7,997 million.

The *Veckans Affärer* list contains some firms in trade, transport, building and construction, and some other industries that are of no interest in this connection. If they are excluded, there remain 117 firms that belong to what might be called the export industries—37 in mechanical-engineering industry, 20 in the forestry industry and 60 in the rest of industry (see Table 2.2). The latter group includes the steel industry and the very old firms that in Swedish are called *bruk,* that is, firms with activities in the steel industry, forestry industry, power production, and agriculture all based on locally owned natural resources. These 117 firms had in 1971 total foreign sales of nearly SKr 47 billion of which 28 billion were export sales. This

Table 2.2. The 117 Largest Swedish Firms in the Export Industry in 1970

| | No. of Firms | Total Foreign Sales, Millions SKr | Percentage of Total Sales | | |
			Total Foreign Sales	Net Sales from Foreign Plants	Exports from Sweden
Mechanical-engineering industry (SKr) Total sales:					
1,000 mill. and more	9	20,290	68.8	37.3	31.5
500–999 mill.	6	2,298	50.2	23.8	26.4
Less than 500 mill.	22	2,180	39.4	15.6	23.8
Group total	37	24,758	62.5	33.0	29.5
Forestry industry Total sales:					
1,000 mill. and more	3	2,335	64.5	7.2	57.5
500–999 mill.	4	2,183	70.4	7.3	63.1
Less than 500 mill.	13	1,137	40.8	—	40.8
Group total	20	5,655	59.5	5.1	54.4
Other industries Total sales:					
1,000 mill. and more	13	12,299	32.0	9.4	22.6
500–999 mill.	11	2,193	26.7	8.8	17.9
Less than 500 mill.	36	1,902	22.7	9.4	13.3
Group total	60	16,394	29.8	9.3	20.5
Total industry Total sales:					
1,000 mill. and more	25	34,924	48.8	20.8	28.0
500–999 mill.	21	6,674	42.0	13.6	28.4
Less than 500 mill.	71	5,219	31.2	9.9	21.3
Total	117	46,817	44.9	17.9	27.0

Source: *Veckans Affärer*, no. 27, 3 August 1972.

amount represented nearly 75 percent of the total Swedish exports.

As can be seen from the table, the shares both of exports and of total foreign sales in general increase with the size of the firm. In a small country like Sweden if a firm in a particular industry wants to expand beyond a certain limit, it has to ex-

plore foreign markets. But in such a typical export industry as
the forestry industry we may also find a firm like the Southern
Sweden Forestry Cooperative that is the third largest but has
foreign sales of only around 39 percent.

In Figure 2.1 the individual firms are distributed with respect
to their total foreign sales, expressed as percentages of their
total sales. Again, we can see that, at least in the mechanical-
engineering and the forestry industries, it is difficult to grow
without penetrating into foreign markets. Firms with total foreign sales of 50 percent or more will be classified here as international firms, and it is these international firms that I shall
deal with from now on. There are several reasons why I have
chosen such a classification. First, I have been influenced by
the availability of data. Secondly, the classification fits the general theme of this paper rather well. As has been mentioned,
the internationalization of Swedish industry has basically been
determined by the struggle for foreign markets. The percentage
of sales abroad reflects pretty well the successes or failures in
this struggle. Thirdly, when we speak of the share of foreign
sales, it is quite clear what we mean. For example, if I had used
as my criterion for an international firm the number of countries in which the firm had foreign subsidiaries, I would have
run into all kinds of interpretation difficulties. Should I have
taken only production subsidiaries or included sales subsidiaries as well? We have seen that many times the borderline between these categories is rather vague, as is the borderline
between sales subsidiaries and independent agents. I have set
the limit at 50 percent and above because a foreign operation
of such a size must certainly have an influence on the firm's
policies and organizational structures.

According to the definitions chosen, there were altogether
thirty-five international firms, but for one of them, Atlas Copco,
separate data on export sales and foreign-subsidiary sales are
not available. Therefore, Table 2.3 contains only thirty-four
firms. Of these, fourteen had total sales of SKr 1,000 million
and more, nine between SKr 500 and SKr 1,000 million and
eleven less than SKr 500 million. But, in spite of the fact that
so many relatively small firms were included, the total exports

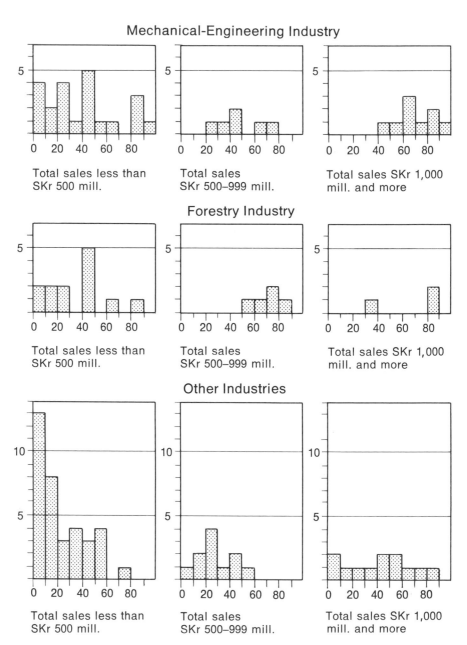

Figure 2.1. Number of firms distributed with regard to their foreign sales as percentages of their total sales

Table 2.3. The International Firms in 1970

	No. of Firms	Total Foreign Sales, Millions SKr	Percentage of Total Sales		
			Total Foreign Sales	Net Sales from Foreign Plants	Exports from Sweden
Mechanical-engineering industry	14	19,327	72.5	39.2	33.3
Forestry industry	9	4,434	73.2	8.0	65.2
Other industries	11	9,462	60.5	24.7	35.8
Total	34	33,223	68.7	30.6	38.1

of the thirty-four firms were approximately half of the total Swedish exports.

In Figures 2.2, 2.3, and 2.4, I have plotted the international firms with respect to (1) total foreign sales, (2) exports from Sweden, and (3) net sales from foreign subsidiaries, which are merely the differences between the two previous items.

The diagrams should be read in the following way. The parallel lines indicate total foreign sales: the horizontal axis, exports and the vertical axis, subsidiary sales. If we are on a particular parallel line, for example, the 50 percent line, and move left and upward, this means that the foreign subsidiaries' share of the same total foreign sales increases. There are lines indicating when these shares exceed 25, 50, and 75 percent respectively, and I shall talk in relation to these lines about the lower, the middle, and the upper sectors of the diagrams.

In examining the diagrams one should remember two things. First, while the phrase "exports from Sweden" says exactly what is involved, the term "sales from foreign subsidiaries" may indicate quite different things for different firms. Swedish Match's operations in India, where it has nearly 10,000 employees—more than it has in Sweden—are, of course, something entirely different from Stenberg-Flygt's marketing and service subsidiaries in Europe or Canada. Second, the diagrams describe the relative positions of the firms only in the year 1971.

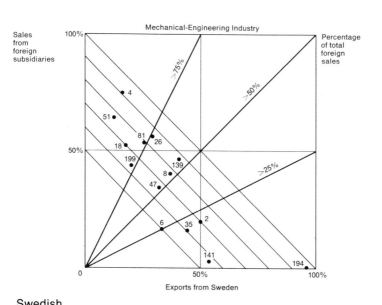

Swedish
Size   European
Ranking   Size
(*Veckans*   Ranking
Affärer)   (*Vision*)   Name of Firm

Total sales SKr 1,000 mill. and more

2	71	AB Volvo
4	88	AB Svenska Kullagerfabriken (SKF)
6	109	ASEA
8	115	Telefon AB L. M. Ericsson
18	187	AB Elektrolux
26	235	Alfa-Laval AB
35	331	Kockums Mekaniska Verkstads AB

Total sales SKr 500–999 mill.

| 47 | 381 | Facit AB |
| 51 | 418 | AB Svenska Fläktfabriken |

Total sales less than SKr 500 mill.

81		Elektriska Svetsnings AB (ESAB)
139		Stenberg-Flygt AB
141		Elema-Schönander AB
194		AB Sundsvalls Verkstäder
199		Billman-Regulator AB

Figure 2.2. Firms in the mechanical engineering industry with more than 50 percent of foreign sales, distributed with regard to (a) their sales from foreign subsidiaries and (b) their exports from Sweden as percentages of their total foreign sales

They tell us nothing about how long it has taken them to reach this position. In order to understand the internationalization process, we would need to make a historical analysis of every firm of the type that Johanson and Wiedersheim-Paul have made. Irrespective of the forces that have led to internationalization, we may expect to find the early starters like SKF and AGA, which have passed through all or most of the stages of the establishment chain on many markets, higher up in the diagrams than newcomers like Volvo or the forestry companies. In spite of these drawbacks the diagrams still seem to illustrate some of the most important features of the Swedish international firms.

First of all, of the thirty-four firms, there are only three that can be classified primarily as producers of consumer goods. The oldest of these is Elektrolux, which started producing vacuum cleaners just before the First World War and, after having built up an efficient marketing organization in the postwar years, became one of the leading, if not the leading, vacuum cleaner manufacturer in Europe with factories first in Germany and France and later in Great Britain (*Affärsvärlden,* 24 May 1928). Utilizing its marketing organization, the company later diversified into floor polishers and refrigerators (the latter based on a Swedish invention, the Platon-Munthe patent) and still later into other consumer durables, such as stoves, dishwashers, and washing machines. In addition, the company operates a considerable commercial and industrial cleaning service, with more than five thousand people employed in seventeen countries (Lundgren 1975, p. 165). Since 1971, Elektrolux has diversified its activities further through the purchase of Facit.

The other two consumer-goods firms are relative latecomers. Wasabröd, which produces hard rye bread, has, after a successful market penetration on the European continent, started production in West Germany. Mölnlycke, a manufacturer of diapers and sanitary napkins, services its foreign sanitary-goods markets from local production units, which seems natural for such bulky products.

Swedish Match has also been a consumer-goods industry from the beginning, having built up match monopolies around

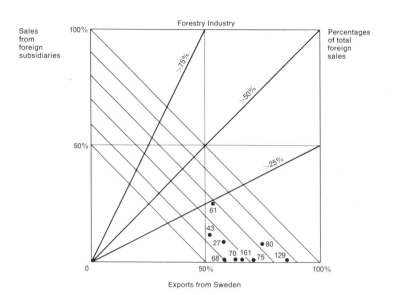

Swedish Size Ranking (*Veckans Affärer*)	European Size Ranking (*Vision*)	Name of Firm
Total sales SKr 1,000 mill. and more		
27	259	Svenska Cellulosa AB (SCA)
43	362	Mo och Domsjö AB (MoDo)
Total sales SKr 500–999 mill.		
61	473	Billeruds AB
68		Norrlands Skogsägares Cellulosa AB
70		AB Iggesunds Bruk
75		Holmens Bruk AB
80		Korsnäs-Marma AB
Total sales less than SKr 500 mill.		
129		Kopparfors AB
161		Rottneros AB

Figure 2.3. Firms in the forestry industry with more than 50 percent of foreign sales distributed with regard to (a) their sales from foreign subsidiaries and (b) their exports from Sweden as percentages of their total sales

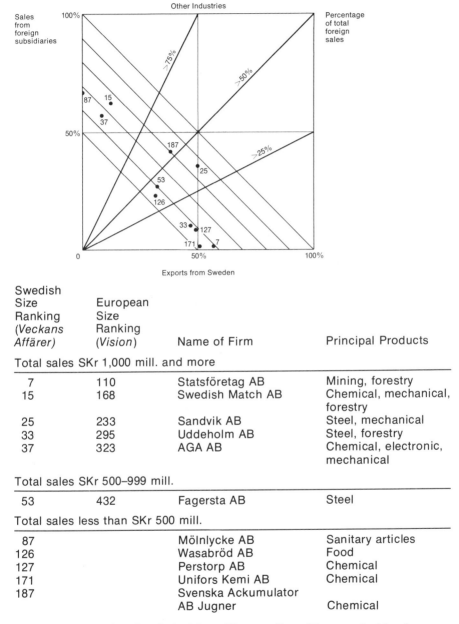

Figure 2.4. Firms in other industries with more than 50 percent of foreign sales distributed with regard to (a) their sales from foreign subsidiaries and (b) their exports from Sweden as percentages of their total sales

Swedish Size Ranking (*Veckans Affärer*)	European Size Ranking (*Vision*)	Name of Firm	Principal Products
Total sales SKr 1,000 mill. and more			
7	110	Statsföretag AB	Mining, forestry
15	168	Swedish Match AB	Chemical, mechanical, forestry
25	233	Sandvik AB	Steel, mechanical
33	295	Uddeholm AB	Steel, forestry
37	323	AGA AB	Chemical, electronic, mechanical
Total sales SKr 500–999 mill.			
53	432	Fagersta AB	Steel
Total sales less than SKr 500 mill.			
87		Mölnlycke AB	Sanitary articles
126		Wasabröd AB	Food
127		Perstorp AB	Chemical
171		Unifors Kemi AB	Chemical
187		Svenska Ackumulator AB Jugner	Chemical

the world. As a result of a series of diversifications, however, matches represent today only 15 percent of the company's business. On the basis of its vast knowledge and experience in the field of international business and foreign marketing, Swedish Match has gradually acquired subsidiaries for the production of building materials, packaging, paper, and mechanical products in a large number of countries.

But the consumer-goods producers, as well as Swedish Match, represent exceptions to the typical internationalization pattern. As has been described above, there are really two patterns, one in the mechanical-engineering and special-steel industries and another in the forestry industry. The difference between Figures 2.2 and 2.3 is striking. While all nine forestry firms are situated in the lowest part of the diagram, only four out of fifteen firms in mechanical engineering are in equal positions. Of these, Elema-Schönander and Sundsvalls Verkstäder are subsidiary companies of foreign concerns and can use their parent companies' marketing organizations. Kockums is mainly a shipyard, and Volvo is a firm that needs an efficient international marketing organization but has, as yet, most of its production located in Sweden. ASEA, finally, specializes in heavy electrical machinery with large unit sales that require technical services directly from the parent company.

If we look at the upper part of Figure 2.2 we find—besides Elektrolux—SKF (ball and roller bearings), Fläktfabriken (air conditioning), and Billman (control instruments), all of which have software-intensive products. SKF, being an old-timer, has large manufacturing plants in West Germany, France, Great Britain, and the United States. ESAB (electrical welding machinery) also has a software-intensive production. One of its products, electrodes, has, in addition, high transport costs in relation to price and often meets with considerable tariff and nontariff barriers.

The latter holds true also of L. M. Ericsson (telecommunications), which is in the middle sector. There we find Alfa Laval and Stenberg-Flygt, which both, like L. M. Ericsson, have software-intensive products, and Facit, which is more difficult to explain. The position of Stenberg-Flygt is interesting, since, like Elema-Schönander and Sundsvalls Verkstäder, it is part of a foreign concern. It kept its independent marketing organization abroad even after it was bought up.

The forestry industry in Figure 2.3 needs no further comment. As can also be seen from Table 3, it has a very high export but a low foreign-subsidiary sales percentage.

Finally, if we turn to "Other industries," Figure 2.4, two of the firms in the upper sector, Swedish Match and Mölnlycke, have already been mentioned. The third firm in this sector, AGA, started to export lighthouses and, in order to supply them with acetylene it had to build gas plants in most of the markets. This was the beginning of an industrial-gas business with production units in Europe and Latin America. AGA also has other product lines, most of which require extensive marketing and technical services. Of the firms in the middle sector, Wasabröd has already been mentioned. Otherwise, we mainly find in this and in the lower sector firms in the steel and the chemical industries.

Company Policies

The company policies that have led to the internationalization of Swedish industry have, of course, been influenced by the characteristics of the country and its citizens. Sweden is a small country with a homogeneous and well-educated population, a highly skilled labor force, and a small establishment in which everybody knows everybody else, not only in industry but also among industry, the government, and the trade unions. The limited home market makes industry dependent on other countries for imports and exports and also for new ideas and intellectual stimulus in general. This dependence is true of the whole Swedish culture. As a famous poet said a long time ago: "Only the barbarian once had a national origin." Contacts with foreign countries and knowledge of foreign languages are essential. Most of the textbooks on technology and economics, for example, were formerly written in German and are today written in English. It seems that technological processes, once they have been started in another country, spread quickly to Sweden. The large foreign trade, the low degree of protection, and the keen competition from abroad, together with the close personal contacts within the Swedish industrial establishment, favor rapid adaptation of technical innovations (Nabseth 1974). The Swedes have sometimes been called the Japanese of Europe.

Both government relations and labor relations have so far been favorable to the internationalization process. Since internationalization mostly meant increased exports and the Swedish government, like most governments, favored export expansion, there has been little interference with the firms' establishment plans. On the contrary, Swedish diplomats and trade commissioners abroad have generally been most helpful in this area. The fact that Sweden has been the leading country in getting bilateral tax agreements with other countries has, of course, also been important. Foreign-exchange control may have caused some inconveniences, but, on the whole, the authorities have shown a great understanding of the firms' establishment plans. Until 1974 only the foreign-exchange and monetary-policy implications of proposed investments had to be considered. Since then, the authorities have also been examining the effects of proposed investments abroad on employment in Sweden, but what consequences this change will have are difficult to predict.

The favorable attitude toward the firms' international expansion plans on the part of the trade unions has, of course, also been of great importance, as have the stable labor relations in general. Swedish labor unions have been uniquely productivity-minded. Their wage-equalization policies have favored the transfer of people from low-wage industries, even though this meant hardships for the individual workers. The successful government retraining program and the low rate of unemployment have made union members much less conscious of redundancy problems than in most other countries. The unions have lately obtained representatives on the boards of directors of the international companies, but this seems not to have affected the companies' plans to expand abroad, at least not as yet. What will happen in the future is difficult to tell. Of course, their close cooperation with the unions has influenced the behavior of the international firms in other ways. Swedish union leaders have often had important positions in the international trade-union movement, and any misconduct with regard to labor relations in a subsidiary abroad has immediately been noted at home.

The most characteristic policy of the international firms has been the desire to grow but to grow in an orderly and gradual way. As has been mentioned above, this international expansion has been carried out in small steps, following a typical "establishment chain." Sudden, large foreign investments have been rare, and when they have occurred, they have come late in the chain. There are exceptions, however, like Swedish Match or the Grängesberg investment in Liberian American Minerals Company (LAMCO) (Carlson 1969, chap. 7). With regard to location policy, at the beginning of the internationalization process firms seem to have preferred markets with a short "cultural" or "psychic" distance (Hörnell, Vahlne & Wiedersheim-Paul 1973 and Johanson & Wiedersheim-Paul 1975). This concept includes such factors as differences in language, general culture and political system, and levels of industrial and educational development. At a later stage, when sales had increased and the time had come to establish wholly owned sales subsidiaries, the size of the market seems to have been more important. The firms started in the large markets when they had a unique and software-intensive product, like Sandvik and Atlas Copco, but when they had products of a less sophisticated character, like Volvo and Facit, they have preferred small markets with less competition from the international giants. Eight years after Volvo started to export cars, Assar Gabrielsson, the founder of the company, said in an interview that countries that produced cars were excluded as export markets. Instead, Volvo had a special liking for small countries that the big automobile companies disdained (*Svensk Exports Jubileumsnummer,* 19 April 1937).

Since the main goal of the Swedish international firms has been to penetrate into new markets or to safeguard market positions already established, they have been remarkably willing to cooperate and to enter into joint-venture agreements with other firms, both Swedish and foreign. To some extent, limited financial resources and the smallness of the Swedish financial market may have been the reason for this eagerness. Some of the early pioneers, like SKF and Swedish Match, have often acted as agents for other Swedish firms for certain periods, and some firms have permanently cooperated in their export operations, for example, Sandvik och Atlas Copco for drills and mining machinery. At the production stage there are many joint ventures between Swedish and foreign firms, in mechanical engineering, forestry, and other industries.

To what extent the policies of orderly and gradual growth that have thus far characterized the internationalization of Swedish industry will continue in the future, no one can tell. As has been mentioned, large and sudden investments abroad have been made but generally they have come late in the establishment chain. By now, the number of firms that have reached this late stage is fairly large, and this may influence the typical development pattern. The number of international firms in other countries has also increased, and it is possible that the gradual penetration of new markets will be more difficult than before. There are also other changes that might affect the firms' internationalization plant—the new exchange-control rules, the changing patterns of labor relations, and the increased public concern vis-à-vis multinational companies, both in Sweden and abroad.

Bibliography

Affärsvärlden, 24 May 1928.

Carlson, Sune. "Ett halvsekels affärer" in *Ett svenskt jernverk. Sandviken 1862–1937.* Uppsala: Almqvist & Wiksell, 1937, pp. 201–249.

_____. *International Financial Decisions. A Study of the Theory of International Business Finance.* Amsterdam & London: North-Holland, 1969.

Forsgren, M., and Kinch, N. *Företagens anpassning till förändringar i omgivande system.* Acta Universitatis Upsaliensis, Studia Oeconomic Negotiorum 1970.

Gårdlund, Torsten. *Svensk industrifinansiering under genombrottsskedet 1890–1913.* Stockholm: Svenska Bankföreningen, 1947.

Hörnell, E., Vahlne, J.-E., and Wiedersheim-Paul, F. *Export och utlandsetableringar.* Stockholm: Almqvist & Wiksell, 1973.

Johanson, Jan, *Svenskt kvalitetsstål på utländska marknader.* Mimeographed licentiate thesis, Uppsala 1966.

Johanson, J., and Wiedersheim-Paul, F. "The Internationalization of the Firm:

Four Swedish Cases," *The Journal of Management Studies* vol. 12, no. 3 (1975).

Kinch, Nils. "Utlandsetableringar inom massa- och pappersindustrin. En studie av olika metoder att hantera en osäker marknad" in J.-E. Vahlne, ed., *Företagsekonomisk forskning kring internationellt företagande.* Stockholm: Norstedts, 1974, pp. 61–84.

Lindahl, E., Dahlgren, E., and Koch, K. *National Income of Sweden,* Part I. Stockholm Economic Studies 1937.

Lundgren, Nils. *Internationella koncerner i industriländer.* SOU 1975:50, Stockholm 1975.

Nabseth, Lars. "Summary and Conclusions" in L. Nabseth and G. F. Ray, *The Diffusion of New Industrial Processes: An International Study.* Cambridge: Cambridge University Press, 1974, pp. 294–315.

Ohlsson, Lennart. *Utrikeshandels och den ekonomiska tillväxten i Sverige 1871–1966.* Uppsala: Almqvist & Wiksell, 1969.

Statistisk Årsbok 1972.

Svensk Exports Jubileumsnummer, 19 April 1937.

Swedenborg, Birgitta. *Den svenska industrins investeringar i utlandet.* Uppsala: Almqvist & Wiksell, 1973.

Söderlund, Ernst. "Svensk industri i historiskt perspektiv" in *Sveriges industri.* Sveriges industriförbund 1967, pp. 13–58.

Veckans Affärer, no. 27, 3 August 1972.

Vision, October 1972, Edition en français no. 23.

Comment

C. J. Maule

The evolution of foreign investment by Swedish firms, discussed by Professor Sune Carlson, presents some important issues in the consideration of investment abroad by small countries. These issues relate to both the theoretical and empirical literature on the subject.

The criterion used by Carlson to identify Swedish international firms—those firms where foreign sales (exports from Sweden plus sales from foreign plants) exceed 50 percent of total sales—does not permit direct comparison with the data of other countries, which use the concept of direct foreign investment when referring to their international firms. Considerable care will have to be exercised by those who use these data to make intercountry comparisons. This problem is aggravated by the fact that official statistics use different percentages of equity ownership to measure direct foreign investment.

Dealing with individual firms rather than aggregate industry data is helpful because it focuses on the dynamic process that led to investment in the first place and to subsequent investment, where the nature of the investment may have changed from sales subsidiaries to manufacturing subsidiaries. The "establishment-chain" concept discussed in the paper is useful in this regard.

A further step in the analysis would be to relate it to the strategy-structure literature in order to determine which management functions are transferable from parent to subsidiary and which are actually transferred and why. Such an analysis would provide an insight into how the parent exercises control and what degree of decision-making autonomy the subsidiary has. This is an important issue for a small capital-exporting country, because, as is pointed out in the paper, firm growth depends on sales in foreign markets. The time may come when the foreign markets are more important to the firm than the domestic market, at which time its national loyalty may change

and its contribution to the capital-exporting economy may
alter.

The individual international firms discussed in the paper are
probably Swedish-owned firms, although this is not stated. In
other countries the ultimate nationality of the parent company
may be different from the nationality of the capital-exporting
country. In Canada, for example, 44 percent of Canadian investment abroad is undertaken by firms controlled outside of
Canada. In the case of small countries, research will have to
pay attention to "piggy-back" investments where the ultimate
owners of the parent company are nationals of some third
country or, in some cases, are nationals of the country where
the subsidiary is located—for instance when Canadian investment in the United States is made by the Canadian subsidiaries
of U.S. firms.

The attitude of government and labor toward investment
abroad is an important consideration. The Swedish case suggests a positive attitude on the part of both government and labor, which is in sharp contrast to some other situations. The
Canadian government has until very recently discouraged
Canadian firms from servicing foreign markets through investment abroad and, instead, has instructed the Trade Commis-
sioner Service to promote exports from Canada. In the United
States the resistance of organized labor, in recent years, to foreign investment by American firms is well known. In the development of a domestic industrial base the Swedish example
shows how cooperation between government, business, and
labor can be of mutual benefit in a small domestic economy.

The explanation of company policies for international expansion has to combine an understanding of factors internal to the
firm and factors related to the domestic and foreign markets.
Professor A. D. Chandler's work on strategy and structure provides a conceptual framework that is especially helpful where
individual companies can be analyzed. One advantage of small
countries is that because they have only a small number of international firms the individual-company case approach is
usable.

Comment

David MacClain

Sune Carlson has written a valuable and comprehensive history of the Swedish multinational experience. I am particularly impressed with the research methodology that he and his associates at the University of Uppsala used, which features the analysis of multinationals' behavior at the most disaggregated level possible. Inferences about direct investment based on this approach seem to me to have the greatest validity.

Let me discuss what I feel are the most significant points of the Carlson paper.

The interconnection of a product's necessary software content and Swedish direct investment behavior is convincingly set forth. It is, of course, consistent with the accepted view that direct investment, at least in highly industrialized economies, tends to occur in industries characterized by a substantial degree of product differentiation. There is a subtle difference, however, in the case of a small-country multinational, a difference that Carlson highlights. It is the importance of qualitative, interpersonal relations in marketing and servicing the differentiated products sold. The history of the Swedish steel industry dramatically indicates the importance to long-term industry survival of gaining the acceptance of a differentiated product as the international standard. High technology and precision workmanship are essential here, but so is continuous visibility in the marketplace. A presence in the market can ensure short-run customer satisfaction and provide intelligence about customer requirements that can be fed back into product redesign.

Carlson reviews the concepts of the "establishment chain" and "psychic distance" that have already been used to describe the Swedish multinational experience in the work of Johanson and Wiedersheim-Paul. The argument that we should observe the establishment-chain phenomenon more closely for those firms selling products with a high necessary software content is a plausible one, but I would submit that the evidence cited comparing the experiences of Sandvik and Atlas Copco, on the one hand, with Facit and Volvo, on the other, is hardly conclusive. In my own research on direct investment by foreign multinationals in the United States, I expected to find that such establishment-chain behavior was more pronounced for investments made in the United States as opposed, for instance, to other European countries because the greater complexity of the U.S. market would produce more "one-toe-in-the-water-at-a-time" behavior. My empirical results suggested, however, that this was not a distinguishing characteristic of direct investments made in the United States.

I find the "psychic distance" concept a useful one, and based on personal experience in private industry, I would submit the hypothesis that it is more important the more technologically complex the product.

I do not agree with Carlson that consumer goods—at least consumer durables—are an exception to the pattern of internationalization of Swedish firms he describes. It is tempting to say that scale economies have required Volvo to concentrate production in Sweden. It is dfficult, however, to reconcile this with Volvo's direct investment in 1963 in Halifax, Nova Scotia, in a plant with an annual capacity for 5,000 cars (15,000 in 1975), or with its investment in Ghent, Belgium, in 1965, where the initial plant had a capacity of 14,000 cars (75,000 in 1975). Lawrence White has suggested that, to realize all scale economies (after eliminating restyling costs, which Volvo has done), a minimum automobile plant size is 200,000 cars per year. Volvo seems to be willing to sacrifice scale economies when marketing considerations, such as those in the European Economic Community, call for it. Indeed, one of the motives for Volvo's direct investment in the United States was the software component of its product: the need to tailor the car to the demand of the American market as far as styling, safety regulations, and inventory availability are concerned.

I believe Carlson should have given more emphasis to the areas in which government and company policies are in conflict. The proposed foreign-investment-review law, which reflected Swedish concern about the effect of multinational behavior on Swedish employment, certainly contributed to Volvo's investing in the United States when it did. Volvo's wage-labor relations are not so harmonious as they are often depicted. At the Torslanda plant, 65 percent of the work force is non-Swedish, and there is high turnover. Pehr Gyllenhammer has said that wage costs were not a determinant in Volvo's decision to invest in the United States, but that is because Swedish unit-labor costs are already equal to those in the United States.

I am surprised that Carlson never mentioned the impact of exchange-rate movements on Swedish direct-investment behavior. Of course, the thrust of the paper is fundamentally historical, when currency fluctuations were much smaller than they are today. Furthermore, Sweden is an associate in the European joint float, and a large percentage of Swedish exports go to the countries in the snake, so the Swedish krona is still fluctuating very little against the currencies of her major trading partners.

In summary, however, I find this to be an excellent and thorough study. I am confident it will become the first place to look when one wants to know more about Swedish multinationals.

3. France as Host to Small-Country Foreign Investment

Gilles Y. Bertin

Introduction

The idea that the behavior of host countries may vary with the size of the home country is a fairly recent one. For a long time, reactions to direct investment took off from the presumption that such investment came from the United States, a dominant country. Much of this reaction was adverse. Lately, however, it has been observed first, that non-American investment has grown substantially over the last ten years; and second, that not all foreign investment reacts in the way that American investment does (see, Vernon [12], Parry [9]) and that, to a degree, the national origin of an investment can explain its behavior and the response of host countries to it.

This paper seeks to give at least partial answers to the following questions. Does host-country behavior toward direct investment from small- or medium-sized countries (SCDI) differ from that toward large-country direct investment, and if so, what is the basis for such differences? How does SCDI react to changes in investment conditions and policies in host countries? How do host countries behave, and how effectively do they carry out their policies?

Before tackling these questions, a few preliminary points may be made.

1. The question of what constitutes a small country is rather imprecise. Should a country be considered small on the basis of an aggregate such as GNP or square miles of territory, or on the basis of its international investment? Switzerland and the Netherlands are small by the first criterion compared with India or Spain, but they are large by the second. In addition, the line between small and large must be drawn arbitrarily since countries can be ranged in size on a continuum.

For present purposes, however, there is little need to address the question theoretically. If we leave aside the United States, which is a large country from all points of view and the only

country that can be considered large in relation to direct foreign investment, the rest of the capitalist world can be divided
into medium-sized countries, like the United Kingdom, Germany, Italy, Canada, or Japan, and the small countries, such as
the Benelux nations, Switzerland, and Sweden. The question
should usefully be considered from the standpoint of three
classes: the United States, medium-sized countries, and small
countries.

2. A more serious problem is the difficulty of isolating the effect of size from other general factors. The economic and financial circumstances that determine the timing of investment
by the United States, medium-sized countries, and small countries differ. So do the general attitudes or conditions that simultaneously affect all three types of investment. General
statistical analysis must, therefore, be supplemented by case
studies at the firm or industry level.

3. Since a general study of the reactions of host countries to
SCDI is out of the question, we must be satisfied with a single-
country study, covering France. France may not be representative of general attitudes, but it has the advantages of being
medium-sized, of having experienced a fairly large but not
overwhelming inflow of foreign direct investment, and of being
so sensitive to the problems of a host country that it has frequently changed its official attitudes toward foreign investment
and has preferred positive, state policies to laissez-faire.[1]

The analysis is divided into three sections dealing respectively with a priori considerations, an account of French experience, and a tentative set of conclusions based upon the two.

A Priori Considerations

Differences of attitude of a host country toward foreign investment coming from large and small countries may be based on
differences in the expected costs and benefits accruing to the
country from it. These differences in expected costs and benefits, though difficult to isolate, may be related to the effects of
the home country's size on the characteristics of the individual
firm, on the nature of the industry, or on the foreign-policy
weight of the home country in a global setting. We call these

the individual (firm), structural (industry), and global (foreign policy) effects.

At the level of the individual firm it is likely that there are differences in firms (in the same industry and of the same general size) that come from different national backgrounds.[2] The differences may lie in the character of their management, which may be more or less aggressive depending upon the vigor and extent of competition in the home market.[3] These differences are apparent in terms of marketing activity, new product introduction, price cutting, and the like. Where two companies are truly international and compete with each other in a series of foreign markets, however, the character of the home market may play a reduced role.

If firms were correlated in size with the size of the home market and large firms offered a wider range of benefits in terms of management skill, research and development, and growth of output, there might be a basis for choosing large-country over small-country firms in terms of cost-benefit ratios. It is likely, however, that the international firms of large, medium, and small countries are more nearly of the same size than are the domestic, sheltered firms. Size of firm is thus likely to differ less widely than size of country.

Let us turn from firms in the same industry to firms in different industries. A large or medium country might appear to offer a wider choice of industries sought for foreign investment than that available from small countries. If a host country wants to attract investment in an industry that it lacks, it is more likely to find it available in large- or medium-sized countries. Direct investment in the automotive industry, for example, is available from the United States, Germany, France, Japan, Britain, and Italy among large and medium countries but only on a limited basis from Sweden among the small. At the same time there is a risk that the larger the country from which direct investment comes, the more firms in that country will undertake direct investment and, to the extent that such firms behave oligopolistically on a national basis, the higher the likelihood of monopolizing the industry in the host country. It may well be that firms engaging in foreign investment compete in the home country and hence in the host country as well. But oligopolistic competition in the home country may be reproduced in the host country with comparable market shares. Such an outcome is unlikely with SCDI, since small countries have only a few investors operating over a limited range of industries. However, the risk remains that a large firm from a small country will enter into oligopolistic relationships with foreign firms in all foreign markets. Such a risk is probably smaller for small countries than for large.

We now come to the global or mass effect. If the country of origin is considered as a single investor, a large country at first sight seems to be a more important and reliable source of the scarce factors sought by the host country: technology, capital, skilled management, and the capacity to combine them productively.[4] Large countries may be in the best position to provide these resources for countries short of them. But for a limited number of activities and small quantities of specialized factors, the smaller countries may not be at a disadvantage since the quality rather than the quantity of resources will count.

If we turn from benefits to the cost of acquiring direct investment, the small home country may be rated more favorably in comparison with the large, though not from the usual economic standpoint. It is likely that the higher level of competition in the larger home market and the greater possibility of economies of scale are likely to make the cost of supplying investment lower in large countries than in small, but the price charged may well be higher because of reduced competition in foreign investment. The investor from a large country may be more willing to supply the host country with high-cost components from the home country and to levy high charges for the management, technology, and other services that are available to its subsidiary. To the extent that relations between the parent, on the one hand, and subsidiary plus national authorities, on the other, partake of bilateral monopoly and the bigger partner gains a preponderant share of the joint product, the host country is better off dealing with small parents in small home countries than with large parents in large countries.

Outside the profit relationship between parent and subsidiary, there are two other possible differences in cost between

investments from large- and those from small-country firms.
The larger the home country, the more extensive the direct investment relationships and the greater the macroeconomic dependence of the host country on the home country. Canada,
for example, is closely linked to economic conditions in the
United States through trade and money and capital markets,
but the linkage is extended by the network of direct-investment
connections. Second, political independence may be compro-
mised by a wide range of connections extending to "strategic"
economic sectors, such as energy, computers, aircraft, and the
like.

In purely economic terms the costs of dealing with small
countries may be higher than those involved with large.[5] Up to
a point, however, the host country may find macroeconomic
and noneconomic compensations in dealing with small partners. Multiplying the number of investors of various origins
widens the range of possible solutions, providing more flexibility and hence greater independence for the host country. If
negotiation over direct investment takes place in a political
environment, the host may thus easily prefer SCDI.

It makes sense to try to calculate the levels of investment
from a large country beyond which a host country might
choose to encourage SCDI.[6] The question may turn not on general considerations, good for all time, but on thresholds and
limits. Such a threshold would depend upon the domestic political climate, the state of foreign relationships, the state of domestic economic activity, as well as on aggregate investment
by the country of origin. This fact makes case studies necessary to understand what really happens.

The French Experience
The analysis of SCDI in France proceeds from three sets of observations: an account of French general attitudes toward foreign direct investment, an assemblage of data on foreign
investment in France from different countries, and qualitative
information based on detailed industrial case studies.

The historical record of French government policy toward
foreign investment in general and specific classes of foreign investment in particular over the period from 1960 to 1975 is one

of frequent changes based on new orientations of foreign policy. Successive French governments have been preoccupied for
most of the period with the problem of dominant American investment. The official attitude toward investment from other
countries was decided as a corollary of policy toward U.S. investment, and the question was given little attention in its own
right until recent years. From the 1970s on, however, a more
active and selective policy toward all non-American investment,
including small countries, can be detected, though it does not
appear explicitly in official texts.

For a full understanding of policy as it evolved, it is important to recall the general conditions affecting foreign investment in France over the period. Four points may be made.

1. The formation of the European Economic Community under the 1957 Treaty of Rome attracted investment in France
from all investing countries but exercised a differential impact
on potential investors, depending upon whether they were inside or outside the European tariff walls. Investors outside were
stimulated to enter because of the investment-creation effect of
customs unions arising from trade diversion. Investors inside
felt some stimulus to reorder their investments because of the
investment-diversion effect.

2. The principle of freedom of capital movement within the
European Economic Community forbade the individual country
members, including France, to reject an investment operation
coming from a European partner country, even though it might
be of non-European origin.[7]

3. The French authorities clung largely to a liberal attitude.
Control over foreign investment had mainly administrative and
statistical purposes and, even in periods of greater stringency,
less than 5 percent of investment applications were rejected,
most of them on purely technical grounds.

4. The international tax structure among European countries
makes it difficult to trace the original source of some investments emanating directly from small "haven" countries, such
as Switzerland and Luxemburg.

Against this background, the period from the Treaty of Rome
to the present can be divided first into two main subperiods—

de Gaulle and post de Gaulle—and, within each, into still
shorter time-segments based on policy differences.

This summary provides the general framework within which
the reactions both of small-country investors and France can
be studied.

Statistical data on foreign investment in France by country of
origin are provided on a continuous basis from the official balance-of-payments accounts (see Ministère des Finances [15]).
Since these data do not give full details of investor behavior
necessary to its understanding, they have been supplemented
by statistics of foreign direct-investment authorizations gath-
ered by the Comité des investissements étrangers (CIE). This
material gives limited coverage of the total investment from
1957 to 1961, 1964, and from 1966 to 1972, but is a highly valuable source on the size, distribution, conditions, and motivation
of foreign investments.

Table 3.1. Chronology of French Policies toward FDI in France

Period	Reason for Change in Attitude or Conditions	Attitude toward Direct Investment	Impact on Foreign Investment
1. The de Gaulle period			
1957–62	Liberalization of French policy	Open	Favorable
1962–66	Tension with a few U.S. investors (Remington-Rand, GM, Chrysler)	More restrictive	Restriction toward U.S. investment not SCDI
1967		New status for investment	
1968	Political crisis		Temporary decline
1969	Refusal of United Kingdom entry into EEC		Temporary decline of U.K. investment
2. The post de Gaulle period			
1969–73	New political conditions	Open	Encouragement to non-U.S. investment
1971	Dollar devaluation		
1973–75	Petroleum crisis, economic recession	Open with qualitative approach	Relative decline in U.S. investment

Finally, industry case studies can be put together from a wide variety of qualitative sources of information, including the reports of the CIE, along with official reports (see Bertin [3], Economic and Social Council [13], and INSEE [14]), business and economic periodicals, and the financial press.

Statistical Analysis

Tables 3.2 and 3.3 set forth the amounts and distinct features of SCDI for two groups of medium- (group II) and small- (group III) sized countries, in comparison with investment from the United States (group I).

As shown in Table 3.2, the net amount of direct investment in France by small countries was 65 percent, divided roughly equally between medium-sized countries (group II) and really small countries (group III) with 35 and 30 percent respectively. The figures are, however, somewhat misleading since a sizeable share of the investment flowing through Switzerland and

Table 3.2. Net Foreign Direct Investments in France Including Associated Loans (by Countries and Group of Countries of Origin) 1961–1973 (Millions Current F)

Country and Group of C.	1961	1962	1963	1964	1965	1966
USA I	490	553	401	670	624	669
Canada	29	55	26	16	23	14
Germany	97	126	148	163	125	121
Italy	68	66	53	51	70	39
Japan						
U. Kingdom	60	118	106	210	246	140
Subtotal II	254	365	332	441	464	314
BLEU	115	128	169	236	224	199
Netherlands	86	57	79	80	110	78
Sweden	4	6	11	20	31	23
Switzerland	429	418	537	608	473	175
Subtotal III	634	609	795	944	838	475
EEC 5 countries	(367)	(376)	(449)	(531)	(529)	(437)
Grand total	1,378	1,526	1,528	2,055	1,926	1,458

Source: Balance of Payments, annual issues.

*Estimated.

the Belgian-Luxemburg Economic Union, amounting to 40 percent in the 1961–65 period, was of American origin. Perhaps a better approximation would be 30 to 35 percent for group II, 25 to 30 percent for group III, and 40 percent for investment coming from the United States. The use of CIE estimates for the 1966–72 phase to correct the balance-of-payments data produces percentages that are broadly similar.

If direct investments are reckoned by number rather than amount and are adjusted to correct for the true nationality of operations, the figures depart slightly from these percentages (see Table 3.3). For groups I, II, and III direct investment, excluding intercompany loans, divides into 35 percent, 31 percent, and 34 percent respectively. The two last figures for medium- and small-sized home countries sum to 65 percent, or a sizeable share of total direct investment in France.

Table 3.3 shows that the average SCDI is significantly smaller than the corresponding investment from the United States

1967	1968	1969	1970	1971	1972	1973
825	208	562	1,415	1,501	1,016	905
−5	−1	37	8	−8	47	43
228	425	638	1,237	734	313	412
145	54	49	211	161	176	34
				9	24	21
228	22	211	417	548	178	1,200
596	500	935	1,873	1,444	738	1,710
233	302	605	790	1,457	1,403	1,722
166	1	214	1,123	449	323	648
6	6	68	60	60*	80*	120*
183	−245	257	793	564	555	476
588	66	1,144	2,766	2,530	2,361	2,966
(772)	(782)	(1,506)	(3,361)	(2,801)	(2,215)	(2,816)
2,009	896	2,589	6,266	5,702	4,289	6,154

(group I). Group II has a larger average size than group III has had in many years (with a higher standard deviation and greater concentration in the first quartile).[8] There is, however, no clear-cut evidence that the medium-sized home countries should be separated from the small-sized home countries on the basis of these data. What we know from other sources, moreover, shows that the difference in the investor groups rests mainly on the number and importance of the largest firms. The relative influence of these seems broadly similar in countries of different size.

The trend in small-country investment is higher than that for the United States, both in number of operations and amounts

Table 3.3. Value, Number, and Distribution of Foreign Direct Investment Operations by Group of Countries 1966–1972 (All Sums in F)

Year	Group of Countries	Value	Number of Operations		Average	Variance
1966	USA (I)	311,180	39		7,979	12,620
	II	91,560	29	92	3,157	3,860
	III	240,220	63		3,813	6,170
1967	USA (I)	209,600	59		3,552	8,390
	II	114,070	32	90	3,565	5,660
	III	194,430	58		3,352	4,570
1968	USA (I)	313,540	35		8,958	13,880
	II	382,200	46	84	8,309	26,720
	III	210,410	38		5,537	7,680
1969	USA (I)	778,650	74		10,522	12,370
	II	570,520	60	126	9,509	2,066
	III	446,020	66		6,758	11,040
1970	USA (I)	644,870	61		10,573	14,650
	II	419,070	52	98	8,059	17,500
	III	234,060	46		5,088	5,980
1971	USA (I)	548,290	56		9,791	12,910
	II	203,580	42	80	4,847	7,380
	III	250,940	38		6,604	7,350
1972	USA (I)	752,440	54		13,934	25,580
	II	668,430	54	108	12,378	23,920
	III	634,480	54		11,750	27,300

Source: CIE.

invested. Over the period from 1960 to 1973, the amounts invested by the three groups show an annual growth rate of 9.9 percent for the United States, 27.6 percent for group II, and 30.6 percent for group III. Even if disguised American investment through Switzerland and Luxemburg is taken into account, it is evident that "small-country" investment (groups II and III) has far exceeded American.

A more detailed observation discloses significant differences between small countries (group III) and medium-sized countries (group II) and U.S. investment in variability.[9] The first two groups show much less variability than group I. Groups II and III, for example, show much less sensitivity to the May–June

Number of Operations (Loans Included)	Average (Loans Included)	Percentages in Quartiles			
		1st	2nd	3rd	4th
52	10,800	79.5	18.5	8	1
39	5,190	68	18	10	4
63	5,600	77	13	9	1
59	4,330	77	12	7	4
37	4,580	70.5	17	7	5.5
62	4,380	65.5	18.5	10	6
36	8,940	80.5	13	5	1.5
46	8,150	87.5	8	3	1.5
40	5,490	66	22	9	3
76	10,500	69.5	20	8.5	2
65	11,360	83	11.5	4	1.5
71	9,720	74	17	7	2
65	16,980	73	16.5	8	2.5
56	10,810	78	13	7	2
53	8,020	61	25	11	3
58	14,020	68	20	8	4
42	7,850	66	19.5	10.5	4
43	7,030	68	18.5	8.5	5
64	13,490	82.4	11.2	4.4	2
60	13,330	77	14.5	6	2.5
53	1,650	78.5	13.5	5.5	2.5

1968 political crisis than do U.S. investors and decline less from the 1969–1970 investment peaks.

The tables reveal two phases that correspond to distinct periods in the integration of the European Economic Community, although the limits of each are rather uncertain. In the first phase from the late 1950s to 1966–1967, and especially during the subperiod ending in 1962–1963, the growth of SCDI on the whole lags behind that of U.S. investment, with part of the rapid gain in group III being the result of what might be called the "Swiss effect"—American investment routed through Switzerland. This phase of investment creation, stimulated by the formation of the Common Market, was accompanied by a sharp growth in the number of investment operations undertaken by France's industrial European partners in the first phase of European integration, during a period when France took a neutral attitude insofar as the origin of foreign investment in France was concerned. During the subperiod—from 1963 to about 1967, this trend continued with some accentuation, however, of industrial European investment and a slower rate of gain in U.S. operations.

In the second period after 1967, however, the position changed drastically. This change was due not only to a volte face on the part of the French government but, more fundamentally, to the completion of the first stage of European integration. Small-country investors no longer limited themselves to nonindustrial investments, nor did the French government forebear from guiding investment operations.

Overall, the figures for numbers of operations and amounts invested show a rising proportion of non-U.S. investments after 1966–1967 (except for 1970–1971). Within the separate groups there were sharply individual patterns. The steady growth in group II, for example, is compounded of two forces: (1) the rise of British investment in France before and after the short period that followed General de Gaulle's second veto of the entry of Britain into the Common Market, and (2) a strong wave of German investments in France representing expanded production at the European level for industrially specialized operations. The wide fluctuations of group III no longer reflect disguised U.S. investment, as in the earlier period,[10] but the pickup in economic conditions in the Common Market, along with the dissolution of the European Free Trade Association (EFTA), which made investment in the European Economic Community relatively attractive to outside investors. France recorded a growing inflow of capital from Switzerland, Sweden, and other small countries outside the Common Market at the same time that investments from the Netherlands and the Belgian-Luxemburg Economic Union leveled off.

It is also of significance that the average size of investment from all three groups tended to converge, as shown in Table 3.3. This convergence suggests that small-country foreign investors were growing in firm size, perhaps at a time when foreign investment from the United States was shifting to medium-sized firms. Whatever the cause, there appears to have been a sharp increase in large-scale foreign direct investment on the part of many European multinational firms after 1967–1968.

The gradual evolution of French official attitude is readily understandable. In the first phase, professed economic priority was given to the strengthening of French industry, which could be more readily accomplished, so far as diversification was concerned, through new entry of U.S. firms. Foreign investment remained welcome, but as the proportion of U.S. control of industry rose—going from 8 percent in 1962 to 15 percent in 1973—there was a growing tendency to call on new sources of investment to provide a countervailing force to American enterprise. Attracting European investors in place of U.S. investors offered two advantages. It conformed strictly to the Treaty of Rome, insofar as Common Market partners were concerned, and it offered the opportunity, through one device or another, to construct much larger, integrated units able to compete more effectively with the U.S. giants.

With the passage of time, this general policy was developed further. In the interest of modernization of French industry, emphasis was placed on technologically advanced and fast-growing industries such as computers, telephonic equipment, nuclear power equipment, and the like where French firms and foreign partners were required to work together to achieve joint solutions. At the same time, however, concern was felt for the national independence of French industry, following the steep increase in British and German investments. The need for modern technology and the fear of domination by Common Market partner-industry together led to a more qualitative approach, which favored diversified sources of SCDI outside of Britain and Germany, including a new source, Japan. The weakness of the dollar and French balance-of-payments difficulties resulting from the energy crisis, contributed further reasons to favor foreign investment from the new sources.

The statistical tables provide little evidence of a strong relationship between the several investment flows and French official attitudes, nor can changes in such attitudes be demonstrated conclusively from the texts of French policy statements. The data, moreover, are strongly affected by the exogenous events of the years 1968 to 1971, and possibly 1973. Nonetheless, it is a safe conclusion that (1) the flow of SCDI increased as a proportion of total direct investment in France over the recent period and that (2) this relative growth may, in some respects, be a consequence of the dominant position previously gained by the large-country investor, the United States.

Case Studies
There is a persistent well-established tradition of the French government intervening in the organization of industry in order to promote or accelerate the achievement of more rational and efficient structures. Actions taken to hinder or encourage particular foreign investments form a part of this overall policy, which has become increasingly more active in the last ten years under two major pressures. First, there has been the increased degree of control of French industry by foreign investors especially American firms, which in the light of the cost-benefit considerations discussed earlier has led the government either to halt all foreign investment or to choose among various potential foreign investors and to discriminate in favor of those from small countries. Second, the French government has pursued a policy of filling gaps in the array of scarce factors or fostering modernization in highly technical industries and, where necessary, searching for foreign invest-

ment partners in the appropriate industries, regardless of their country of origin.

In a number of industries such considerations have resulted in an increase in investment by non-American firms, not only from the traditional investing countries but also from "younger" investors like Japan, Sweden, and the Arab petroleum-producing countries. The motivation for governmental intervention—whether initiating or responding to investor action—is often rather complex and is not always self-evident. The motives can perhaps be classified under two headings.

Industry Structure   The intervention may be negative, such as breaking up actual or potential monopoly by American or domestic firms and increasing production and competition in a given industry; or it may be positive, such as the promotion of higher concentration and increased size to achieve an efficient scale of operations.

International Economic Policy   In oil, for example, the objective may be to obtain secure access to raw materials; or the intervention may be based on balance-of-payments considerations, especially vis-à-vis the oil-producing countries.

It is important to bear in mind that because of the special status of foreign investment from the European Economic Community, the main policy weapon is positive attraction. The negative path of restriction is available to the French government only for investors domiciled outside the EEC. But, of course, even in the EEC it is possible to adopt indirect resistance through postponing or raising difficulties for unwanted foreign investment or to obtain a better bargain for French parties. By and large, it is fair to say that the policies of the French government with respect to foreign investors, EEC, and others have reflected some hesitation and less than careful forethought and steadiness of purpose and have been, by and large, only partly successful. A few case studies illustrate these points.

The computer industry furnishes the best known and most controversial example of active governmental policy to achieve national technical independence, to develop for France a modern productive tool, and to limit the overwhelming power of U.S. firms—mainly IBM. When the French government decided to produce large computers, primarily for strategic reasons like the building of a thermonuclear military force, it soon came to realize that the task lay beyond French resources and that it was necessary to work out an alliance with partners in Europe to share the large investment burden necessary to construct the required minimum size of equipment and to capture enough of the market—roughly 5 percent—to make a viable producing firm. Negotiations were started with three firms: British ICL, Philips of the Netherlands, and Siemens of the German Federal Republic. ICL soon dropped out, however, mainly because of the cost of the heavy investment it was called upon to make. Negotiations were then resumed with the two continental partners and a plan devised: the French would put up 50 percent of the cost of the plant, and, in turn, the larger part of the manufacturing, the assembly, would take place in France. When estimates predicted very heavy operating costs, and some doubts about economic performance, the European partners showed great reluctance to go along, especially as they feared the dominant French role. Therefore, the French government abandoned the partnership operation and sought an alternative "national" solution in association with Honeywell of the United States. As of this writing, the governmental objective has not yet been achieved, and the French taxpayer has borne a substantial financial burden.

A more successful example is furnished by the telephone-equipment industry in which two U.S. controlled firms, LMT and CGTT, both affiliates of International Telephone and Telegraph (ITT) accounted for a sizeable (55 percent) share of the entire market in 1973. At that time the French government initiated a seven-year plan that was intended (1) to treble the capacity of production and to overcome the lag in French telephonic capacity, (2) to increase the share of the market of domestic firms, and (3) to reduce artificial monopoly prices drastically by increasing competition and adding to the number of producers. Since the entry of new U.S. firms was not wanted, the French government sought new investments in Europe. British firms proved not to be competitive; so the French sought proposals from Philips, Siemens, and Swedish Ericsson, the last of which had a presence on the French market dating back to the 1930s but a limited one amounting only to 5 percent. Siemens was temporarily ruled out for various reasons, largely political. It proved to be impossible to reach an agreement with Philips. Only with Ericsson was an agreement possible, and the company was allotted an increased share—almost 15 percent—of the greatly enlarged market. This expansion has had the result of maintaining the overall foreign share.

A similar situation of a foreign investor from a small country playing the role of an additional competitor exists in the automobile industry where Volvo engages in joint-production activities with Peugeot and Renault. In electronics Siemens is involved with French firms, and Japanese firms participate in several mechanical projects.

The paper industry furnishes a rather different case. Here the French industry was in the process of concentration, and a foreign presence in the industry was felt to be necessary to assure access to overseas sources of pulpwood and wood pulp. For this reason and because at least one French group (Beghin) was of international size, American and British investors were not discouraged, but were only permitted to enter limited and specialized branches of the industry, such as thin or special papers, paperboard, and the like. The British group Bowater contemplated an investment in France at the time, undertook it, and then gave it up. Negotiations were then undertaken with Swedish and Canadian firms. These last finally declined to enter large-scale production projects, the profitability of which looked uncertain in comparison with serving the EEC market in the traditional way through exports. However, Canadian and Swedish firms did take over small, specialized firms with high rates of return, and finally one Canadian producer, Moore, agreed to enter a joint venture on a wider basis with French associates.

Other joint ventures with state-owned firms from Iran, Saudi Arabia, Kuwait, and Qatar were planned in 1974–75 following the energy crisis.

A good example of investment decisions taken with global considerations in mind is provided by the plans for building catalytic crackers to enlarge the French supply of basic feedstocks for the petrochemical industry. Five of the six projects

submitted to the French government for acceptance were proposed either solely by foreign firms or in association with
them: the Phillips Petroleum Co. of the United States, Rhône-
Poulenc with an American partner, Royal Dutch Shell, ATO with
AKZO of the Netherlands, and Charbonnages de France with a
governmental corporation from Qatar. Two of the proposals
from ATO and Rhône-Poulenc were withdrawn on the basis of
financial considerations. Another was postponed. Of the two
left, the French government gave the preference to the Charbonnages de France-Qatar proposal, since it could finance a
larger share of the total investment needed with outside
sources, agreed to supply oil under long-term contract, and reduced the level of dependency on American investment. In the
light of the recent conditions set forth by the Ministry of Industry to potential foreign investors, which may be summed up as
requiring investors to bring in capital and new technology from
abroad and to conform to official regional policy, the decision
to favor the Qatar proposal has set a precedent for the future.

These examples show policies favoring SCDI. Policy can be
negative toward SCDI, however, if the potential entrant has already taken or will take too large a position in the French market. In the biscuit industry U.S. firms acquired control of all the
large French firms but one as early as 1966. Thereafter the
French authorities vetoed any further acquisition from abroad
by United Biscuit, General Biscuit, or Parein and worked out a
purely French solution. Again, when the German chemicals giant Hoechst purchased a major interest in the French Roussel
UCLAF from the Roussel family—the firm being the second
largest in the French drug industry—there was official reaction.
The acquisition could not be canceled since official consent
had already been given to the deal, but the French authorities
became active in promoting concentration of the industry under the leadership of the French firms ATO and Rhône-
Poulenc. A similar reaction occurred when Nestlé, the Swiss
giant firm, announced that it would take control of l'Oréal, the
leading French cosmetic company, within the next six years in
spite of the fact that the president of Nestlé was a Frenchman.
Finally, the Belgian oil producer Petrofina in late 1975 was denied the right to buy a major interest in France's third largest

producer of paint—Ripolin—on the ground that the first two paint producers are partially under foreign control.

These examples suggest that French policy toward foreign investment is highly pragmatic and that the size of the country of origin plays a role, but not a decisive one.

Conclusions

The statistical material and case studies offer conclusions that may be briefly summed up. SCDI can be seen as a specific class of foreign investment, but not a homogeneous one. As a class, it differs from the dominant U.S. investment in respect to average size and standard deviation, though the distributions overlap. Despite the fact that the differences in the two sorts of investment decline over the period of study, there is an adequate basis for treating the two populations of investors as different.

SCDI is not a homogeneous class of investment. On the basis of behavior, however, the size and distribution of small-country investments are not particularly related to the size of the country from which they come. Country makes a difference, as was shown by the fact that countries within the European Economic Community behave more similarly with respect to investment than countries of the same size outside the EEC.

In the host country France, SCDI is perceived as different from U.S. investment. This difference is partly concealed in the particular rules applying to investment from the EEC and by the events of the last five years, which have had a particular impact on U.S. investment. The case studies make clear, however, that French policy distinguishes SCDI from American investment and uses the former as a counterweight to the latter. American investment still accounts for the preponderance of foreign investment in France, to be sure, and specific American proposals are almost never specifically rejected.

For these reasons, small-country foreign investment appears to have been for France a way to counteract U.S. dominance rather than a means of attracting specific foreign resources. The case of raw materials is different, however.

Both the statistics and the case studies confirm the strong impact of external factors on the origin of direct investment in

France. The rise of European investment in France may be the result more of the increased competitiveness of Europe vis-à-vis the United States than of conscious French policy.

On the whole, France cannot be said to have had a specific policy toward SCDI so much as to have used it as part of a general policy aimed at counterbalancing the overwhelming influence of U.S. investment, especially prior to 1970, and increasing competition among all foreign investors.

The host-country model that emerges from the French experience rests on several propositions:

1. The smaller the total foreign-investment position in a given industry and the larger the relative share in that industry of the dominant, large-country investor, the more favorable will be the attitude of the host country to SCDI.
2. The attractiveness of SCDI or, indeed, of any foreign investment also depends on the overall position of the host country, including its defense posture and its balance of payments. A country with a strong, adverse balance of payments may well not pay attention to the origin of foreign investment but, indeed, may welcome it from wherever it comes.
3. The host country will prefer to attract investors from countries with which it can successfully conduct negotiations on investment conditions. These may well be countries of equal or smaller size that, from an industrial standpoint, will not endanger the existence of national industries but, indeed, will strengthen them.

To what extent this model holds true for other countries is uncertain. Casual observation suggests it may be applicable at least to Mexico and Iran. It is possible that the smaller the host country, the less chance it has of imposing regulations of its own on foreign direct investment, even on investment from still smaller countries. But with a growing awareness in all countries of their national interests and their independence, the probability runs high that small-country direct investment will play an increasing role in the future and enjoy favorable treatment from host countries.

Appendix

Note on the Statistical Data from the Comité des investissements étrangers (CIE)

The CIE is empowered to examine all foreign investment projects above a minimum size that have varied over the years. Its statistics, however, have two possible causes of major error. (1) They refer to projects some considerable proportion of which —perhaps 10 percent—never reach completion. (2) They include only a part of total direct investment since some of the very large projects are handled in the office of the prime minister and since projects below the minimum size are not subject to control.

It is likely that over the period 1960–1971, the statistics on foreign investment in France issued by the CIE cover 70 to 85 percent of the total with a size distribution that closely approximates the total. The quality of coverage declined after 1972. Only rough global estimates were collected for the years 1961 to 1965. There is also no record of operations that are carried out through the capital market when the amount of stock purchased by foreigners represents less than 20 percent of the company's total equity.

Notes

1. It is not a matter of pure coincidence that France has called forth more case studies of foreign investment than any other developed country with the exception of Canada. See the bibliography.

2. The main expected gain can be measured in terms of increased efficiency resulting from a more appropriate concentration of firms and/or from livelier competition. The costs arise from structural losses—the costs of halting operations—or from increased monopoly practices of either foreign or large, local firms.

3. This was the case in the 1960s when the American international firm was universally considered the most efficient. Conversely, Japanese firms sometimes encountered negative reactions owing to their style of management.

4. Consider, for example, the oil-exporting countries, most of which can supply large amounts of capital for investment though they lack all other complementary factors.

5. See Johnson [7].

6. The curve of net benefits for the host country from direct investment by a

single investing country may well take the shape of a reverse U, reaching a maximum for moderate amounts and then declining as control extends over more and more industry.

7. This has been increasingly the case over the last ten years.

8. The existing data do not furnish a quantitative picture of investors by number, but their distribution by size should not be very different from that of the amounts invested.

9. Correlation coefficients to the trend line for groups I, II, and III are 0.38, 0.62, and 0.58 respectively. See the appendix.

10. U.S. and German investment flowing into France through Switzerland declined steeply after 1966.

Bibliography

1. Behrman, J. N. *National Interest and the Multinational Enterprise.* Englewood Cliffs, N. J.: Prentice-Hall, 1970.

2. Bertin, G. Y. *Les investissements des firmes étrangères en France (1945–1962).* Paris: Presses universitaires de France, 1963.

3. Bertin, G. Y. *L'industrie française face aux multinationales, Rapport au commissariat général du plan, la documentation française.* Paris, 1975.

4. Bonnaud, J. J., and Bosser, A. *La politique economique des pouvoirs publics et les grandes firmes internationales en France,* in C.N.R.S., *La croissance de la grande firme multinationale.* Paris, 1973.

5. Dickie, R. B. Foreign Investment: France—A Case Study. Leyden, 1970.

6. Hahlo, H. R. *Nationalisation and the Multinational Enterprise, Legal, Economic and Managerial Aspects.* Leiden: Sijthof, 1973 (especially contributions by Leleux, H. Johnson, J. Fayerweather, and A. Litvak).

7. Johnson, H. G. "The Efficiency and Welfare Implications of the International Corporation," in C. P. Kindleberger, ed., *The International Corporation.* Cambridge, Mass.: The M.I.T. Press, 1970.

8. Johnstone, A. W. *United States Direct Investment in France.* Cambridge, Mass.: The M.I.T. Press, 1965.

9. Parry, T. G. "The International Firm and National Economic Issues: A Survey." *Economic Journal* (December 1973).

10. Schmill, E. *Les investissements étrangers en France.* Paris: Cujas, 1966.

11. *Symposium sobre las empresas transnacionales y los paises receptores,* C.I.D.E., Mexico, 1975 (especially articles by G. Bertin, J. Dunning, and Gilman R. Newfarmer).

12. Vernon, R. "L'influence des origines nationales sur la stratégie des entreprises multinationales." *Revue économique* (Juillet 1972).

13. *Reports to the "Conseil economique et social"* (Economic and Social Council), Vallon, 1960; Charvet, 1966; Moch, 1972.

14. INSEE, *Données essentielles sur l'industrie: rapport par la commission de l'industrie du VII Plan,* vol. 2: *Les relations avec l'extérieur.* Paris, 1974.

15. Ministère des Finances, *La balance des paiements* (annual issues).

16. Litvak, I., and Maule, C. J., eds. *Foreign Investment, the Experience of Host Countries.* New York: Praeger, 1970.

17. Cohen, J. C., and Fondanaiche, P. "Les participations étrangères dans l'industrie française en 1971." *Economie et statistique* no. 52 (Janvier 1974).

18. Gabet, C. "La pénétration du capital étranger en 1971, dans les sociétés de plus de 2 millions de francs de capital social." *Economie et statistique* (Octobre 1975).

4. Technology Transfer:
The Australian Experience

Helen Hughes

Australia has had a long experience of foreign investment, both as host and as investor. Indirect investment dominated the inflow of capital into the Australian colonies in the nineteenth century, but private direct foreign investment in Australia began almost as soon as British firms established trading, financial, and later manufacturing subsidiaries. Australian investment abroad also began in the nineteenth century, mainly in New Zealand and the Southwest Pacific, although Australia's role as host has always far outweighed that of investor. Not surprisingly it is the host role that has dominated the considerable discussion of the impact of foreign investment on Australian development. However, even in this context, questions of the relative efficiency of technological transfers by foreign firms have not received a great deal of attention, and there has been even less interest in Australia as a technological intermediary to adapt existing technology, to innovate, and to apply such technological developments abroad through trade and direct foreign investment. The first part of this chapter is concerned with the Australian experience of the transfer of technology through the inflow of direct foreign investment; the second examines the Australian transfer of technology abroad; and the concluding section suggests that the highly protected host conditions in Australia tend to limit Australia's potential as a technological intermediary and investor abroad.

Technology Transfer to Australia

Australia continued to pursue with particular vigor its traditional policies of welcoming direct foreign investment without conditions in the 1950s and 1960s as a complement to its immigration and growth policies.[1] Britain remained the principal source with about 44 percent of the investment inflow, and the United States and Canada accounted for 39 percent. Japan became a significant, albeit still small participant (Table 4.1).

Table 4.1. Cumulative Net Flow of Private Direct Investment to Australia by Home Country of Investment, 1947–48 to 1970–71

	Undistributed Income		Other Investment		Total	
	$A million	Percent	$A million	Percent	$A million	Percent
United Kingdom	1,406	13.7	3,149	30.7	4,555	44.4
United States and Canada	1,210	11.8	2,781	27.1	3,991	38.9
Other countries	134	1.3	1,583	15.4	1,717	16.7
Total	2,750	26.8	7,513	73.2	10,263	100.0

Source: Australia, Commonwealth Treasury, *Overseas Investment in Australia*, Treasury Economic Paper no. 1 (Canberra, May 1972), p. 16.

Note: The totals recorded are sums of annual flows valued in current prices so that they must be viewed with considerable caution. The category "other investment" consists of other direct investment in Australian branches and subsidiaries, portfolio investment, and institutional loans. Separate totals of these were not available until 1962–63.

There was some direct foreign investment in agriculture and service industries, but the proportion of production attributable to foreign ownership in those sectors was small. The bulk of direct investment went into mining and manufacturing. By the end of the 1960s foreign ownership accounted for some 58 percent of mining production and 26 percent of manufacturing production with considerably higher proportions in some groups (Table 4.2). It is in these sectors that the transfer of technology through foreign investment has been of importance.

The transfer of technology has several aspects. The direct costs in terms of patent and license fees may not be the most important ones. First, there is the "appropriateness" of the product being transferred.[2] To be appropriate to the tastes, income characteristics, and climate of a host country, the transfer of technology may require product adaptation or innovation, and this, in turn, may require changes in the production process. The production process may require adaptation or innovation even if the product is appropriate. Technology transfers among countries at similar levels of development, with similar cultural, income, and factor-price characteristics, usually require least adaptation. This is generally true of the transfer of technology from Europe and North America to Australia. However, even in these circumstances transfers from countries with relatively large markets to countries with relatively small markets (whether resulting from natural or policy constraints) often do require adaptation rather than mere transfer of technology. Such adaptation may also require product changes. It has been well established that "high technology" is an important component of the package that gives rise to direct foreign investment. Because high technology is also usually capital-intensive and capital intensity is another important aspect of the direct foreign investment package, many of the industries in which direct foreign investment operates most effectively are subject to economies of scale. But while increases in scale are, in such cases, generally relatively easy to achieve in the transfer of technology, "scaling down" is usually very difficult and requires considerable adaptation if unit costs are indeed to fall. Thus, in Australia the transfer of technology has not presented

Table 4.2. Direct Foreign Control of Australian Manufacturing and Mining Industries, Effective Protection and Concentration of Ownership

	Share of Production Attributable to Foreign Ownership (%)	Effective Rates of Protection (%)	Share of Industry Sales by Largest 5 Firms (%)
Motor vehicles, construction and assembly	88	50–86	60–84
Nonferrous metals— rolling and extrusion	84	100–281	n.a.
Oils, mineral	82	(−9)–26	80
Industrial and heavy chemicals, acids	78	0–53	57
Pharmaceutical and toilet preparations	76	32–64	31–71
White lead, paints, varnishes	70	81	83
Musical instruments	65	n.a.	n.a.
Other chemicals	58	11–115	57
Wireless and amplifying apparatus	46	49	n.a.
Electrical machinery, cables, and apparatus	42	38–84	27
Agricultural machines and implements	32	34	n.a.
Other food, drink, and tobacco	31	(−15)–164	47–100
Meat and fish preserving	31	0–34	38
Jam, fruit, and vegetable canning	29	10–12	53
Rubber	23	48–53	73
Plant, equipment and machinery	22	26–81	26
Other industrial metals, etc.	22	1–189	n.a.
Miscellaneous products	20	2–82	28–45
Textiles and textile goods (not dress)	16	(−1)–73	39–97

Table 4.2. (continued)

	Share of Production Attributable to Foreign Ownership (%)	Effective Rates of Protection (%)	Share of Industry Sales by Largest 5 Firms (%)
Bakeries (including cakes and pastry)	15	(−8)–12	52
Paper, stationery, printing, book binding, etc.	14	10–136	
Treatment of nonmetallic mine and quarry products	12	(−5)–67	55
Bricks, pottery, glass, etc.	10	8–49	53–93
Clothing (except knitted)	6	42–152	14
Sawmills, joinery, boxes, etc.	5	5–57	29–37
Furniture of wood, bedding, etc.	5	51–68	24
Skins and leather (not clothing and footwear)	5	46–93	33
Heat, light, and power	1	n.a.	n.a.
Total manufacturing	26	—	—
Metal mining	69	n.a.	n.a.
Fuel mining	40	n.a.	n.a.
Nonmetal (excluding fuel) mining	20	n.a.	n.a.
Total mining	58	—	—

Notes on sources: The data were collected from two separate sources and even within these sources industry aggregations are not compatible. They also refer to various years, and must therefore be interpreted with caution as suggestions of orders of magnitude. Foreign control percentages for manufacturing are an average for 1966 and 1967, and for mining they are for 1968. They are taken from Table 17, Overseas Ownership and Control of Individual Manufacturing Industries, 1966–67, p. 23 and Table 18, Overseas Ownership and Control of Australian Mining Industry, 1963 to 1968, p. 25, Australia, Commonwealth Treasury, *Overseas Investment in Australia*, Treasury Paper no. 1 (Canberra, May 1972). Effective protection ranges refer to 1969–70. They are taken from Table 1.2.10, Characteristics of Employment in the Manufacturing Sector, by Industry: Australia—30 June 1971, pp. 78–90, Australia, Industries Assistance Commission, *Annual Report*, 1974–75 (Canberra, September 1975), mimeo. Concentration of sales ranges refer to 1973–74. They are taken from Table 4.3.1, Concentration, Profitability and Sales: Manufacturing Sector, 1973–74, ibid., pp. 248–249.

problems in mining where development has been on much the same scale as in other countries, but scaling down is a critical issue in manufacturing where natural and policy constraints exacerbate the relative smallness of the markets represented by the country's thirteen million people.

The efficiency of technology transfers to Australia has only recently begun to be seen in these terms.[3] In the past, moreover, evidence about technology transfer was collected without reference to the comparative efficiency of foreign and domestic firms in the transfer of technology.[4] Foreign firms have undoubtedly been instrumental in introducing new designs and techniques, but so have domestic firms. Because the transfer of technology is a long-term, continuous process, a systematic approach to the relative efficiency with which foreign firms transfer technology requires, at least initially, case studies in which the process may be examined and foreign and domestic firms' experience may be compared.

The motor-car industry is the Australian industry group with the highest share of foreign investment (Table 4.2). Three major manufacturers—General Motors, Ford, and Chrysler—dominate production with more than 80 percent of the output of motor cars. With the exception of 3.14 percent of Chrysler shares owned by Australians, the three companies are wholly owned by the parent corporations in the United States. Leyland, 100 percent owned by British Leyland International Ltd., assembled motor cars in Australia until recently. Motor Producers, 100 percent owned by Volkswagen AG and with a Nissan affiliation, Renault (Australia) 100 percent owned by Renault (France), and Australian Motor Industries, 50 percent owned by Australian shareholders, 25 percent owned by Toyota Motor Sales Co., and 25 percent by Toyota Motor Company have assembly lines that produce the other 20 percent of the Australian output. Local production is maintained at about 90 percent of the Australian market supply. The industry accounts for about 6 percent of employment and 7 percent of value added in manufacturing,[5] and, as in other countries, carries a considerable psychological weight in Australian economic well-being.

The motor-car industry has almost as long a history in Australia as in Europe and North America. In the 1900s and up to

World War I the made-to-order car business flourished. In the 1920s demand expanded rapidly with motor-car ownership rising to 571,000 (including about 104,000 commercial vehicles) by 1929–1930. Only the United States, Canada, and New Zealand had a higher per capita ownership of motor vehicles than Australia, and, in spite of the smallness of its population, its motor-vehicle market was the sixth highest in the world.[6] Considerable scope for the development of local motor-car and component production thus existed in the 1920s.

The first steps toward an indigenous body-building industry were, in fact, taken toward the end of World War I. Once American and British manufacturers began to turn from individual to series production, it became cheaper to import chassis than to produce them locally, but freight costs protected body building, thus stimulating local production. This production was accentuated when a "luxury embargo" in 1917 prohibited the imports of motor bodies, allegedly to boost the war effort. Australian manufacturers could not handle the rush of orders immediately, and the prohibition had to be modified, but body building was well established when the tariff took over the protective function with a 40 percent British preferential and 55 percent general duty rate. Holden's Motor Body Builders Ltd. of South Australia quickly emerged as the most efficient and largest of the four or five principal car-body manufacturers in Australia. First-class management persuaded the trade unions to agree to the retraining of skilled coach makers for the semiskilled, moving-line method of production for which equipment was imported from the United States. Cost accounting was introduced and materials controls were instituted.

The Liberal (conservative) government of the time, eager to see more local production than just body building, introduced a lower tariff for unassembled than for assembled chassis, underlining an existing freight advantage by some 5 to 7 1/2 percent. To stimulate competition, both Ford's (of Canada, taking advantage of imperial preferences) and General Motors' proposals for Australian manufacturing were encouraged. The production of Model Ts, Chevrolets, and Buicks for the Australian market represented a direct transfer of product designs. Ford began to build bodies in a plant similar to that established by Holden's as well as assembling chassis. The Australian body builders replaced by Ford were resentful, and some switched to support for British chassis suppliers, thus diversifying body production. Holden's secured the General Motors body market to assure itself of competitive runs. The contract was on a cost-plus basis, and General Motors assisted Holden's by providing a permanent liaison officer, supplying production engineers to instruct Holden's staff on advanced American production methods, assisting in the purchase of tools that could not be bought locally, informing the firm in ample time of prospective chassis changes, and buying supplies for Holden's when it could do so more cheaply through its American organization. By 1929 Holden's unit labor costs were a fifth of what they had been in 1917–1918, and were considered to be no higher than in the United States. General Motors took 50 to 60 percent of Holden's annual output. The second largest body builder, T. J. Richards & Sons Ltd., secured a similar arrangement with Chrysler, a small assembler, accounting for 10 to 15 percent of the market. Motor-vehicle prices, however, remained high, utilizing the tariff protection available. It seems likely that the high prices were, to some degree, a reflection of high costs resulting from the shortness of production runs without adaptation for "scaling down." The shortness of runs was, of course, exacerbated by the very competition the policy framers were so eager to encourage.

How much of Holden's and Richards's success was due to their own capacities and how much was contributed by General Motors and Chrysler technology transfers it is impossible to judge in retrospect. It is equally impossible to know whether the encouragement of only one body builder, with total runs of some 70,000 units or so annually (rather than Holden's 35,000 car bodies, Ford's 20,000 or so bodies, and Richards's and other sundry small body-builders' outputs), could have substantially lowered total unit costs further, thereby allowing lower tariffs and prices closer to international competitiveness.

Whether the chassis-assembly technology was most efficiently acquired as part of three foreign investment packages must now also remain an open question. Domestic chassis assemblers were in production in the 1920s although their volume of output was reduced, and most were to be driven out of business in the 1930s by the three North American firms. Whether the best of the domestic producers might have been strengthened and encouraged to join with a combination of Holden's and Richards to build up a domestic motor-vehicle industry and what the possible or likely outcome of such a policy might have been can again not be known.

Australian firms were also active in motor-vehicle component and tire manufacture in competition with imports in the 1920s. Replacement-component production grew spontaneously, but the government, again eager to build up local production, hastened local component manufacturing by threatening Ford and General Motors with further preferences for British importers if they did not use Australian components whenever possible. The threats were successful, and Australian component production increased apparently without direct, foreign technical assistance. But when tariffs were raised in 1930, U.S. and British producers accelerated their move into Australia to protect their markets, the former through subsidiaries and the latter as shareholders often with majority control. Australian tire manufacturing lasted somewhat longer, remaining competitive with imports by a series of mergers of local firms, but this strength attracted defensive British participation in the foremost Australian firm and led to the entry of the United States into the field. There was thus apparently sufficient domestic technological and managerial ability to adopt internationally accepted "best practice," but foreign firms came in nevertheless to protect their share of world markets. Such entry, reversing the domestic firms' trend to consolidation, resulted in renewed fragmentation of production. Another conservative government attempted to rationalize the motor-car industry and reduce prices in 1939 by reducing the number of models and concentrating production in the hands of a domestic firm, Australian Consolidated Industries, with a proven record of efficiency in the glass industry, but World War II intervened.

In contrast, for several industries in which domestic producers predominated, the high protection of the 1920s and 1930s provided a sheltered infancy from which they emerged internationally competitive in the mid-1930s. Basic iron and steel production, where the principal producer, the Broken Hill Proprietary, forced a rival firm to merge with it during the Depression to achieve economies of scale and to further them through exports, is perhaps the best example.[7] The steel industry engaged in considerable "scaling down" of technology to meet international competition. To some extent this scaling down was achieved at the cost of product variety, the timeliness of deliveries, and other unfavorable aspects of a monopolistic supplier; relying on imports also had costs, however, and, on balance, Australian steel consumers appeared to benefit. Domestic producers achieved similar results in glass and sugar production, scaling down technology to become more competitive and consolidating production on a monopolistic basis to make the most of a limited market.

During World War II, body-building and assembly facilities were turned to the production of trucks and armored vehicles and even some tanks. At the end of the war, a Labor government saw the manufacture of an all-Australian motor car as the culmination of the industrial growth stimulated by wartime production needs, as the spearhead of economic self-sufficiency, and as a stimulus for a new phase of industrial development. It called on existing producers to submit proposals for the manufacture of a completely Australian motor car and suggested the setting up of a publicly owned corporation as an alternative if established producers did not come forward. Ford, Chrysler, International Harvester, and General Motors responded, and the General Motors proposal contained the highest local content without requesting additional protection. This proposal was accepted, and the government assisted General Motors by helping it to secure a $A2 million overdraft with the publicly owned Commonwealth Bank to begin production.[8]

This move was again a crossroads decision. Wartime vehicle-manufacturing experience suggested that there was in Australia the technology, including design, production engineering, plant management, labor skills, and financial expertise, to design and manufacture a passenger car. Indeed, much of the initial General Motors design adaptation and production planning was done in Australia with existing resources. Enough was now known of economies of scale in motor-car production to indicate that the Australian market, even on the most optimistic assumptions, could economically sustain only one motor-car production line. Something of this reasoning indeed lay behind the government's negotiations with General Motors.

However, as the new Australian car, a slightly modified Chevrolet somewhat ironically called the "Holden," came on-stream, and—backed by General Motors sales resources with the help of import licensing—began to capture a sizeable proportion of the market, the two other American firms operating in Australia and the other major participants in the world market, including Austin and Morris (later to become the British Motor Corporation and then Leyland) and a series of vigorous newcomers to international motor-car markets—Volkswagen, Renault, Toyota, and Nissan—clamored for entry. The conservatives were back in power, and in the name of competition they responded to the transnationals operating in the motor-vehicle market by creating a cost-plus made-to-order tariff system to suit several classes of car, each with a predetermined level of local content and an anticipated share of the market. Tariffs of 35 to 45 percent were reinforced by a complicated bylaw system of limited imports by the manufacturers who had become established in Australia. Import licensing has also been used to keep down the proportion of wholly imported cars to about 10 to 20 percent of the market.

Although Australia is a high-income country in which distance and suburban life styles have led to a rapid rise in car ownership, total annual sales of passenger cars (including light commercial vehicles) have not kept pace with the minimum scale of production considered economic for a conventional production run. The annual Australian passenger-car market rose from about l00,000 units in the early 1950s to 300,000 in the early 1960s, grew again to some 500,000 in the early 1970s, and, with a reduced growth rate, is expected to reach 600,000 by the early 1980s. In the past thirty years rising labor costs have led to rapidly increasing capital intensity in high-income countries' production and consequent economies of scale in the principal manufacturing stages: stamping, casting, machining, and even in assembly.

The unit cost of production for stamping is generally thought to begin to fall in the range of an annual output of 400,000 to 600,000 units, but not to bottom out until annual outputs of 1,000,000 plus units are reached. In casting, the cost curve begins to flatten out at 100,000 or so units a year, but economies do not become significant in machining until 250,000 or so units are made, and the average cost per unit continues to fall until 1,000,000 units plus of production. Economies are less marked in assembly. Some recent European innovations suggest that annual outputs of 25,000 to 50,000 may be economic with a complete reorganization of the assembly line, at least for high-quality cars. However with the conventional lines used in Australia, minimum economic outputs are considered to be about 100,000 units a year, and costs continue to fall to volumes of at least 200,000 units a year.[9] To illustrate the orders of magnitude involved, in the early 1960s, when Volkswagen production reached its peak in Australia, the plant manager claimed that his annual output would not make a three-shift, one-day's run at the parent company's Wolfsberg plant.

The effect of product diversification and production fragmentation on prices is illustrated by Table 4.3, which indicates the price disadvantage of Australian cars compared to landed, duty-free prices in Australia of Japanese and European cars. Because freights average very roughly 10 percent on top of duty-free imports, the figures underestimate the cost differential by that amount.[10] Assuming average pricing for the

Table 4.3. Price Disadvantage of Australian Motor Vehicles

	Japan	Europe
Small light	40–65	–40[a]
Large light	25–50	5–25
Medium	20–35	–20[a]
Upper medium	n.a.	40–85
Light commercial and 4-wheel drive	55–75	n.a.

Source: Australia, Industries Assistance Commission Report, *Passenger Motor Vehicles, Etc.*, 10 July 1974. Parliamentary Paper no. 72, p. 82.

[a] Advantage.

Japanese and European car exports, this also suggests the magnitude of cost differentials. The data indicate, and managers claim, that there has been some technological adaptation to the small scale of production. Otherwise the price differentials would be even higher. However, such adaptation has been very limited, and Australian practice has been far from the vanguard in spite of its small market. Instead, it lags markedly behind the smaller European producers. The nature and high level of tailor-made protection have made the lack of adaptation possible. The ratio of operating profits to funds employed in the motor-vehicle and component industries, in comparison to those for all manufacturing, shows that profitability has not suffered from production fragmentation (Table 4.4). Protection has in fact been so high that relatively large-scale producers have made large intramarginal profits. Profit repatriation by General Motors has caused an almost annual embarrassment.

The motor-car industry is not unique; it is rather typical of a variety of industry groups in which transnationals have a worldwide influence in the transfer of technology in manufacturing. Other industry groups marked by the lack of scaling down and production fragmentation include other motor vehicles, nonferrous metal processing (particularly aluminum), almost the whole range of consumer durables and electronic equipment, pharmaceuticals, rubber, and chemicals. A recent study of the chemical industry concluded that

there have been a few cases of technological adaptation of derivative technology resulting in the development of smaller scale plants conforming to market size while approaching international cost competitiveness. Unfortunately more commonly the international firm entrant, taking advantage of the economies of technology transfer behind tariff walls, has pursued a policy of installing replicas of overseas plants, with some scale down, waiting for market growth to absorb excess capacity. For the life of the plant, however, the unit costs are considerably in excess of the larger and growing plants overseas. This is compounded by the additional costs and misallocations of excess capacity. Further, on an industrywide basis, and in the context of international oligopolists competing within a small market, the industry fragmentation of sub-optimal and under utilized plant conditions the nature of the "performance" of the industry.[11]

Table 4.4. Ratio of Operating Profit to Funds Employed in the Vehicle Industry and All Manufacturing Industries

	Vehicle Manufacture and Assembly[a]	Component Manufacture[a]	All Manufacturing Industries
1967–68[b]	17.7	14.5	11.4
1968–69[b]	20.2	16.7	12.6
1969–70[b]	17.9	15.3	13.0
1970–71[b]	13.0	14.4	12.1
1970–71[c]	13.0	14.4	12.1
1971–72[c]	7.8	14.6	11.5

Source: Australia, Industries Assistance Commission Report, *Passenger Motor Vehicles, Etc.*, 10 July 1974. Parliamentary Paper no. 72, p. 56.
[a]Data include commercial vehicles.
[b]Tariff Board industry classification based on factory subclass classification employed by ABS prior to 1968–69.
[c]Australian Standard Industrial Classification.

It is not known whether the Australian firms in these industry groups have performed similarly, better, or worse.

In other industry groups in which the Australian market is relatively small so that scaling down is of importance, Australian firms have continued to be more adaptive. Steel, glass, and sugar remain important in this regard. Adaptation has also been important in some industry groups with particularly fragmented regional and local markets. The low density of the Australian population means long distances between the principal urban centers, and state government incentives to local producers exaggerate such fragmentation. Here scaling down has usually resulted from price competition. Ready-mix concrete and other concrete products, asbestos and plaster products, and various types of builders' hardware have seen adaptation and innovation both of products and of production methods to meet Australian geographic conditions.

In a large group of industries, product adaptation and scaling down have not been a major problem. For such products as processed foods, tobacco, beverages, and many engineering products, Australian markets have been large enough for many of the technological production practices introduced by transnationals from Europe or North America to be economic without adaptation. Australian firms also compete effectively in many of these industry groups apparently with technology equivalent to that of the transnational firms. The Australian firms keep abreast of overseas developments through a variety of channels, including visits abroad, patent and licensing arrangements, and their own technological endeavors. Managers complain, however, that their efforts to adapt products and production technologies are limited by the necessity of competing with transnational firms whose research and development costs are absorbed by worldwide sales. Overall the situation is far from clear. Transnationals appear to spend more on research and development in Australia than Australian firms, but most such expenditures are confined to minor adaptations and include market research for sales techniques. Australian firms appear to focus their attention on the adaptation, and particularly the scaling down of production processes. Overall, there is a growing fear that the relatively high level of direct foreign investment in Australian manufacturing, under protected conditions that limit the necessity of adaptation, has tended to reduce the resources devoted nationally to research and development. A recent comparison with research and development efforts in other Organization for Economic Cooperation and Development (OECD) countries was unfavorable to Australia and reinforced this view.[12]

Technology Transfer from Australia

The total net flow of private direct investment from Australia between 1947–1948 and 1970–1971 was $A663 million, or about 6 percent of the inflow of foreign investment.[13] Net income receivable from abroad was a small proportion of income payable abroad (Table 4.5). In 1973–1974 New Zealand, which had been the principal market for Australian investment from the nineteenth century, still accounted for about a quarter of the stock of Australian investment abroad, and there was investment in the United Kingdom, the United States, Canada, and South Africa. However, Papua-New Guinea represented 30 percent, indicating the increased importance of Australia's neighboring

Table 4.5. Private Direct Investment Income Payable Abroad by Companies in Australia and Receivable from Abroad by Australian Companies, 1970–71 to 1973–74[a]

	Income Payable Abroad $A million	Income Receivable from Abroad $A million
1970–71	639	49
1971–72	680	65
1972–73	872	127[b]
1973–74	1,003	185[b]

Source: Australia, Bureau of Statistics, *Overseas Investment, 1973–74* (ref. no. 5.20), pp. 19 and 32.

[a] Includes undistributed income.
[b] Includes returns to the Bougainville copper investment, mostly payable abroad.

developing countries (Table 4.6). Papua-New Guinea and Southeast and East Asia began to increase in importance for Australian investment in the 1950s, and this trend was accentuated in the 1960s. Papua-New Guinea has clearly been the most important developing country for Australian investment, particularly in the early 1970s when a major mining investment—in the Bougainville copper mine—took place. Investment in developing countries has accounted for nearly 60 percent of the investment outflow between 1964–1965 and 1973–1974, with Papua-New Guinea making up about 48 percent of the total (Table 4.7).

Australian investment in high-income countries (including South Africa) has been very varied. There has been some investment in backward-linked raw materials and components to ensure supplies. Investment in South Africa and New Zealand, however, has been principally in manufacturing, and it has at least partly exploited Australian firms' scaling down of technology expertise for these small markets. In investment in the large high-income markets of Europe and North America, Australian firms have taken advantage of their sales and organizational ability, notably in shoe polish and pharmaceuticals. In at least one case, however, in the introduction of ready-mixed concrete to European markets, Australian firms followed their

Table 4.6. The Stock of Australian Private Direct Investment Abroad by Principal Host Countries, 1973–74

	$A million	Percent of Total
United Kingdom	132	11
New Zealand	306	25
United States and Canada	95	8
Papua-New Guinea	377	30
Other countries	331	27
Total	1,241	100

Source: Australia, Bureau of Statistics, *Overseas Investment, 1973–74* (Canberra ref. no. 5.20), Tables 21–34 covering overseas branch liabilities to head offices, intercompany indebtedness of overseas subsidiaries to head offices, and other liabilities of overseas companies to Australian parent or related companies, pp. 33–34.

adaptation of a technology widely used in North America by becoming foreign investors.

Australian investment in developing countries was traditionally in plantations, trade, and minerals, but in recent years most of the ventures have been in manufacturing. The number of enterprises established is relatively large, but most Australian investment has been small-scale. It is estimated that in manufacturing there are about fifty Australian-associated firms in Singapore, thirty in Malaysia, twelve in Thailand, nineteen in the Philippines and more than one hundred in Indonesia. There are also a relatively large number of Australian consulting firms in these countries, although compared with European, U.S., and Japanese investment, Australian investment is low.[14]

Investment in manufacturing has included a large variety of products with investment typically following export trade.[15] Up to the 1950s, before the major transnationals became seriously interested in Southeast Asia, Australian firms created branches in these countries and in Fiji and Papua-New Guinea to take advantage of natural protection given by freight costs and perishability. Building materials, glass bottles, and perishable food products were among this group of investments. With the introduction of tariffs and other incentives Australian producers

Table 4.7. The Cumulative Net Outflow of Australian Private Direct Investment to Southeast and East Asia and Oceania, 1964–65 to 1973–74[a]

	$A million	Percent of Total
Hong Kong	24.01	2.6
Indonesia	15.35	1.6
Malaysia	11.60	1.3
Philippines	2.53	0.3
Singapore	5.01	0.6
Thailand	1.50	0.2
Total, Southeast and East Asia	60.24	6.6
Fiji	11.11	1.2
Papua-New Guinea	441.99	48.3
Total, Oceania	469.82	51.3
Total net private direct investment abroad	916.00	100.0

Source: Government Statistics and Australia, Bureau of Statistics, *Overseas Investment, 1973–74* (Canberra ref. no. 5.20), Table 35, p. 34.

[a] In current prices.

moved into a wider range of nondurable and durable consumer goods (including flour milling, canned milk, and wall-to-wall carpeting), based on Australian raw-material exports, and into producer goods. Investment in most "branded" products and in producer goods such as heavy chemicals, petroleum refining, and nonferrous metal processing, where the U.S. and European transnationals dominate, has been closed to Australia. Only a handful of Australian firms have had the resources to compete with the major transnationals, and in one instance a public authority took the initiative. The Australian Dairy Board provided an investment package—funds, management, and technology—for the establishment of powdered-milk processing plants in Southeast Asia to ensure a market for Australian powdered milk to counter the European and U.S. transnationals' practice of using their home-country raw materials, often regardless of price. In spite of its geographic proximity, the transnationals have used Australia as a base for investment in Southeast Asia only in exceptional cases, mainly where an associated firm has had significant Australian domestic participation. Yet the cost of air fares from Sydney to Djakarta is lower than those from Sydney to Perth. Conzinc Riotinto, Australia's investment in copper mining in Papua-New Guinea on behalf of its parent company, the Riotinto Zinc Corporation of the United Kingdom, is the only major exception. The investment was undertaken while Papua-New Guinea was still an Australian colony, and most of the major decisions, including those determining incentives for Conzinc's entry, were made in Canberra.

Australian resentment of the transnational corporations' reluctance to give Australians the opportunity to participate in the profits and control of subsidiaries operating in Australia together with the feeling that transnationals in Australia used foreign managerial staff for control rather than for genuine management purposes led to an early acceptance of local participation and management in Australian investment abroad. Long established branches have been turned into locally registered firms with local share participation and board representation, and in recent years most Australian investments have taken the form of joint ventures. In accepting local participation Australian managements have felt themselves to be not only upright but smart. Like most Japanese corporations investing in Southeast and East Asia, they saw the advantage of a local partner or board member in dealing with labor and political issues and also in being able frequently to take advantage of existing marketing channels. The smallness of the Australian parent often made a considerable degree of local participation essential.

The smallness of the Australian parent firms, and the absence of international departments taking care of foreign investment, also made the early training of local managers imperative. Most Australian firms could not spare managers from Australia for any length of time, and the cost of maintaining expatriate managers in developing countries was high for firms with small volumes of production. Australian firms have, moreover, been able to find many of their managers, particularly those requiring advanced technical skills, among the Asian

graduates of Australian universities. Some 3,000 to 4,000 overseas students, mainly from Southeast and East Asia, have
graduated from Australian universities annually during the last
twenty or so years. Many of these graduates have difficulty
finding employment at home and welcome a continuing association with Australia. This situation has many advantages for
both employers and employees. Potential staff members are
sometimes picked out while still in Australia and trained in the
parent factory. There are also disadvantages, however. The
training the students receive is designed for a high-income,
high-labor-cost country. Not surprisingly it lacks an appreciation of the need to design products appropriate to low-income
countries and to produce them by labor-intensive production
techniques that will take advantage of the factor costs prevailing in these countries. Changes in product design and the use
of greater labor intensity would not only lower costs but would
generally make substantial scaling down of production possible
without a commensurate increase in unit costs. Unlike the difficulties of the scaling down of technology with high labor costs,
scaling down with low labor costs can, by a simultaneous reduction of capital intensity, lead to substantial unit-cost reduction, and such a reduction is obviously of critical importance to
low-income countries with limited markets for the relatively
sophisticated goods that require the import of high-level
technology.

Australian firms have been transmitting the scaled-down
technology developed for Australian conditions through their
investments in developing countries, and in a few cases a product developed for Australia has also been appropriate for the
developing countries. For example, window louvres are particularly suitable for tropical countries. But Australian firms are
only now becoming aware of the desirability of product and
process adaptation for developing-country income levels and
factor-price relationships. The growing awareness of the need
for adaptation is partly an outcome of the firms' experience in
developing countries and partly the result of changing policies
in the developing countries. In the past a combination of trade
policies, licensing measures, and income-tax incentives favored

the production of Western goods for local, upper-income consumers. Employment needs were given little real attention. The
desire to produce sophisticated products often made capital-
intensive production methods necessary, so that labor/capital
substitution opportunities were largely confined to material
handling and packing. The use of second-hand equipment was
frowned upon, partly because of maintenance difficulties, but
often simply for prestige reasons. Similar to Australia, the desire to encourage competition led to oligopolistic practices and
production fragmentation, and to ever increasing demands for
protection. Neither the ideological climate nor the prices facing
the Australian investors encouraged the questioning of the appropriateness of product design or of production techniques
for the host countries.

An Australian shoe-polish manufacturer, for example, came
into Indonesia in the late 1960s in response to the incentives
for foreign capital-intensive investment in import-substituting
industries. Given Indonesia's per capita income and climate,
the demand for shoe polish could not be expected to be very
large, and the investment was accordingly modest. A small
modern factory was constructed from structural steel and other
duty-free imported materials. An Australian manager and a
handful of workers were enough to handle production. In
granting the Australian investor "pioneer" privileges, the Indonesian government was apparently not aware that a local manufacturer had for some twenty years, in spite of the vicissitudes
endured by private enterprise during the Sukarno years, supplied the Indonesian market. His factory was built of timber and
cheap local bricks, and production was hardly mechanized. Because he made his own containers as well as the polish itself,
he employed more than two hundred workers until the foreign
firm came into the market. The Australian firm had a duty ex-
emption on all of its imported inputs; the local manufacturer
had to pay duty on imported Carnauba wax from Brazil, and local sales taxes on all other inputs. The Australian company had
a five-year income-tax holiday; the Indonesian manufacturer
had to pay taxes according to the tax inspector's determina-
tion. The Australian company had access to international

capital markets; the Indonesian firm had to pay street-market interest rates. The Australian manufacturer had an international brand name; the Indonesian producer had an Indonesian one.

Australian firms, like most high-income country investors in developing countries, have typically not been able to handle labor-intensive technology opportunities. When an Australian canned-milk factory started to produce in Indonesia, the cans were boxed in small crates made of wooden slats by subcontractors working on the factory site. As production grew, the subcontractors could not keep up supplies, principally because poor transportation from the outer islands made the supply of wood irregular. The milk-processing firm accordingly encouraged another Australian company to take advantage of the "pioneer" investment incentives to produce corrugated cardboard boxes to replace the wooden crates. Another "modern" factory was built from imported materials and the production process was also capital-intensive, but the imported inputs were duty free, and the firm had a tax holiday that enabled it to depreciate its investment quickly. Its market grew rapidly because other foreign firms were also unable to handle the wooden-crate problem, and local manufacturers followed their example to be "modern." The relatively simple alternative steps that would have been required to support the subcontractors' capacity to supply the wooden crates on a sustained basis were not beyond the Australian manager's capability, but the desirability of doing so was beyond his understanding. As in Australia, it seems that in a wide range of products, domestic firms are likely to be more adaptive than even the small Australian foreign investors.

The Australian firms operating in developing countries pride themselves on their pragmatic approach to production, and the relative smallness of their plants tends to encourage a situation in which the expatriate manager spends a great deal of his time in overalls. While this does encourage a healthy attitude to manual labor and ensures that equipment is properly installed and maintained, it does not necessarily indicate that the product and production technique will be "appropriate" for the developing country. However, when such firms expand their operations after some experience in developing countries, they tend to be more sensitive to local needs and to adapt products and production methods accordingly.

Most Australian investment has been for import substitution. However, one measure of some Australian firms' relative efficiency is their early position as exporters of manufactured products from Singapore, Malaysia, and Thailand in the 1960s before these countries became seriously concerned with exports. A handful of Australian firms have started to manufacture in Southeast Asia for the Australian market, but Australian tariffs are high, preferential tariff treatment for developing countries is limited, and there is an almost total absence of interest in restructuring the Australian economy to improve the international division of labor so that progress in this direction is likely to be very slow indeed. One or two firms have also gone abroad to produce for third-country markets, but they are, to date, quite exceptional and of minor importance. Most Australian manufactured exports are resource-based and relatively capital-intensive so that there is little movement likely in this direction.

Australia as an Intermediary in the Transfer of Technology

The costs and benefits of the transfer of technology by direct foreign investment cannot be gauged in isolation but must be seen in relation to alternative ways of transferring technology. In Australia this means in relation to the domestic firms' experience. In the absence of detailed case studies that include both foreign and local firms and in the absence of quantitative data any conclusions at this stage can be regarded only as hypotheses for a research agenda. It can thus be postulated that while foreign firms have undoubtedly contributed to the transfer of technology to Australia, they have perhaps been less effective than domestic firms in adapting European and North American practices to Australia's market size.

The degree to which technological adaptation, and particularly scaling down, occurs is apparently affected by the nature of competition in an industry group, and this competition is, in turn, influenced by the "rules of the game" prevailing in Australia and particularly by trade policy. Although a detailed industry subgroup breakdown by foreign ownership and effective protection is not available, existing data (Table 4.2) suggest a relationship between foreign ownership and protection levels. A historical perspective, moreover, indicates that this relationship is complex. Protection attracted foreign investors for "defensive" reasons, creating an oligopolistic structure of competition and tending to fragment production. Economies of scale grew as technology became more sophisticated and capital-intensive, but, backed by strong parent corporations interested in world market shares, the Australian subsidiaries resisted mergers and, instead, pushed for higher tariffs and other subsidies. Product proliferation and differentiation became more important than price competition, and there was relatively little pressure on the firms to lower costs by scaling down production techniques. The data available are again only suggestive (Table 4.2). The concentration of sales, moreover, does not distinguish between monopoly and oligopoly. However, it is known that the industry groups and subgroups with the highest levels of foreign investment—motor vehicles, nonferrous metal rolling and extrusion, petroleum refining, petrochemicals, pharmaceuticals and toilet preparations, and paints—are oligopolistic and have relatively high levels of effective protection.

In other technologically complex and capital-intensive industries in which transnationals have been traditionally less active, development has been somewhat different. Competition among domestic firms led to merger and monopoly, exposing the firms to a great deal of public attention. Lobbying for higher protection became awkward, and, in fact, there was pressure on the firms to cut costs. Product adaptation, mainly in the direction of simplification of product ranges, and the scaling down of imported production technology were means of cutting costs, alleviating the need for higher protection, making existing protection redundant, and then, in some instances, making reductions in protection possible.

There is some evidence of similar trends in price-competitive industry groups, notably in building construction materials. Wide substitutability among building materials within small markets led to pressures to lower costs, permitting adaptation to local conditions and the scaling down of production, particularly where relatively low levels of technological sophistication and capital intensity created high returns for such efforts.

The structure of Australian industry has in turn affected its capacity to act as a technological intermediary. High levels of protection have directly and indirectly been the most important factor. Australia, together with New Zealand, has by far the highest protection levels among high-income countries (Table 4.8) and this protection has encouraged socially uneconomic foreign investment in Australia since the 1920s. It is true that in spite of some continuing foreign parent-corporation restrictions on their Australian subsidiaries' capacity to export manufactures, foreign subsidiaries have been quite important contributors to Australia's growing exports of manufactures, which have, in recent years, represented 20 to 25 percent of total exports, and they have, of course, been dominant in mineral exports. However, transnational corporations have used their Australian subsidiaries as headquarters for third-country operations only in exceptional cases, thus limiting Australia's capacity for investment abroad and for directly passing on such technological adaptation to small-scale market conditions as the foreign firms have done in Australia. Protection also ensures an inward-looking orientation by most Australian firms and limits their need for technological adaptation. The majority of Australian entrepreneurs clearly prefer the low but relatively secure earnings of a highly protected small, domestic market to the potential gains of investment abroad. Predictably, although some of the monopolistic firms and some of those in the most competitive industries have ventured abroad, Australian foreign investment remains negligible in spite of the smallness of the home market and in spite of proximity to the rapidly growing and potentially vast markets of Southeast Asia. Australian foreign-investment levels thus contrast sharply with such vigorous small, high-income countries as Sweden, Switzerland, and the Netherlands, contributing to lagging per capita productivity and income growth and limiting Australia's technological potential.

Table 4.8. Average Tariffs on Dutiable Most-Favored-Nation Imports of Industrial Products, 1970

	Percent
Australia	20.7
Austria	12.3
Canada	7.1
Denmark	4.6
EEC	6.9
Finland	6.4
Japan	10.7
New Zealand	20.3
Norway	7.2
Sweden	4.6
Switzerland	3.2
United Kingdom	8.1
United States	7.1

Source: General Agreement on Tariffs and Trade, *Basic Documentation for the Tariff Study*, Geneva, 1972. The average tariff was calculated in two steps. First, a weighted average based on a country's own most-favored nation (MFN) imports up to the Brussels tariff nomenclature (BTN) heading level was calculated. The results in individual BTN headings were then weighted by the total (MFN preferential, and intra-area) combined imports of the industrial countries covered by the study in calculating an average of each category.

Notes

1. However, investment conditions existed in media, commercial banking, coastal shipping, domestic airlines, railways, telephone, telegraphic and postal services, and atomic power production.

2. The terms "appropriate products" and "appropriate technology" are obviously very loose approximations for the complex conditions that would maximize the private, marginal utilities of "consumers" and minimize the "social marginal costs of production." In spite of their evident looseness they represent a useful shorthand for important concepts and are used here in this sense.

3. T. G. Parry, "Plant Size, Capacity Utilization and Economic Efficiency: Foreign Investment in the Australian Chemical Industry," *The Economic Record* (June 1974).

4. For example even so highly competent and persuasive a discussion of foreign investment as Donald T. Brash's *American Investment in Australian*

Industry (1966) does not indicate what was simultaneously taking place in domestic firms. While the positive influences of American investment on the Australian economy outlined by Brash cannot be denied, similar developments were taking place in Australian firms.

5. Australia, Industries Assistance Commission, *Annual Report,* 1974–1975, Canberra 1975, mimeo, Table 1.2.10, pp. 86–87.

6. See Colin Forster, *Industrial Development in Australia 1920–1930* (1964) chap. 2, "Mass Markets for Consumer Durables: The Impact of Motor Vehicles" for the growth of the Australian motor-car market in the 1920s.

7. Helen Hughes, *The Australian Iron and Steel Industry, 1848–1962* (1964), pp. 129–131.

8. Brash, *American Investment in Australian Industry*, pp. 289–291.

9. Australia, Industries Assistance Commission Report, *Passenger Motor Vehicles, Etc.,* 10 July 1974. Parliamentary Paper no. 72, Appendix 8, Cost Studies of the Motor Vehicle Industry, summarizes recent cost studies and adds information based on the Australian industry.

10. Australia, *Policies for Development of Manufacturing Industry,* A Green Paper, vol. I, Report to the Prime Minister by the Committee to Advise on Policies for Manufacturing Industry (October 1975), p. 71.

11. Parry, "Plant Size," p. 239.

12. Australia, *OECD Examiners' Report on Science and Technology in Australia* (Canberra 1974).

13. Australia Commonwealth Treasury, *Overseas Investment in Australia,* Treasury Economic Paper no. 1 (Canberra 1972), p. 148.

14. J. B. Reid, "Australian Industry Relations with South East Asia," address delivered at the Australian Academy of Science Forum on Science and Industry, 17–18 October 1975.

15. Helen Hughes, "Australians as Foreign Investors: Australian Investment in Singapore and Malaysian Manufacturing Industries," *Australian Economic Papers* (June 1967).

Comment

Jose D. Epstein

Despite its higher per capita income Australia shares, as an investment and technology recipient, more characteristics with the advanced developing countries than with its industrialized OECD associates. Its experience is similar to that of Argentina, Brazil, or Mexico, rather than to that of "vigorous small, high-income countries, like Sweden, Switzerland, and the Netherlands." Indeed, most advanced, developing countries evidence many of the main features concerning technology absorption that Dr. Hughes describes. Foreign investments in Australia have tended to be concentrated in mining to the degree that almost 60 percent of mining investment is foreign-owned. This proportion is higher than that of almost any Latin American nation. In this regard it would appear that the transfer of technology is easier where there is less local value added to be incorporated into the final product. Again, this is not too different from the experiences of intermediate, developing countries elsewhere in the world. The paper explains that adaptation of foreign technology is not problematic when scaling-down processes are involved, as seems to be the case in mining. The implication is clear, however, that in the manufacturing sector size of market—and Australia does have a limited market—often conspires against successful adaptation processes. It should be added that a goodly proportion of technology transfer, precisely in the mining sector, has to be scaled up, often considerably, to suit conditions in the recipient countries. It seems that scaling upward is much less of a problem than the reverse. With regard to Australia's successful absorption of technology, immigration to Australia from Commonwealth countries probably deserves a larger share of credit than is given in the paper. Naturally, the commonality of language also immensely aided the process of technology transfer from the United Kingdom and the United States, as it does when the flow is reversed and Australian investment, albeit modest, flows toward countries such as South Africa, New Zealand, and Singapore.

Although the author calls for more case-study material, she makes a good contribution to the inventory for both inflows and outflows. Her study of steel and automobiles is a welcome addition to the not very plentiful material available in that branch of recent economic history. The special contribution of the Commonwealth Bank of Australia, that unique institution combining features of central and commercial banking, adds luster to the spirit of venture which has distinguished that bank as an example for innovative government banking.

The description of the genesis and current status of automobile manufacturing in Australia gives credence to the suspicion that there must be a secret worldwide conspiracy of finance ministers who probably have established an international clearing house on how best to complicate custom tariffs and regulations for car imports.

A more important part of the paper deals with outward transfer of technology. Although only a small proportion of the inflow figures is represented by direct private investment abroad, it is here that we would expect to find the most significant contributions to the subject of the MIT seminar. Australia's performance as an investing country and as a source of capital outflow and technology transfer is, so far, not very distinguished. In this respect Australia seems to behave, mutatis mutandis, like an eighteenth century United Kingdom. The majority of its investments are devoted to mining and production of raw materials abroad, partly to assure its own supply. Although there is also some manufacturing investment in New Zealand and South Africa, the (until recently) quasi-colony of Papua and New Guinea and the Southeast Asian heartland have been the prime recipients of Australian investment and technology. One would think that having recently gone through the birthpangs of absorbing technology, Australia would also be a good intermediary for its transfer. Although this may be so in the future, it is not yet noticeable. In fact, where the paper could have been more explicit is precisely in explaining how to make the transfer of technology into low-income and high-labor supply countries more efficient; scaling down with low labor cost by the use of greater labor-intensive projects is really a great challenge, but it is not described, much less resolved, in the paper. The empirical evidence presented on Australia's potential as a technological intermediary, embodied in Table 4.2, appears to point to relationships between foreign ownership, market shares and tariff protection. Given the dynamic nature of the process, as evidenced by the table comparing firms at different stages of their life cycles, such an analysis might require a deeper investigation, and the author is correct about the pervasive nature of tariff protection, especially in the case of mature products. This protection would certainly create an inward-looking attitude, detrimental to Australia's potential as a technological intermediary and investor abroad.

One of the saddest case studies I have ever seen described in papers dealing with foreign private investment and with transfer of technology is that of the Indonesian shoe-polish manufacturer. It is not surprising that this sort of event, more often attributable to ignorance of governments than to the conspiracies of multinational firms, is one of the main sources of complaints against foreign private investment. It is also the type of subject that has prompted the establishment of filtering mechanisms to which foreign private investment should be subjected. Some countries are experimenting with such mechanisms. Venezuela has created a division of technology transfer within the Ministry of Development, and Chile has an equivalent department in the Industrial Planning Division of the Corporación de Fomento de la Producción. Most Latin American countries and several associate members of OECD, such as Turkey, Greece, and Spain, have similar entities.

The paper is at its most interesting when it deals with the choice of Australia as a base of operations for transnationals. In fact, it would be very interesting to have a good overview of the attitude of Southeast Asian countries whose trust in technology might tend to gravitate to the original source, the United States or Europe, rather than toward an intermediary transfer agent. The paper's comment that transnationals have only used their Australian subsidiaries in exceptional cases as headquarters for operations in their countries does nothing but reaffirm the experience elsewhere. In the framework of the 1970 OECD Conference of Transfer of Technology, I had occasion to show similar experiences with potential intermediary countries in Latin America, whose foreign-owned subsidiaries of transnationals were not allowed to compete with their headquarters for export markets.

The paper is well researched, but it fails to answer an implicit question that could have served as the theme of a seminar on small-country multinationals: Does an MNC based in a small country become less objectionable to receivers of investment and technology transfer? Of all the case studies brought to the seminar, Australia might have been expected to bring the best credentials, for it has no important metropolitan colonizing past, no international political ambition, no deep-rooted commitment to ideologies or to rigid models of development.

There is no reaction to this frustrating question in the study, but perhaps we should leave this field to sociologists and political scientists.

5. The Internationalization of Firms from Developing Countries

Louis T. Wells, Jr.

In Asia, the Middle East, Latin America, and parts of Africa a number of local firms are moving abroad to establish manufacturing plants in other developing countries. Indian companies have subsidiaries in Sri Lanka, Malaysia, and Kenya. Argentine firms have established production facilities in Brazil, Chile, and Uruguay. Countries, such as Indonesia, find themselves hosting subsidiaries of companies headquartered in the Philippines, Korea, Taiwan, Singapore, and Hong Kong.

For some developing countries that are looking for technology or management from abroad, investment from other developing countries appears to offer a politically and perhaps economically attractive alternative to the multinational enterprise.

Size of Flows

The few data that exist give only hints as to the importance of the investment flows from one less developed country (LDC) to another. In a list of the 441 largest nonfinancial firms in Latin America, 10 Brazilian firms are listed as owned in Argentina.[1] Two Argentine parents, Sociedad Industrial Americana di Maquinaries (SIAM) and Bunge y Born, account for several of these firms. In Indonesia, investments approved by the Foreign Investment Board since 1967 contain a significant number of investments from other developing countries. When the mining and petroleum sectors are omitted from the list of foreign investments, Hong Kong stands in second place as a source of foreign investment by total dollars of investment.[2] (Japan holds first place.) The Philippines is in third place, with Singapore and South Korea in the seventh and eighth positions. Asian LDC investors together account for more investment than either Japanese, North American, or European investors.

Although many developing countries like Indonesia report their incoming investments by national origin, the reports of most countries bury many of the projects undertaken by firms from developing countries under the classification of "other" nationalities. Nevertheless, a few hints appear in the reports of several governments. The "other" category presumably has some upper limit on the magnitude of the flows from developing countries into the countries that do not report investment from developing countries separately.

Consider Thailand, one of the better documented cases but almost certainly one of the largest recipients of LDC investment. Of the 360 foreign firms granted promotion status between 1966 and 1973, 93 were from Taiwan, 10 from Malaysia, 5 from Hong Kong, 15 from India, and 16 from Singapore.[3] In addition, 36 fell into the "other" category. No doubt, many of these were also from developing countries.

The Philippine government reports data by value of investment. Non-Philippine Chinese investors accounted for 413 million of the 2,829 million pesos of foreign investments approved by the Board of Investments between 1968 and 1974.[4] The "other foreign" category made up 1,146 million pesos, but it covers much more than the developing nations, since it includes all nationalities except Taiwanese, Japanese, and American.

For Latin America the available data appear to be even less complete. For example, Mexico reports only Venezuelan investors as a separate class, among the developing countries.[5] But the "other" category amounts to only a small percentage of investment in Mexico; so one suspects that incoming investment from other developing countries is small. In fact, Mexico seems to be a source rather than a destination for such investment. Mexican entrepreneurs apparently have important holdings in Central America.

Brazil does not report the investments of developing countries separately. (Panama and the Netherlands Antilles are listed, but no doubt these countries serve only as residences for tax-haven subsidiaries, not as the ultimate home country of the investing companies.) The "other" category accounts for 4 percent of incoming investment in 1973 in a table that lists thirteen countries of origin.[6] No doubt a significant amount of that figure represents investment from other developing countries, especially Argentina.

Somewhat more detailed data are available for the countries of the Central American Common Market. Of 572 reported foreign projects, the vast majority, 413, were from the United States.[7] Twenty eight were from Panama and the Bahamas and thus of uncertain origin. However, other Latin American countries were the homes of 43 investors.

Even when figures are available from host countries, they probably do not adequately indicate the importance of the investment from other developing countries. The reported figures generally show only the sum of the capital actually contributed by the foreign firm. However, the foreign investor from a developing country generally contributes relatively little capital to the project. (I will return to this point.) For the investments from developing countries a local partner in the host country usually puts up a major portion of the funds. Thus, the data as reported by host countries generally understate the total value of industry that is linked to foreign investors from other developing countries, as compared with the investors from the advanced countries, who generally insist on a larger percentage of equity.

On the home-country side, the data appear to be even more sketchy, although some developing countries do collect data on outgoing investments. India, for example, requires her firms to obtain approval before they undertake foreign investments. Thus, government data are available that give some indication of the number of Indian firms involved in overseas activities. By 1974, about 100 firms had received permission to invest in 185 projects abroad.[8] Fifty five of the approved projects were in the construction stage and forty six were in production by this time.

Some Drives behind Foreign Investments

There are some factors that act to encourage foreign investment by a wide range of firms from developing countries. In some cases, the influences arise from government policies. In countries with strict foreign-exchange controls, entrepreneurs see foreign investments as a way of accumulating foreign-exchange holdings. Thus, they can provide themselves with some security in case they have to flee their home.

Sometimes home countries (India, for example) require that firms which desire to import earn their own foreign exchange. Foreign subsidiaries provide an opportunity for some enterprise to earn the needed exchange.

A number of countries place constraints on the growth of their private firms at home, in the form of antitrust action, capacity licensing, or policies that discriminate against large enterprises. For the firm faced with such policies, the only possibility for continued growth may be foreign investment.

Where the size of the home market provides a constraint on potential growth, the entrepreneur may be encouraged to devote his energies abroad, even in the absence of government constraints. The rewards from applying known technology abroad may be more attractive than those that are anticipated from diversification at home. Moreover, some firms find that they can reduce their risk by diversifying across borders. The boom-or-bust environment of construction facing the firm in one country, for example, might be modified if the firm operated in several countries.

Although these and other factors act to encourage the internationalization of LDC firms, it is clear that only certain firms respond to the pressure and are able to survive in foreign markets. These appear to be the firms that have some kind of competitive edge over the multinationals from the advanced countries and over the domestic firms in the countries hosting the LDC investors.

Data are not yet available to provide much empirical evidence about the comparative advantage of LDC investors. Nevertheless, there are some tantalizing hypotheses.

Which Firms Invest?

Research on the activities of firms from advanced countries demonstrates that their foreign investments are made most fre-

quently in industries in which some firms have built an oligopolistic position.[9] The strength of the well-known multinationals
from advanced countries may be based on technology, marketing skills, or some type of economies of scale. To exploit the
competitive edge, whatever its source, the firm from the advanced country extends its interest to foreign markets. For a
time it may be able to exploit that edge by exporting products
that embody its particular know-how, but after a period, freight
costs, tariffs, and the actions of competitors lead the entrepreneur to establish manufacturing plants in those markets.

When the oligopolistic position of the firms is built on technological know-how or on marketing skills, firms from the advanced countries are able to avoid tough price competition.
With some flexibility in the prices they can charge, firms find
that production costs are not generally critical to their success.
Rather than allocating scarce management time to reducing
production costs to a minimum, the major multinationals appear to devote their managerial attention to other matters.[10]
The lack of attention to cost minimization leaves a market
niche for the firms of developing countries, as we shall see in a
moment.

Although technological advantages may provide the major
multinationals with an edge for a while, that edge tends to disappear with time. For some multinational enterprises the ero-
sion of their technological lead means a loss of market share
as local competitors are able to supply similar products at
competitive costs. But those multinationals that have or can establish a particular skill in marketing are able to retain an advantage over local competitors. A well-known trade name, for
example, may protect them from local competition.

There are paths other than marketing by which the major
multinationals extend these competitive advantages. Some multinational firms manage to maintain their oligopolistic strength
by depending on exploiting economies of scale to give them an
edge over producers who might manufacture for a single market. Sometimes the advantages of scale are established
through the construction of a system of specialized plants in
different countries that manufacture long runs of parts and

models so that production costs are minimized. Turning to such strategies, multinational firms in certain industries can contain potential local competitors.

If the multinationals are unable to contain price competition in a particular product line through innovation, marketing skills, or economies of scale, they appear to move on to new product lines where they can establish some oligopolistic position. The old product lines are sometimes spun off to others; in some cases, the multinationals simply allow their market share to be eroded in these products as they devote their attention to other product lines.

In contrast to the multinational firms, the foreign investors based in the developing countries appear to thrive in industries or segments of the market where cost competition is severe and the advantages of economies of large scale do not overwhelm small-scale manufacturers.

The data available suggest that most LDC investors operate in industries that have mature technologies. The technology for the products these investors manufacture has become rather standardized in the advanced countries. Although the manufacturing technologies for the products are generally not characterized by major changes in the advanced countries, an opportunity remains for innovation of a very special kind. The technology used in the advanced countries to manufacture these products is usually based on large-scale manufacture for a mass market. When that technology is applied to manufacture for the market of a developing country, costs are usually high since the market is small. The firm that employs the technology used in the advanced countries for production in the developing countries usually finds itself saddled with excess capacity in various stages of the production line.

In such a situation, there is an opportunity for innovation. That opportunity, it appears, is particularly likely to be seized by the developing-country entrepreneur beginning the process that leads to foreign investment. Many of the developing-country investors appear to have gained their initial advantage when they adapted large-scale technologies of the industrialized countries for manufacture at small scale in their home countries. Once mastered, the ability to manufacture efficiently for small markets gives firms from developing countries a skill that is exportable to other countries with small markets.

Note that the entrepreneur from the developing country may have obtained his original know-how from an industrialized country. In fact, it appears that a major portion of the firms that do go abroad from developing countries were earlier licensees of firms from the advanced nations.

The story of SIAM, today an Argentine-based international firm, illustrates such growth.[11] SIAM went to Brazil in 1928 to manufacture gasoline pumps for the same British customer it served in Argentina. The Brazilian subsidiary never gained its feet with gasoline pumps because the British firm's management was changed and the new management did not back the Brazilian venture. This subsidiary was on the verge of liquidation in 1937. In 1933 the Argentine parent tried to produce refrigeration equipment at home by copying foreign equipment. These efforts were not terribly successful. Finally, SIAM turned to Kelvinator for a license in 1937, and to Westinghouse in 1940. The know-how obtained from these licenses was eventually taken by SIAM to Brazil, and the factory that was to be liquidated in 1937 became an important producer of refrigeration equipment by 1957. The refrigeration technology was introduced in Chile as well, where SIAM's know-how enabled it to take the lead in establishing a compressor plant to supply other assemblers of refrigeration equipment.

In fact, refrigeration equipment is an industry in which developing-country investment seems to be particularly common. For example, Malaysian investors applied and received approval for five ventures for the manufacture or assembly of refrigerators, air conditioners, and household appliances in Indonesia.[12] A Lebanese firm is interested in manufacturing refrigerators in Egypt.[13] A Caribbean investor has established refrigerator plants in other Caribbean countries.[14]

The importance of scale is evident in the Indian firms that have invested abroad. Preliminary work by Balakrishnan is suggesting that Indian foreign investors tend to be firms with a plant size at home similar to that required in the foreign market.[15] Other firms in the same industries, but with much larger or smaller plants in India, do not establish plants outside India.

The emphasis on scale on the part of developing-country investors suggests that they concentrate on a strategy that is based on cost cutting so that prices can be reduced. Cost cutting is not always a viable strategy for market entry, of course. The special technology offered by LDC investors is likely to give them an edge in foreign markets only if price competition is a viable strategy for the particular product in those markets. If the consumer is interested primarily in brand names, for example, LDC investors usually have no edge over multinationals, which are often very skilled in promoting a trade name. In fact, the firm from the developing country is likely to be at a serious disadvantage in competition with multinational firms with sophisticated marketing skills and trade names that are already well known.[16]

The advantage that a firm can gain by having small-scale technology is greatest when the penalties are largest for using the manufacturing processes of the industrialized countries to supply a small market. An optimal plant for the manufacture of refrigerators in the United States, for example, has an output of some 500,000 units annually. There are few developing-country markets that could absorb a major fraction of that output. It is hardly surprising that some entrepreneurs have found a niche for small-scale technology.

The adaptation of technology to small-scale manufacture generally results in a technology that is more labor-intensive than the large-scale technology employed by most multinationals.[17] In fact, the small-scale technology may be competitive only where labor rates are relatively low. In addition, the machinery that is employed tends to be simpler, requiring fewer specialized repair personnel and using more standard parts that can be obtained "off the shelf."[18]

One cannot avoid wondering why multinational enterprises from the advanced countries abandon the market captured by the firms from developing countries. In fact, some multinationals have made efforts to innovate small-scale technology.[19] But for various reasons, the adaptation is usually very limited. Most multinational enterprises appear to be satisfied if they can hold a market niche that is relatively insensitive to price changes.

The managers of multinational firms appear to find that the return to their own time is higher if they devote their attention to technological and marketing innovations that will continue their oligopolistic position, rather than devoting their attention to ways of entering a price-competitive market. As a result, there is a niche left by the multinationals for the developing-country investor to exploit.

In fact, the ability to manufacture efficiently at small scale appears not to be the only cost advantage of the LDC investor. Some appear to have an edge over potential competitors from the advanced countries through their ability to reduce the costs of management and engineering personnel. Although the multinational enterprises generally move expensive managers and engineers from the advanced countries to their subsidiaries, the LDC investors draw theirs from their own home countries. In fact, the manager of an overseas subsidiary is likely to be a relative of the owner-manager of the parent. SIAM, for example, sent a nephew of the founder to Brazil in 1937 and a brother-in-law to Chile in 1933.[20] The typical salary for an Indian manager abroad is only a small fraction of that for an American stationed overseas. Low costs for management and engineers appear to enhance the advantage of the LDC investor over the multinationals in market segments where price competition is a viable strategy.

The developing-country investors seem to have an edge over host-country firms as well, at least in certain industries. LDC investors possess a technology not in the hands of local investors. True, in many cases the purchases of the machines would probably enable a local manufacturer to begin production. However, it appears that the international market for machinery made in developing countries is particularly poorly developed. It would rarely occur to a potential Indonesian manufacturer to seek his machinery in India, for example. Yet, an Indian investor knows about that machinery; and, as I will point out, he has a way of finding out about the market and its output.

As we have noted, to exploit the advantages offered by lower management and manufacturing costs, the usual LDC investor appears to concentrate on serving a price-sensitive market. In fact, few firms from developing countries seem to have the skills to survive in a market dominated by marketing competition.

Identifying industries for which price competition is a viable strategy poses problems. Some efforts have been made to classify industries by their barriers to entry in the advanced countries. Although this work provides a useful start in looking at LDC investors, it is clear that price competition is an attractive alternative in some industries in the developing countries, even though there is little price sensitivity evident for those same industries in the advanced nations. The proportion of consumers sensitive to price appears to be higher for some products in poor countries than in the wealthier ones. In addition, the LDC firm may consider a small market share sufficiently attractive; a multinational firm from an advanced country might well ignore that segment.

Detergents illustrate such a situation. Bain describes detergents as being characterized by significant product differentiation.[21] The big three detergent manufacturers hold 95 percent of the U.S. market. Their strategies rely on heavy advertising budgets to convince the consumer that their products are better. With consumers in the advanced countries, price appears not to be at issue. But in several developing countries a segment of the market for detergents is much more price sensitive than the U.S. market appears to be. Thus, there is a market segment open in developing countries that can be captured by low-cost producers.

The opportunities to exploit cost advantages may be taken up by two different types of LDC firms. In most cases, the firm that ventures abroad is probably a manufacturer of the same product in his home country. In other cases, the investor is a manufacturer of machinery, who has adapted Western machinery technology to the needs of local markets. For the machinery maker the alternative of direct investment is often more viable than that of simply exporting machinery to a firm in the other country, because the marketing links that would allow him to make the sale are usually so poorly established. The would-be entrepreneur in the host country does not have access to information about the machinery available in other developing countries. In fact, where I found LDC equipment in use in locally owned plants in Indonesia, almost invariably the local firm was owned by a Chinese Indonesian who had discovered the machinery supplier through his family contacts in Singapore, Taiwan, Hong Kong, or the Philippines.[22] Where this type of family network does not exist, export opportunities are likely to remain unexploited unless the manufacturer himself or a firm from his own country takes up the overseas project.

Operating Policies

The vast majority of LDC investors enter foreign markets through the use of joint ventures with partners of the host country. The data illustrate this entry. For advanced-country investors in Indonesia, 20 percent of the projects were wholly owned by the foreign investors. In contrast, only 13 percent of the projects of LDC investors were wholly foreign-owned.[23] This pattern appears to be typical of LDC investors elsewhere.

In some cases, the reasons why the investor from a developing country prefers joint ventures, and even minority ownership, are strikingly apparent. India, for example, allows its firms to export no capital except machinery. The plant, some equipment, and working capital are generally supplied by a local partner. As in India, exchange controls in other countries no doubt make it difficult for their investors to gain a large portion of the shares in an overseas project.

There are probably other reasons for the preference for joint ventures. One possibility is that investors are conditioned by the political sensitivities they know in their home countries. Aware of the feelings raised by wholly foreign ownership in their own countries, investors from developing nations may be more sensitive to this issue when they invest elsewhere than are their counterparts from the advanced countries. In addition, one of the major reasons that some major multinationals avoid joint ventures does not apply to LDC investors. The single most important source of conflict between multinationals and joint-venture partners does not affect most LDC investors. Unlike their multinational counterparts, the LDC investor has little fear of having his strategy disrupted with disputes over marketing policies with a local partner, since sophisticated marketing strategies do not usually play a role in the firm's success.[24]

There are probably other important differences in management style between the LDC investor and the multinational enterprise. Prime among these is the nature of the relation between the subsidiary and its parent.

It is usually important for the multinational enterprise from the advanced country to maintain a close relationship with its subsidiary. Typically that subsidiary has a role to play in the global strategy of the parent that extends beyond contributing dividends. It may provide raw materials or parts for manufacture or processing elsewhere. Or it may provide a market for components manufactured by the multinational enterprise in other countries. Its prices and the quality of image it creates can, management usually believes, affect the prices or image of products sold by the firm elsewhere. In addition, the subsidiary may serve to reduce the risk of other parts of the operation by providing a threat to international competitors.[25] And so on. In such a situation the parent feels compelled to keep a tight boundary around the subsidiary's freedom of action. In addition, the subsidiary is likely to be rather dependent on the parent for a continual input of technology or marketing know-how to retain its competitive edge. If the edge is based on technological skills, new skills are needed as the old ones are copied by competitors. If marketing skills provide the advantage, new developments elsewhere must be transferred to the subsidiary. When new inputs are required to maintain a competitive edge, some kind of close link to the parent is likely to be essential. If scale is the competitive weapon, the subsidiary may have to remain integrated into the trade system of the multinational enterprise. This integration requires careful control of quality and delivery dates by the parent.[26]

In contrast, the subsidiary of the LDC investor is often, I suspect, "on its own" after a brief period of assistance from the parent at the outset. In fact, the links between the subsidiary and the parent may wither away with time. After a few years, the subsidiary of the LDC investor may be hardly distinguishable from a local enterprise. There may, of course, be exceptions. Some LDC parents may be able to keep up a regular flow of newly adapted technology.

Direction of Investment Flows

Not surprisingly, investment among the developing countries appears to flow primarily from the larger or wealthier developing countries to smaller or poorer ones. Primary sources of manufacturing investment seem to be India, Mexico, Argentina, Lebanon, Taiwan, Singapore, and Hong Kong. Several years ago, these countries provided sufficiently large home markets for many products. In these countries with larger markets, local businesses acquired the necessary technology and adapted it to the special needs of developing countries. The products are only later demanded in sufficient quantities in the poorer or smaller countries to support local production. The pioneering firms from the larger or wealthier countries then find an opportunity to exploit their know-how elsewhere.

There are small investment flows from the developing countries to the advanced countries and "horizontally" in the developing world. But these appear to be the result of special product innovation or vertical integration, matters which I will deal with later.

Theory

One might conveniently view the internationalization of developing-country firms simply as a stage in the product-life-cycle or technological-gap models to explain trade and investment flows.[27] According to one version of the models, countries can be considered to fall into a "pecking order."[28] They can be ranked by when they first produced a particular product. The countries currently manufacturing the product export down the "pecking order" to those countries that do not yet have plants. Not only might the source of exports in world trade move down that order as a product matures, but the source of foreign investment might follow a similar pattern. The advanced countries provide the early foreign investors. Later, some of the more advanced developing countries appear as exporters of capital to countries further down the list.

The "pecking order" approach has a well-developed rationale to explain why the source of exports might move down the order. That explanation is based on the availability of technology plus the differences in production costs.

It is less clear why the source of investment should move down the order. Once European or Japanese firms manufacture a product, there is no immediately obvious reason why those firms should have any edge over the American investors in setting up plants in the next round of countries. But the data that exist support two possible explanations. First, the product may have gone through a subtle change by the time it was manufactured in Europe or Japan. Many products have been adapted to the needs of a somewhat lower-income consumer as they have been produced abroad. Mass-produced automobiles in Europe were smaller and more economical to operate than their North American counterparts. Refrigerators and freezers were more suitable to less spacious living arrangements.[29] The adaptation gives the firm from Europe or Japan an edge for certain products in the poorer markets. At this stage the adaptations appear to be primarily in product design rather than in production technology.

Another explanation of the role of the European and Japanese firms in a "pecking order" lies in the willingness of the later producers to offer more attractive terms than the first North Americans could offer to the countries in which they manufactured. Not bound by agreements elsewhere that might be upset, the later investors do not hesitate to offer joint ownership or even straight licensing arrangements to countries further down the pecking order. If the U.S. multinationals were to offer similar terms, they would find many of the host countries where they had earlier established subsidiaries clamoring for the new, better deals. Thus, it was European manufacturers, such as Fiat, that first showed a willingness to enter licensing arrangements for automobile plants, at a time when U.S. manufacturers were still insisting on large equity positions.

While the Japanese and European firms sometimes gain an

edge over the Americans by adapting products to lower-income needs, changes in the product do not appear to be a very important factor for the developing-country firms. The critical change appears to be in manufacturing technique. It is the edge that comes from this kind of development that enables the developing country to compete abroad in certain markets. Thus, although the "pecking order" continues, there is a shift in the source of the competitive edge that investors exploit.

There are other elements involved, however, especially in the movement of factors of production. First, in the case of developing-country investment, managers tend to move. They move in the case of multinationals as well, but there their role is primarily as conveyors of know-how or as part of the control function. In the case of developing-country firms, their low wages play a role in the cost competitiveness of the firm. Thus, a part of the factor-cost advantage that would influence trade in the absence of investment flows actually moves when investment flows are allowed.

Machinery provides an example of a similar phenomenon. In the case of multinationals, machinery is often moved from the advanced countries to the developing countries. However, the machinery is not necessarily "appropriate" to the factor costs of the recipient country. In the case of the LDC investor, machinery may also move from one developing country to another. However, for the LDC investor that machinery is adapted to the needs of the host country and provides a part of his competitive edge.

Other Factors in the Investment Flows

Needless to say, the discussion thus far does not capture all the factors that influence investment by LDC investors. Some of the other factors that influence developing-country firms appear to be similar to those that lead firms from the advanced countries to go abroad.

Some firms from developing countries innovate in ways other than the development of small-scale technology. As the Americans innovate for high-income, labor-saving products, and the

Europeans innovate raw-material saving and capital-saving technologies, some developing-country firms innovate products, as well as technologies, suited to their own markets. The spread of noodle manufacturers from other Southeast Asian countries into Indonesia can hardly be explained as an adaptation of Western technology. It must be seen as a product or marketing innovation suitable for local tasks. There are also a few examples of LDC investors carrying their products to the industrialized countries. Such examples appear to be primarily cases of serving ethnically related markets with products from the home country.

Like the multinationals a few LDC investors have established overseas operations as sources for exports. However, it does not appear that many developing-country firms are establishing foreign subsidiaries to obtain low-cost labor to supply their home market. Rather, costs at home are low enough and the import barriers are sufficiently high so that such moves are not necessary. Only a few LDC investors seem to be looking for low-cost labor to supply markets in other countries that they used to supply from home like some Japanese investors who moved abroad to protect their export markets in the United States. However, a number of LDC firms have set up subsidiaries abroad to escape "voluntary" export controls. Garment manufacturers have been on the move for a number of years. First, they tended to be centered in Hong Kong. Faced with export quotas in Hong Kong, some established subsidiary operations in Singapore.[30] As exports there were restricted, they gradually sought bases in Thailand, Indonesia, and elsewhere.[31]

The need for raw materials has provided a challenge to LDC firms similar to that faced by firms from the industrialized nations. Many LDC firms have built manufacturing operations at home based on what appeared to be secure sources of raw materials. These sources have, on occasion, turned out to be less reliable than was originally anticipated. As a result, the firms have sought sources of raw materials elsewhere. For example, Korean and Philippine firms that manufactured wood products from timber sources in the Philippines have begun to invest in alternate sources of timber, especially in Indonesia. Philippine and Korean investments have accounted for 69 percent of the forestry projects approved in Indonesia since 1967.[32]

At times, the need for captive overseas sources of raw materials has been obvious from the outset. It was rumored, for example, that some recent proposals for an Iranian steel mill included plans for the Iranian firm to hold an interest in Indian iron-ore sources. (The Indians, it appears, would also have a holding in the Iranian steel plant.) Similar proposals have been put forward for the development of the Mutún iron-ore deposit in southern Bolivia. To assure a market, the Bolivians would seek equity participation from Argentine steel firms. To provide an offset for the financial flows, Bolivia might take an interest in the Argentine plants. In another case, a major Argentine investment has already taken place in Brazil, as an Argentine firm sought a source of manganese.[33]

The drive for vertical integration probably affects LDC investors in another way. There are, apparently, some cases of LDC firms that have established subsidiaries abroad, in more advanced countries, to provide outlets for their products produced at home.

Like firms from the advanced countries, some LDC service companies have also established international operations. The Bangkok Bank Limited, for example, has offices in Singapore, Kuala Lumpur, Jakarta, and elsewhere. Osman Ahmad Osman, an Egyptian contractor, operates in a number of Middle East countries, I understand.

Financial institutions apparently respond to the same challenges as their counterparts from the advanced countries. As their customers' needs have required contacts overseas, some banks from the developing countries have established overseas offices to serve those needs. I suspect that the foreign offices are concerned primarily with the needs of exporters from the home country. In the absence of local banks with overseas facilities, the exporting firms would probably have turned to advanced-country multinational banks to meet their needs. But there are no data available, as far as I know, that cover the activities of these banks.

Contracting firms probably have certain advantages over competitors. The Egyptian contractor has the experience in

large projects that is lacking in several other Middle East countries. But the question remains how he competes with the large
international contractors from the advanced countries that are
also active in the region. Some local observers suggest that local firms are better at the cheap, unsophisticated construction
work that is so common in the commercial buildings constructed in the area. No doubt, the ability of an Arab firm to deal with
Arabic-speaking workers is another edge. Similar advantages
may exist for contractors from other developing countries
where a region speaks a common language and shares related
cultures.

Other service investments provide a more mixed bag. Language and common culture probably play a role in most cases,
as in construction firms. But common standards of performance may also be important factors that enable service firms
to expand beyond their home countries.

The Attractions of LDC Investors to Governments

Attitudes in the developing countries toward foreign investments by LDC firms vary from antagonism through indifference
to enthusiasm. Antagonism is most common on the part of the
governments of countries that tend to be sources of such investments. Indifference or mild encouragement is more typical
of the governments of countries that receive the investment
flows. And enthusiasm appears to be strongest on the part of
international organizations, several of which view the internationalization of projects in a region as a step that encourages
regional cooperation and integration.

From the point of view of host countries, investment from
other developing countries may have certain advantages over
the alternative of multinational enterprises. Probably the most
attractive advantage lies in the nature of the technology. If
the investors do indeed bring in a small-scale technology, their
plants are less likely than plants based on other technologies
to suffer from idle capacity, and LDC technology is more likely
to be labor-intensive than the technology brought by the
multinationals. Thus, the contribution to dealing with unem-

ployment problems may be greater than that brought by multinationals.

Investors from developing countries may offer other advantages to host countries. If they respond to the pressure to take
local partners into projects, they will be considered attractive.
In fact, most LDC investors may seek out local partners even
without government pressure. In addition, any sensitivity on the
part of LDC investors to the special political problems of business in developing countries is considered as an advantage
over multinationals. If projects from developing countries are
actually less dependent on continuing foreign ties, the local
control that develops is politically attractive to most developing-country governments. Allowing a foreign firm to invest
need not be an almost permanent surrender of an industry segment to foreign control.

There are several possible advantages on which virtually no
data are available. For example, developing-country investors
may be more likely than the multinationals to source their inputs locally. It is possible that the overall costs of projects from
developing countries is less than the costs of multinationals.
Management and engineers apparently cost less. However, no
data are available on dividends, royalties, and other payments
abroad.

Not surprisingly, LDC investors may also have certain disadvantages in comparison to the multinationals. The LDC investor
is perhaps less likely to be able to provide a continuing stream
of technology, although there are a few examples that suggest
this may not always be the case. It is likely, however, that the
LDC investor has less ready access to a significant export market. There is some evidence to suggest that he pays lower
wages to local workers.[34] While some countries would view this
as a disadvantage, others apparently do not.

Many developing countries probably will tentatively conclude
that the economic and political benefits outweigh the economic disadvantages for a wide range of industries. The exception
will probably be where a continual flow of new technology
seems particularly important or where it appears that the multinational will indeed provide access to a foreign market that

another firm could not reach. But a definitive answer, or even an approach to classifying the firms by their potential net benefits, will have to await the collection of more empirical data.

The social issues provide special problems in certain regions of the world. I have suggested that the original contacts for LDC investments are often provided through ethnic ties. In many areas this connection means that LDC investors are closely linked with a local minority group that already poses a social problem. Indian firms in East Africa and Taiwanese or Singapore firms in Indonesia receive only a cool welcome, in spite of economic advantages. They are sometimes perceived as contributing to the strength of a locally unpopular minority group. In East Africa and Indonesia the possible conflicts are apparent. In contrast, in many other parts of the world the LDC investor is likely to provide a welcome relief from the familiar U.S. firm or investor from the former colonial master.

From the point of view of the developing country that is a source of foreign investment, the advantages are less apparent. Many home governments view the projects suspiciously because they export scarce foreign exchange and divert the attention of entrepreneurs that are desperately needed at home.

In most developing countries, governments cannot be very confident that the price mechanism will lead business people to make decisions that are in the national interest. If local entrepreneurs calculate the returns they would receive on a domestic project, their private calculations may lead to a decision that is not optimal from the social point of view. The returns from the local project may, for example, be influenced by tariffs on inputs and other distortions. As a result, the private return may be greater from foreign investment, even though the social return may be greater from a local investment.

Only a project-by-project evaluation can fully answer the questions involved. However, there is some evidence to suggest that the home country may benefit more than it suspects from foreign investment. First, little foreign exchange is used in most cases. The investment by the LDC firm apparently typically consists largely of machinery supplied from its home country. To the extent that this machinery would not have been exported in the absence of the investment, there is no foreign-exchange cost. Second, the net return to the home country from the foreign investment may be reasonably high. The entrepreneur may be capturing rents on know-how with little or no opportunity cost. In fact, the home country may have paid for the know-how in the past through licensing fees to an industrialized country. Now it is simply reselling the modified know-how to another country without diminishing the benefit it has received.

The cost in terms of entrepreneurs presents a more difficult case. The issue is whether the managers sent abroad and the time devoted to the project by those at home would have been used as productively in the home country in the absence of the foreign project. My guess is that in quite a few cases the answer is no. The managers at home are often not fully occupied with a single business. Fears of government reaction if they expand their business at home restrict them in countries such as India. In addition, family members who would not strike out on their own may provide the overseas management in many cases.[35]

There is certainly not enough evidence yet available to draw any kind of definitive conclusions on the attractiveness of LDC investors to their home and host countries. There are some investments for which the net benefits are particularly apparent. Overseas bank offices may, for example, provide major benefits to the home country in the form of facilitating local exports. However, in most cases the benefits are less apparent. The few data do suggest that the more common manufacturing investments might well benefit both the home countries and the host countries. A final answer will have to await further research.

Notes

I have benefited greatly from the ideas of K. Balakrishnan and from the comments of Jagdish Bhagwati and Stephen Kobrin.

1. "Directorio de las mayores compañías de América Latina," *Progresso* (January/February 1974): 30–48.

2. Indonesian Foreign Investment Board, *Investment Applications and Approvals: 1967 through 1973,* mimeo, Jakarta. As in most data on foreign investments, the stated country of origin can be misleading. A Philippine investor could be the subsidiary of a U.S. firm, for example. Although several such cases have been identified, the problem does not appear to be sufficiently

widespread to affect the data seriously.

3. Mimeographed documents provided by the Board of Investment, Bangkok.

4. Government of the Republic of the Philippines, *Four-Year Development Plan: 1974–77* (Manila, 1973).

5. Data reported by the Banco de Mexico.

6. Data reported by the Brazilian government.

7. Gert Rosenthal, *The Role of Private Foreign Investment in the Development of the Central American Common Market,* Table 27 (forthcoming).

8. Data collected by K. Balakrishnan for doctoral dissertation (in progress) at Harvard Business School. See also Indian Investment Centre, *Joint Ventures Abroad,* New Delhi (date unknown).

9. See, for example, Raymond Vernon, *Sovereignty at Bay* (New York: Basic Books, 1971), chap. 3; Stephen H. Hymer and Robert Rowthorn, *Multinational Corporations and International Oligopoly* (New Haven: Yale University, Economic Growth Center, 1959); and Stephen H. Hymer, "The International Operations of National Firms," unpublished dissertation, M.I.T., 1960. For the Europeans, see Lawrence G. Franko, *The European Multinationals: A Challenge to American and British Big Business?* (New York: Harper and Row, 1976).

10. See, for example, Louis T. Wells, Jr., "Economic Man and Engineering Man: Choice of Technology in a Low Wage Country," *Public Policy* (Summer 1973). A complementary explanation of why multinationals ignore the price sensitive market is found in Nathaniel H. Leff, "Multinational Corporate Pricing Strategy in the Developing Countries," *Journal of International Business Studies* (Fall 1975): 55–64.

11. Thomas C. Cochran and Ruben E. Reiner, *Capitalism in Argentine Culture: A Study of Torcuato di Tella and S.I.A.M.* (Philadelphia: University of Pennsylvania Press, 1962).

12. Indonesian Foreign Investment Board, *Investment Applications and Approvals.*

13. Private interviews.

14. Private interviews.

15. Balakrishnan, doctoral dissertation in progress.

16. See Ralph Z. Sorenson, II, "An Analysis of Competition among Local and International Firms in Two Central American Industries," unpublished dissertation, Harvard Business School, 1967.

17. Donald LeCraw, "Determinants of Capital Intensity in Low Wage Countries: The Case of Thailand," thesis in progress at Harvard University, suggests the technology of LDC investors was more labor-intensive than that of other foreign investors. The relation between scale and labor intensity has not been well established, as far as I know. However, there are suggestive data, such as those for sugar in James Pickett, *A Report on a Pilot Investiga-*

tion of Technology in Developing Countries (Strathclyde: University of Strathclyde, David Livingstone Institute of Overseas Development Studies, December 1975), p. 96.

18. Wells, "Economic Man and Engineering Man." The observations are from forty-five factories studied in Indonesia.

19. The work of N. V. Philips, the Dutch multinational, is frequently cited by scholars. See also, Wayne A. Yeoman, "Selection of Production Processes for the Manufacturing Subsidiaries of U.S. Based Multinational Corporations," unpublished dissertation, Harvard Business School, 1968.

20. Cochran and Reiner, *Capitalism in Argentine Culture.*

21. See Joe S. Bain, *Barriers to New Competition* (Cambridge: Harvard University Press, 1956).

22. See Louis T. Wells, Jr., "Men and Machines in Indonesia's Light Manufacturing Industries," *Bulletin of Indonesian Economic Studies* (November 1973).

23. Indonesian Foreign Investment Board, *Investment Applications and Approvals.*

24. For the importance of marketing disputes in the decisions of multinationals with regard to joint ventures, see John M. Stopford and Louis T. Wells, Jr., *Managing the Multinational Enterprise* (New York: Basic Books, 1972), chap. 8.

25. See Fred T. Knickerbocker, *Oligopolistic Reaction and Multinational Enterprise* (Boston: Harvard Business School, 1973).

26. The nature of the ties required affects the overall organizational structure of the multinational enterprise. See Stopford and Wells, *Managing the Multinational Enterprise.*

27. See Raymond Vernon, "International Investment and International Trade in the Product Cycle," *Quarterly Journal of Economics* (May 1966) and Vernon, *Sovereignty at Bay.*

28. Gary Hufbauer, *Synthetic Materials and the Theory of International Trade* (Cambridge: Cambridge University Press, 1966).

29. See, for example, Louis T. Wells, Jr., "Test of a Product Cycle Model of International Trade: U.S. Exports of Consumer Durables," reprinted in Louis T. Wells, Jr., ed., *The Product Life Cycle and International Trade* (Boston: Harvard Business School, 1972).

30. See, for example, Helen M. Hughes, ed., *Foreign Investment and Industrialization in Singapore* (Madison: University of Wisconsin, 1969).

31. In 1972 Indonesia had at least half a dozen proposals from Hong Kong firms to establish government facilities to serve export markets. My interviews in Hong Kong suggested that the major reason for establishing facilities in Indonesia was to escape the strict export controls imposed in Hong Kong.

32. Indonesian Foreign Investment Board, *Investment Applications and Approvals.*

33. Case study developed by the Institute for Latin American Integration (INTAL), Buenos Aires.

34. See Wells, "Economic Man and Engineering Man," p. 323.

35. Family managers in Chinese firms are examined in John Lee Espy, "The Strategies of Chinese Industrial Enterprises in Hong Kong," unpublished dissertation, Harvard Business School, 1970.

Comment

Stephen J. Kobrin

Wells's paper deals with three sets of issues relating to the internationalization of firms based in the developing (or perhaps more correctly, the less industrialized) countries. The first is the empirical question of the nature and the extent of the phenomenon. The second concerns its theoretical basis, and the last discusses the relative advantages and disadvantages of the internationalization of developing-country firms for both home and host countries. I shall only comment on the first and second issues in the context of the paper, but I should like to expand upon the third to discuss a subject covered only tangentially: the political ramifications of foreign direct investment (FDI) by firms based in the developing countries.

The Extent of the Phenomenon

In attempting to determine the extent of developing-country FDI, one is limited to anecdotal evidence and inadequate data. Unfortunately, even the existing data are ambiguous. Sources of flows of FDI provide no information about who ultimately controls the investment. While Canadian subsidiaries of U.S. firms have served as the parent for other subsidiaries in the Commonwealth, one would not assume that the resulting flows actually represent Canadian FDI in any but a nominal sense. Similarly, one wonders how much of what is recorded as Philippine-based FDI is really controlled by Philippine nationals and how much is a "retransmittal" of investment originating in the industrialized countries. It thus appears difficult, if not impossible, to determine the extent of foreign direct investment by developing-country firms.

The question has qualitative as well as quantitative implications. If developing-country FDI is an occasional and limited phenomenon, it may well be explained by environmental factors such as the existence of a large, transnational community of overseas Chinese or Indians. If FDI originating in the developing countries is a more general phenomenon, it should either be consistent with theories of FDI or suggest modifications to the latter.

The Theoretical Basis of Developing-Country FDI

The paper posits systematic differences between FDI that originates in less and more industrialized countries. It is assumed that subsidiaries of less-industrialized-country firms are not integrated into a global system, that joint ventures with local partners predominate, that little capital is transferred, and that organizational structure and control are polycentric. Perhaps most importantly, Wells hypothesizes that investors mediate between the large-scale, automated, capital-intensive technology found in the industrialized nations and the needs of the less industrialized countries for smaller-scale labor-intensive processes. They develop and export intermediate technology.

The last contention is crucial and much of the paper's conclusions turn on its acceptance. The ability of less-industrialized-country investors to develop and transfer technology that is appropriate for the conditions found in a small labor-intensive country could provide a major source of benefits to host countries. In addition, it could provide the basis for competitive advantages with regard to both industrialized-country multinationals and host-country competitors that the investors need to survive. However, while the successful development of intermediate technology is a hypothesis, it is taken as an assumption of Wells's argument. It is interesting and certainly not illogical. However, at this point it remains conjecture supported by only limited anecdotal evidence.

The paper raises an interesting theoretical issue. How do foreign investors from developing countries compete with local firms? As foreigners they face added costs imposed by geographical and cultural distance and by unfamiliarity with local conditions that must be somehow offset. The industrialized-country firm is typically found in an oligopolistic industry where their technological and/or managerial advantages can be contained to generate rents to offset the added costs imposed by distance. As Wells points out, developed-country FDI is typically not found in industries where price competition is the norm.

However, if investors from developing countries are found in industries where price competition is typical, how do they off-set their added costs versus local competitors? One could argue that the magnitude of the disadvantage is smaller in contrast to the disadvantage to an enterprise from an industrialized country, as a developing-country investor is familiar with a somewhat similar political and socioeconomic environment. However, there are still major differences in language and culture and in social and political systems. Furthermore, it is not clear that the developing-country investor will be more welcome than his industrialized-country counterpart. The Chinese in Asia and the Indians in Africa serve as examples.

As the paper notes, developing-country investors may have several advantages over competitors from industrialized nations. Their technology may be more appropriate and their costs, especially in terms of wages paid to expatriates, may be lower. But if, as Wells suggests, they operate in industries where technology is mature, where price competition is the norm, and if "after a few years, the subsidiary of the investor may be hardly distinguishable from local enterprise," how do they generate, much less retain, a source of rents? The wages paid expatriate managers are not likely to be lower than those paid to local managers. Even if developing-country investors bring a technological advantage initially, how can they keep from losing that advantage through competition? In summary, given that developing-country investors lack the technological and managerial advantages of industrialized-country firms and given that they operate in industries where competition makes it difficult to retain any advantage that does exist, it is hard to see how they can hold their own against local enterprise. Perhaps the phenomenon is more accurately described as immigration rather than as foreign investment.

The Benefits of Developing-Country Investment
The paper thoroughly reviews many of the costs and benefits of developing-country FDI to both host and home countries. If one assumes that developing-country investors are net contributors of appropriate technology and/or management to host countries (Wells acknowledges that they are unlikely to transfer much capital), I would contend that their advantage over their

industrialized-country counterparts may lie in the political rather than the economic or technical sphere.

FDI has the potential to contribute much needed technological and managerial resources to the process of development and industrialization. However, it is obvious that FDI is viewed as less than universally beneficial by many in the developing countries. As Barbara Ward notes: "Private investment is valuable. It does provide indispensible technological inputs. But it can be too powerful and it can stay too long."[1]

Many of the concerns about FDI in developing countries can be subsumed under two headings: control and dependence. Policy makers recognize the need for the transfer of resources that FDI can provide. However, they often express concern over the fact that these resources come embodied in a corporate entity responsible both to a headquarters located in, and to a government of, a significantly more powerful industrialized country. One response has been to seek "unbundling": the direct purchase of management and technology through contractual arrangements. If Wells is correct, if FDI flowing from one developing country to another can provide appropriate technology at a reasonable cost, it may well provide an alternative to unbundling. Given that political and economic relationships between LDCs—what Rosenbaum and Tyler call South-South relations[2]—are less likely to be asymmetrical than those between developing and industrialized countries, problems of control and dependence should be alleviated.

Concerns of developing-country governments over the loss of political and economic control as a result of FDI can be expressed as a function of two related factors. First, the subsidiary is a unit in a global system whose objective, at least in theory, is optimization on a global basis. There is no reason to assume that this will result in the subsidiary's maximizing output, employment, or exports on a local basis. The multinational enterprise (MNE) and the host country view the same subsidiary as an instrument for executing different objectives that may, or may not, be compatible.

Second, even in countries where "arm's-length" business-government relations are the norm, subsidiaries are clearly responsive to the home-country government. The fact that the MNE's headquarters, and often the single largest concentration of its assets, are located in a specific political unit is obviously important. The U.S. government, for example, has extended its domestic laws extraterritorially through indirect pressures (via the headquarters) on the subsidiaries of its multinational corporations. The Trading With the Enemy Act has been used to prevent subsidiaries from dealing with China or Cuba, even when the transaction was both legal and desired in the host country.[3] In other instances U.S. antitrust laws have been extended extraterritorially through the subsidiaries of multinationals.

Given asymmetrical power relationships, it is difficult to see how FDI does not at least entail a serious potential loss of political and economic control and a loss of sovereignty for host-country governments. It is clear that the MNE mediates between home- and host-country governments; their relationship would be significantly different if MNE were absent. However, one does not need to assume a state-centric paradigm, a view of states as unitary international actors, to perceive threats to host-country control arising from FDI. The recent literature abounds with discussions of MNEs as significant transnational political actors in their own right.[4] They, as well as various government departments, the armed forces, and the Vatican, may "make foreign policy," linking interest groups in a number of political jurisdictions. A flagrant and unfortunate example can be found in Lockheed's attempt to influence Japanese rearmament policy in a direction diametrically opposed to the preference articulated by the U.S. State Department.

It should be noted that the emergence of MNEs as significant transnational political actors may constrain the freedom or restrict the control of home as well as host nations. As Samuel Huntington has noted, a transnational organization "has its own interest which inheres in the organization and its functions, which may or may not be related to the interests of national groups."[5] To function transnationally, an actor must obviously command significant resources. However, such functioning also requires a global view, a "broader than national perspective with respect to the pursuit of highly specialized objectives through a central optimizing strategy across national boundaries."[6]

A second major set of problems that are viewed as unwanted baggage accompanying FDI by many in developing countries can be classed under the heading of dependence: the political, economic, or cultural control of one nation by another. While political dependence or neoimperialism is a controversial and much debated subject and one in which multinationals are seen by some to play a significant role, technological and cultural dependence are more logically associated with FDI.

In essence, dependence entails a restriction of indigenous freedom to choose future paths of development. (The traditional dependency-theorists would claim that it constrains the process of growth per se and that it results in underdevelopment.[7]) By supplying a sophisticated, capital-intensive and closely held technology, multinational firms may make developing countries dependent on industrialized nations for maintenance, spare parts, and repairs. A more simple machine might be repaired and maintained with local skills and materials. A more sophisticated piece of equipment will probably require continuous transfers from advanced countries.

MNEs can also act as a cross-cultural vehicle for the transfer of attitudes and values.[8] Advertising, for example, may create a consumer mentality, increasing demand for nonessential luxury goods that require both a concentration of income to generate demand and a production technology inappropriate for the level of industrial development. The argument is far from settled. What some call cultural dependence is viewed by others as merely responding to local demand. More important, perhaps, is the comparison some theorists make between the MNEs and an idealized scenario where an identical level of industrial development and resource transfer are achieved indigenously. However, one does not have to be a Marxist to recognize the potential for technological and cultural dependence. FDI involves a trade-off for the developing countries, although the risks—to both parties—may be reduced through an appropriate regulatory framework and through entry negotiations.[9] Furthermore, whether one accepts dependence as a reality or not, it is accepted as such by a broad range of individuals in the developing countries who view FDI as a mechanism through which industrialized countries maintain economic and technical, and thus political control over the developing countries.

FDI from the Developing Countries

All of the potential problems discussed above, which are associated with flows of FDI from industrialized to developing countries, are a function of two characteristics of multinational enterprise. First, there is a marked asymmetry in terms of wealth and political and economic power between home and host countries. Second, multinationals tend toward optimization on a global basis. However, asymmetry and global optimization are not typically characteristics of foreign investment flowing from developing countries.

While there are significant differences in both wealth and power among the less industrialized countries and while, as Wells notes, one would expect FDI to flow down a "pecking order," differences within the group of less industrialized countries are less marked than those between less and more industrialized countries. South-South economic and political relationships are more symmetrical than are North-South relationships.

One would not expect foreign investors from the developing countries to have either a global horizon or operations that are global in scope. The Wells model posits quite the opposite. FDI flows from one developing country to another are based upon the ability to develop an appropriate intermediate technology and low managerial costs, and they are polycentric in character. Global optimization and concern over suboptimization do not appear to be relevant objective functions.

There are numerous political and economic conflicts between less industrialized countries. Furthermore, concerns over imperialism are not absent from Third World relationships. Iran's growing military strength and Brazil's increasing power in Latin America are not viewed with equanimity by all Third World countries. However, within the context of concerns arising from FDI, it appears reasonable to conclude that flows originating in less developed countries carry a smaller potential for restraints on host-country (and perhaps home-country) sovereignty and/or technological and cultural dependence.

The absence of a global horizon and attempts at global optimization should mitigate conflicts over objectives between the enterprise and the host country. Few developing-country firms possess either the resources or the global span to function as transnational political actors. Finally, it appears less than likely that developing countries would attempt to use subsidiaries of their companies as vehicles for the extraterritorial application of their laws and regulations.

The nature of the investment and the relative symmetry of home and host countries make it unlikely that South-South FDI will result in either technological or cultural dependence. Again, the Wells model posits a transfer of intermediate technology that is consistent with the resources and capabilities of the host society. One would expect that most maintenance and repair could be handled locally. Similarly, one would expect that the products transferred would generally be appropriate for the state of development of the host country rather than luxury consumer products that require intensive advertising and promotional support. The cultures of home and host countries, when both are less industrialized societies, should be more similar than those of a less and a more industrialized nation.

Thus, some of the political problems that inhere in FDI flowing from more to less industrialized countries should be alleviated when FDI originates in a developing nation. However, some of the potential benefits, in terms of transfers of management and technology, are also reduced. A trade-off is involved the dimensions of which, in part, depend upon the capability of developing-country investors to mediate between the advanced technology of the industrialized countries and the needs of developing nations. That capability—to develop and transmit an intermediate technology—is an important and interesting hypothesis that deserves much further attention.

Notes

1. Barbara Ward, J. D. Runnals, and Lenore D'Anjou, *The Widening Gap* (New York: Columbia University Press, 1971), p. 242.

2. H. Jon Rosenbaum and William G. Tyler, "South-South Relations: The Economic and Political Content of Interactions Among Developing Countries," in C. Fred Bergsten and Lawrence B. Krause, eds., *World Politics and International Economics* (Washington: The Brookings Institution, 1975), pp. 243–274.

3. See William L. Craig, "Application of the Trading with the Enemy Act to Foreign Corporations Owned by Americans: Reflections on Fruehauf V. Massardy," *Harvard Law Review* 83 (January 1970): 579–601.

4. An excellent introduction to the topic can be found in Robert O. Keohane and Joseph S. Nye, eds., *Transnational Relations and World Politics* (Cambridge: Harvard University Press, 1971).

5. Samuel P. Huntington, "Transnational Organizations in World Politics," *World Politics* 25 (1973), p. 338.

6. Ibid., p. 340.

7. The argument is presented in Paul A. Baran, "On the Political Economy of Backwardness" and Andre Gunder Frank, "The Development of Underdevelopment," in Robert I. Rhodes, ed., *Imperialism and Underdevelopment: A Reader* (New York: Monthly Review Press, 1970). For a view of capitalist industrialization leading to development see Bill Warren, "Imperialism and Capitalist Industrialization," *New Left Review* 81 (1973), pp. 3–44.

8. For a discussion of foreign investment as a vehicle for the cross-cultural transfer of attitudes and values, see Stephen J. Kobrin, "Foreign Direct Investment, Industrialization and Social Change," *The Journal of Conflict Resolution* (December 1976).

9. See Richard D. Robinson, *National Control of Multinational Corporations—A Fifteen Country Study* (New York: Praeger, 1976).

6. Foreign Direct Investment by Latin Americans

Carlos F. Diaz-Alejandro

Introduction

Latin American firms appear to have been going international at an increasing rate during the last few years. Although this is an area where practice is far ahead of theory and academic interest, the topic of "joint enterprises" by Latin American organizations is, at least, attracting increasing attention within the region.[1] It will be seen that into this category one can place very different kinds of firms. Therefore, this paper will attempt to be a wide, exploratory survey. It will try to say something about foreign direct investment (FDI) either by public or private Latin American (LA) organizations, within or outside Latin America. It will examine the formation of both transnational corporations (TNCs) and "true" multinational corporations (MNCs) owned and controlled by Latin Americans.[2] In keeping with the exploratory spirit of this essay, comparable experiences of non-LA, but semi-industrialized countries (whether small or not), will also be discussed.

Quantitative evidence that may be used to convince the skeptic that we are dealing with an important phenomenon is not easily found. Some of what is happening is at the fringes of local law or of recent origin. National and international statistics have traditionally worried about measuring inflows rather than outflows of FDI for countries that concern us here. The paper will have to rely on the documentation provided by some pioneering work, bits and pieces of data, and much hearsay. A look at recent *Balance of Payments Yearbooks* of the International Monetary Fund is instructive regarding data problems: nothing is recorded in the debit column of direct investment for countries such as Argentina, Mexico, and Venezuela whose firms are often reported in business publications to have invested abroad. Table 6.1 shows direct investment outflows for some semi-industrialized countries for which data are provided. These data are very likely to involve substantial underestimation of the actual flows. Furthermore, it can be argued that at the early stages of "going abroad" the actual flow of funds across frontiers will be quite small; focusing exclusively on them would miss much of what the process is about. This, of course, is true about FDI in general. The hypothesis is that it is even more so for countries that concern us here. Two reasons may be given: entrepreneurs will be especially cautious in their first ventures abroad, putting out as little of their own capital as they can, while exchange-control authorities, for reasons of their own, will encourage such behavior.

Why should one be interested in looking into the cluster of topics hidden under the title of this paper? There is, first, the positive interest in recording what is happening and why it is happening. In particular, a look at FDI by semi-industrialized countries may cast new light on theories regarding FDI, TNCs, and MNCs. One may simply be curious to see whether the same theories regarding FDI among the rich apply for cross-investments among the not-so-rich (yet not-so-poor). What are the differences and the similarities regarding the way the decision to invest abroad is made by a U.S. firm going to France in contrast with an Argentine firm going to Brazil? Is a Latin American Vernon really necessary? Second, most policy-oriented people who have become interested in these issues in Latin America have done so both as a way of reacting against the excesses of TNCs operating from politically dominant states and as a way to encourage LA political and economic integration (or more generally, Third World cooperation) free of

Table 6.1. Direct Investment Abroad of Selected Countries (Million SDRs)

	Brazil	Colombia	Italy	Spain
1969	11	4	283	13
1970	14	4	110	43
1971	1	3	399	25
1972	25	1	198	52
1973	31	1	216	67

Source: International Monetary Fund, *Balance of Payment Yearbook, 1969–73* (Washington, D.C., 1974–75).

extra-LA dominance.[3] One must worry that there will be a tendency to regard all LA MNCs as "good things." There is room, therefore, for normative analysis in this area, particularly if one wants to avoid disappointments later on. In fact, there are already some unfortunate precedents.

Latin American Firms That Have Gone Abroad

This section will review some of the characteristics of LA FDI that have not emerged primarily as a deliberate result of efforts to promote joint ventures or other types of FDI as such. This kind of investment may be classified as being private or public and subclassified geographically depending on whether it takes place inside or outside Latin America. Not all FDI will fall neatly in clear categories, of course. Besides the ambiguity regarding what is really private, the public-private mix is likely to cover a wide range. Who is a Latin American, or what organization is really Latin American, is also open to debate. Is Fiat-Argentina operating in Venezuela or Bolivia different from Fiat-Italy operating in those countries? Remember also that Mr. Onassis carried an Argentine passport and that Mr. Vesco is a species of Costa Rican. Other examples of multinational families and individuals could be given. Finally, while Panama and the Bahamas are geographically within Latin America, LA FDI there appears quite different in nature from that going, say, to Bolivia.

The central hypothesis is that as capitalistic, semi-industrialized, and somewhat-open LA economies move up the per capita income ladder, one will begin to observe some outflow of FDI, either from private or from market-oriented public enterprises, even as those countries continue to be net receivers of FDI. The hypothesis can be extended to countries such as Spain and Ireland. Indeed in these countries the apparent paradox of cross-investment may appear in sharper relief than in Latin America, because even as they offer generous incentives to FDI inflows (often justified by references to their alleged scarcity of local savings and entrepreneurship) some of their local firms go abroad without any kind of government support. Finally, even in socialist countries such as Yugoslavia and Hungary one may expect tendencies for some firms active in foreign markets to set up plants abroad. In short, many enterprises in semi-industrialized countries may be expected to go through a cycle that starts with production for the home market, typically enjoying some form of protection, then moving toward exporting an increasing share of their output, and finally setting up production facilities abroad. A look at evidence on private LA FDI may shed some light on this hypothesis.

Argentine firms, not surprisingly, appear as pioneers in this field. During the 1920s SIAM di Tella first began exporting metallurgical products to Uruguay, Brazil, and Chile. In 1928 it set up plants in those countries, while establishing commercial agencies in New York and London.[4] Bunge y Born, which started as a grain dealing firm, appears to have turned into a TNC before SIAM di Tella and certainly has gone beyond Latin America in its investment interests.[5] Alpargatas, also an Argentine firm, appears to have invested in other Latin American countries before the Second World War. During the 1950s several Argentine firms set up plants elsewhere in Latin America, particularly in Brazil; examples include Bagó, Yelmos, Grassi, Wobron, Sibra, Semperer y Cohen.

There is a shadowy borderline between non-FDI forms of foreign interests (exporting, financial, marketing, and commercial agencies abroad) and FDI proper, but it is likely that unusual LA entrepreneurs and their firms, such as the Bolivian Patiño interests and the Cuban Bacardi company, also engaged in the latter before the Second World War, particularly within countries of the region. Comparison of their histories with those of other small-country mavericks, such as the Irish Guinness, may eventually prove fruitful. One may note in passing that the transition from reliance on domestic markets to a rather high degree of multinationalization happens very rapidly for these small-country mavericks.

While these historical examples are of some interest, the bulk of LA FDI within the region seems to have arisen during the early 1960s, and its expansion appears to have accelerated during the 1970s. Between 1930 and about 1960, exchange

controls and inward-looking foreign trade policies no doubt
hampered the development of this phenomenon. Spontaneous
private LA FDI, a good share of which occurs behind the backs
of public agencies charged with administering remaining
exchanges and trade controls,[6] is concentrated in several geographical patterns, such as Argentine and Brazilian cross-
investments and investment in their neighboring countries;
Colombian and Venezuelan FDI in each other's markets as well
as in bordering and nearby countries; and Mexican FDI in Central America and the Caribbean. Two tentative descriptive gen-
eralizations may be offered on these patterns. First, a large
share of the FDI goes from a relatively advanced (and large) LA
country to a relatively less developed (and smaller) LA country.[7]
Second, certain geographical propinquity is apparent. Brazilian
FDI in Paraguay is more likely than in Honduras, and the opposite is true for Mexican FDI. "Sphere of influence" enthusiasts
already call attention to this trend.

Why Do Private LA Firms Go Abroad?

Why do private LA firms decide to invest in other countries of
Latin America? Those familiar with positive theories of direct
foreign investment will find no surprising answers, although
the mix of motivations may be different for the Latin American
variety. First of all, as emphasized by the Hymer theory, one
finds a "special asset" in LA firms engaged in horizontal FDI,
typically some kind of firm-specific adaptation of foreign technology to a relatively small scale of operation and/or some adaptation of product design to Latin American conditions.[8] Such
a "special asset" is the result of accumulated learning by the
firm, which can be applied in new markets at low marginal
costs. It emerges as a necessary condition for the firm going
abroad. Some examples may amplify what is meant by a "special asset."

1. An Argentine firm developed machinery to adapt exhaust
pipes for automobiles, of a generic type, to specific models of
cars without the need of large production runs. Uruguayan entrepreneurs heard about it and sought to form a joint venture

with the Argentine firm in Uruguay with the Argentine firm providing the technology and some used machinery as its capital share (and little or no foreign exchange).

2. Another Argentine firm gave up making radio cabinets with the techniques requiring large-scale operations, and in the process it redesigned many aspects of the radio itself. When a new radio plant was set up in Bolivia, the Bolivian producer sought the Argentine (adapted) technology and eventually they formed a joint venture.

3. When Fiat-Italy entered the Venezuelan market it called upon Fiat-Argentina and its engineers, who had adapted the Fiat models to Latin American conditions. (This may or may not lead to formal association between the Argentine and Venezuelan subsidiaries.)

This type of LA FDI may be interpreted as part of a two-step diffusion of technology involving either product or process adaptation. One can speculate that it occurs mainly in activities where the world technological frontier is not advancing very fast, allowing LA firms to keep pace with it. The closer the LA firms are to the world technological frontier, the easier it is for them to compete with traditional TNCs. In that competition, they benefit from the lower salaries earned by domestic engineers and semiskilled labor as well as from a more flexible attitude that is due to the lack of a worldwide organizational structure.

As suggested in the Argentine-Bolivian example, much of the LA FDI into smaller countries is triggered by the erection by those countries of barriers against goods imported from the larger ones. The Argentine firm facing loss of the Bolivian market for its radios tried to preserve a market for its radio components by setting up a joint venture in Bolivia, just as previously U.S. and European FDI went to Argentina following the erection of Argentine import restrictions. Flows of machinery, parts, technology, and profit payments in these circumstances act as substitutes for trade in some commodities. Whether such a substitution is desirable from the viewpoint of either regional economic efficiency or regional integration is a moot question. Even when tariff barriers are held constant, the desire to be closer to an important market previously serviced by exports may motivate outflows of FDI from the largest semi-industrialized countries of Latin America.

The transfer of adapted technology to activities where fresh technological changes are becoming less frequent in industrialized economies is likely to involve institutional arrangements somewhat different from those surrounding investments that transfer rapidly changing technology. Indeed, it appears that horizontal LA FDI involves joint ventures, rather than the creation of fully owned subsidiaries, to a greater extent than FDI from industrialized countries. Some observers even detect a natural tendency for horizontal LA FDI within the region to "fade out," and for investors from the host country to take a majority share in the equity from the start.

Like U.S. FDI in Canada and Mexico (but unlike U.S. FDI in Europe) horizontal LA FDI within the region is not the exclusive preserve of very large companies. A good share of this investment is carried out by medium-sized firms. The same characteristic has been noted for Spanish FDI. Indeed, in this case the absence of large firms in a rapidly expanding outflow of Spanish investment has caused some wonder.[9] Contrary to the typical LA case, Spanish FDI, while not given special incentives, is fairly easily registered with the authorities; so it cannot be argued that it is the quasi-legal (or downright illegal) channels used for outflowing investment that discourages firms with high profiles. An obvious hypothesis to cover these observations is that medium-sized firms have been on the whole more active than larger firms in adapting technology to conditions in semi-industrialized countries. In fact, most LA private FDI within the region has occurred in manufacturing branches such as light engineering—including automobile parts and machine tools, domestic appliances and other consumer durables, and textiles—activities in which medium-sized LA-owned firms have been active in import substitution for several years. These investments typically involved equity participation by nationals of no more than two countries, and their size has been modest by international standards.

Export-promotion policies in the major semi-industrialized Latin American countries, as in the case of Spain, are an intermediate step preceding significant outflows of private FDI. An Argentine firm, for example, exporting most of the machinery for a "turn-key" plant ordered by a foreign customer naturally considers the possibility of taking some equity into that plant. The several economic-integration efforts within Latin America, even when modest in actual results, also focus entrepreneurial attention on nearby markets and multiply contacts among businessmen. Accelerated improvements during the 1960s in intra-LA communications (air links, telephones, etc.) also help explain the not-surprising fact that most horizontal private LA FDI has stayed within the region. One may wonder how far this type of investment will roam in its search for new markets where its technological insights can be best exploited through setting up local plants. Spanish FDI, it may be noted, can be found in the United Kingdom and the United States, besides its more predictable location in Portugal, Latin America, and Africa.[10]

Private LA entrepreneurs have historically invested part of their portfolio outside the region but usually in liquid form or in real estate. Cuban investments in Florida, for example, were substantial and well-known even before 1959. Only a few entrepreneurs, such as Patiño and the Cuban Julio Lobo, appear to have actually moved into FDI outside the region. However, the outward orientation of economic policy in major Latin American countries could change this situation. Some scattered activity has recently been reported on this front. Manufacturing LA firms are said to have set up plants in Spain and Africa. A Brazilian firm has found its way to Texas; Irish officials of that country's Industrial Development Authority report interest on the part of a Mexican textile firm and an Argentine engineering company in taking advantage of Irish incentives for inflowing direct investment. But the magnitudes involved here are likely to be a small fraction of those for FDI within Latin America. Joint enterprises with Arab countries might be the most likely candidates for rapid expansion of purely private LA manufacturing FDI outside the region in the near future.

The desire to diversify as a motivation for FDI has received on the whole little emphasis in the literature on industrialized countries. One may conjecture that the smaller the home market, the more important diversification will be as an additional motivation for FDI. A United States firm, confident in local political stability and skeptical of foreign business cycles that diverge greatly from those in the United States, will be less interested than Spanish or Argentine firms in spreading risks globally. Indeed, much recent Argentine FDI into Uruguay and Brazil, as well as Peruvian FDI into Venezuela, can be regarded more as capital flight than as FDI. In some cases, both capital and capitalists leave the home country. In cases where entrepreneurs belong to social groups deemed culturally marginal in their home countries, such mobility, as well as the desire for diversification, will naturally be greater. Leaving aside extreme cases of economic and political instability, it remains plausible that a desire for diversification will push many firms based in small or semi-industrialized countries into going international. Firms particularly vulnerable to the local business cycle, such as those involved in construction or other forms of capital formation, will naturally look abroad to offset instability, first by exporting goods or services, and then by setting up plants or large agencies. As LA FDI becomes more generally accepted in home countries, it is conceivable that individuals who historically diversified their portfolios by buying foreign real estate or liquid claims will instead (at least partly) purchase available stocks and securities in local firms that have plants abroad.

Discussion of horizontal FDI has focused primarily on that within manufacturing. Latin American banks, not all private, are showing great dynamism in their expansion abroad. Many are flocking to international money centers, such as London, Panama, and the Bahamas, as well as to other Latin American countries. Much of this expansion can be explained as a result of the relatively new, outward-looking policies of the major semi-industrialized countries in Latin America that have been leading to increasing use of world private capital markets as well as growing servicing needs of LA exporting firms. The publicly owned Banco do Brasil has been listed among the top fifty international banks. With assets of US$23 billion it ranks eighteenth place—ahead of such well-known banks as the Chemical New York Corporation, Lloyds Bank, and the Bank of Tokyo.[11] Another publicly owned bank, the Banco de la Nacion

Argentina, has substantial interests abroad. Venezuelan banks as well as the ubiquitous Banco do Brasil are reported to be competing actively with U.S. banks in the Chilean market.[12] Venezuelan and Colombian banks have formed joint ventures, with parallel activities in Bogota and Caracas.[13] Colombian banks are reported active in Ecuador and Panama. Those left behind are getting itchy; the president of Mexico's second largest private, commercial bank has called for changes in that country's regulations to permit local financial institutions to operate internationally. The claimed advantages to the Mexican economy of internationally active domestic banks are that such banks can "support the opening of new export markets, support and activate the search for new capital sources for Mexican industrial growth and support the international expansion of Mexican companies when this requires joint-venture investment in foreign countries."[14]

Mexican, Argentine, and Brazilian consulting firms have also multiplied their regional activities. While not directly generating FDI themselves, they act as important catalytic agents in the promotion of LA joint ventures. The "marriage-broker" activities of some consulting firms in the Brazilian northeast between firms located there and those from the rich Brazilian south are noteworthy. While strictly speaking they refer to intra-Brazilian investment, the problems they deal with are very similar to those of LA FDI within Latin America. Engineering consulting firms show much promise for the diffusion of adapted technology.

The motivation for vertical FDI, involving both forward and backward integration, is quite straightforward, and can be expected to apply to profit-oriented firms anywhere. There are some examples of private LA FDI going elsewhere in the region, and even outside, to secure access to raw materials as well as to seek safe "downstream" customers for their output. But purely private investments in this category appear less important than vertical FDI by public enterprises. We turn to these issues now.

Direct Foreign Investment by Latin American Public Enterprises

Public enterprises play an important role in most Latin American economies, even (or especially) in those, such as the economy of Brazil, with international reputations as havens of capitalism.[15] The public sector, more generally, accounts for a good share of capital formation, typically above 50 percent in the largest LA countries.

The projection abroad of some public LA enterprises, involved in commodities for which the home country is a net importer, is best described as following the path of Italian, Spanish, and French state oil companies, or what might be called a public TNC model. For example, a recent report on Braspetro, the foreign trade and investment arm of the Brazilian state company, Petrobras, states that it is exploring for oil in half a dozen Middle East countries, plus Madagascar and Colombia and that it has joined a consortium of non-LA oil independents to bid on North Sea concessions off Norway.[16]

Other public LA enterprises involved in commodities for which the home country is a net exporter follow the practice of private TNCs from industrialized countries that, having gained control over mineral deposits or other raw materials, have integrated forward to assure themselves of steady buyers and some knowledge of the changing technology in material use. A good illustration of this practice is the Brazilian state enterprise, Cia. Vale do Rio Doce, which is involved in iron ore mining and steel production and may be building a new steel mill in Egypt with Kuwaiti financing.[17]

Such backward and forward vertical integration of the great LA state enterprises in raw-material exploitation and in basic sectors such as steel and aluminum is to be expected, whether within or outside Latin America and whether alone or in joint ventures with other LA or non-LA firms. Projects in this area are likely to be large and perhaps too spectacular. State corporations such as the well-established Pemex or newcomers like the Venezuelan state oil company and the Chilean state copper company are likely to become prominent in various types of vertical FDI. An interesting example of a binational joint venture involving two public oil corporations is the agreement between the Argentine and Bolivian enterprises (YPF and YPFB, respectively) to build a pesticide plant in Bolivia. It is expected that majority in equity holding will gradually be transferred from YPF to YPFB.[18]

It is generally accepted that uncertainty regarding availability or price of the upstream good and the consequent need for information by downstream firms will provide a powerful incentive for vertical integration, even when futures markets exist.[19] However, the use of explicitly public enterprises as national agents for the buying or selling of the upstream good seems to appear more often in semi-industrialized than in fully industrialized countries that were early comers. As with public banks, those organizations establish close links with small and medium-sized local, private manufacturing firms.

Public LA enterprises have gone abroad in areas other than that of natural resources. An early example of a joint venture involving both public and private capital is the Flota Mercante Grancolombiana, created in 1946 with the participation of Colombia, Venezuela, and Ecuador at a time when extraregional shipping companies exerted substantial monopoly power. This enterprise has suffered several ups and downs, including the withdrawal by Venezuela in 1953, pressures from the U.S. State Department on charges of discrimination, and treatment by other LA countries as if it were just another foreign shipping line.

A more recent, but also far from successful example of a mostly public LA joint venture is Monómeros Colombo-Venezolanos, a highly capital-intensive petrochemical project, which started operations around 1972 and which has been plagued by technical and management problems. Monómeros operates behind substantial protection, and its demand for unskilled labor is negligible. It stands as a warning that the type of mistakes made at the national level under import-substitution policies can be repeated at the multinational level under the banners of integration and joint enterprise.

More encouraging are the binational public companies recently set up between Paraguay and Brazil, Paraguay and

Argentina, and between other countries in the River Plate basin to exploit common hydroelectric resources there, which may be compared with the authorities for the Ruhr and the Tennessee valleys. These projects typically involve substantial investments. Also noteworthy are the Central American public company Cocesna, which is active in air navigation, and investments by the public Chilean steel corporation in Ecuador in joint venture with investors from that country. Proposals abound for new binational or multinational ventures involving LA public enterprises whose basic motivation is often noneconomic, but before looking at the future, explicit discussion of normative criteria is called for.

Gains and Losses from Latin American Foreign Direct Investment

Evaluation of the economic and social consequences of outflowing or inflowing LA FDI of the spontaneous variety raises all the complicated issues that such an evaluation has raised elsewhere. In particular, many Latin American public officials are learning to evaluate FDI from a home-country viewpoint, thus deepening their understanding of the phenomenon. Is Argentine FDI in Uruguay and Brazil good or bad for the Argentine balance of payments? For Argentine employment? Should it be part of Argentine export-promotion policies? Are Argentine exports and royalty earnings understated? Are Argentine entrepreneurs taking more money out than they bring back in? The issues (and problems) are familiar ones. Eager investors will highlight how their activities promote exports of machinery and parts; worried public officials will devise schemes to encourage profit repatriation.

Even more familiar are the preoccupations of Bolivian and Honduran officials who may wonder whether it is a good idea to have so many Brazilians and Mexicans in their country and whether they are trading a first-rate imperial power for a second-rate one. Such preoccupations could lead Ecuador to treat FDI from Germany more kindly than that from Peru.

More than cost-benefit analyses of specific investment projects may be at stake. As firms in the major semi-industrialized countries of Latin America expand their exports, either to the region or elsewhere, barriers to their establishing plants abroad on their own or in joint ventures may weaken their ability to compete with firms from extraregional countries where such foreign investment is, if anything, subsidized. Indeed, some cases have already been recorded in which the formation of, for example, an Argentine-Uruguayan joint venture was the result of competitive pressure from an extraregional TNC.[20] Having gone this far in competitive struggles for world markets, the logic of such competition could dictate growing FDI for LA firms.

At this point a methodological parenthesis is in order. If FDI and the creation of joint ventures were viewed primarily as mechanisms to move capital from one country to another, Brazilian investments in Uruguay or Europe or Colombian investments in Venezuela would appear abnormal. When the home country has employment or balance-of-payments problems, many would challenge the desirability of outward flows of FDI.

One may view corporations, of which MNCs and TNCs are particular examples, as a type of organization that emerges to replace arm's-length markets. The well-known reasons for such substitution are several: (1) markets may not work well because of uncertainty regarding input sources, or because of uncertainty about sales that endangers large fixed investments; (2) investors may wish to benefit from increasing returns from developing or collecting information and knowledge including firm-specific adapted technology; and (3) investors may wish to exercise market power in buying or selling.

This view implies that the creation of LA MNCs or TNCs may improve on real-world markets, or it may not. However, such a view says little on how gains and losses from improving or destroying markets are shared between home and host countries or inside each country. It should also be clear that the creation of new LA MNCs or TNCs is neither the only, nor necessarily the best way to deal with uncertainty, need for information, or lack of market power from either the private or the social viewpoint, where the social viewpoint may involve several associated countries. Contractual arrangements of various sorts that are limited in time can often function better than new, permanent organizations.

Observers in Latin America have noted with interest the reluctance of governments in industrialized countries to allow their large corporations either to go broke or to be taken over by OPEC money. To some theorists this reluctance suggests that even purely private organizations become charged with a social or national interest after reaching a certain size, particularly in a world where other countries have their own heavyweight champions. The idea is that for a given Latin American country, or a group of them, locally controlled TNCs or MNCs act as reliable scanners, searchers, and bargainers in uncertain, rough, and unreliable world markets.[21] They become their group's team out in the cold, an attitude not unlike that of some foreign ministers in industrialized countries who view even their purely private TNCs, particularly those involved in raw-material exploitation abroad, as very much a part of the national team.

The complex, symbiotic relation between the state and large private or public enterprises raises issues beyond the scope of this paper. But it raises another doubt about the merits of LA MNCs or TNCs. In evaluating these organizations, how much depends on what kind of state lies behind them and on what groups actually control their activities? (Consider South African TNCs.)

When outward FDI involves medium-sized firms exploiting their technological wrinkles, even home countries with serious employment or balance-of-payments problems could benefit because such an activity might have higher returns abroad than the best alternative at home for the firm.

It does not seem very fruitful to talk in general about the optimum amount of outflowing FDI for Latin America, or for any individual LA country, nor to seek general rules regarding the optimum organization of joint ventures. It may perhaps be more helpful to look first for possible artificial barriers and distortions hampering the flow of LA FDI and the creation of LA MNCs and TNCs on the presumption that there should be more. Enthusiasts of LA joint ventures and LA MNCs list so many advantages to be derived from them that one is tempted to ask: If such ventures are so good, why are there not more? Possible answers include: (1) they are on the way, and with a vengeance, in which case arguments for additional public promotional efforts lose much of their force and indeed one may begin to worry about their going beyond the social optimum; (2) there are barriers imposed by archaic legislation or foolish public officials, which should be removed; or (3) some social pump priming is socially desirable on a kind of "infant-organization" basis. It is the second answer that interests us now.

Lawyers were early comers to the topic of joint LA enterprises, particularly lawyers associated with the Institute for Latin American Integration (INTAL), and many were influenced by the European debates and experience in this field.[22] A key preoccupation was whether lack of uniformity in LA company laws was a significant obstacle to the formation of joint LA enterprises. They concluded that "the creation of foreign affiliates does not represent a serious difficulty from the viewpoint of [LA] company laws. This is especially due to the similarity in the way the [LA] countries regulate the structure and functioning of commercial enterprises. Therefore, in Latin America there do not exist the legal and psychological barriers which in the European Economic Community have been blamed on the diversity of legislation in this field."[23] In all LA countries it seems possible to find more than one satisfactory legal mechanism to organize LA MNCs, even in the more difficult case of public enterprises.

Barriers arising not from company laws but from economic legislation are another matter. A turbulent and not always profitable history of dealings with foreign investors, as well as a history of balance-of-payments crises, has been reflected in most LA countries in regulations that complicate capital movements in general and FDI in particular whether incoming or outgoing. The traditional targets of such rules have been the exploitative non-LA, foreign investor and the local entrepreneur seeking to take his capital abroad. Such a defensive attitude is reflected in a hundred ways throughout the economic legislation of most LA countries and now, somewhat ironically, creates a barrier to LA joint ventures and intra-LA FDI. Indeed, the twists and turns of restrictions, exemptions, and incentives in some LA countries may have the net effect of favoring FDI from outside Latin America relative to that from other countries in the area. A given LA country, for example, may have a smoothly working treaty with the United States to avoid double taxation of foreign investment but none with neighboring countries. Countries within the Andean group have shown a special preoccupation with existing differences in the treatment given to national and other Andean firms in such matters as access to domestic credit and taxation, especially in public enterprises.

Neutrality between home and foreign investment, regardless of its geographical destination, and nondiscrimination among sources of inflowing FDI will be rejected in Latin America as undesirable policy guidelines for a mixture of economic and noneconomic reasons that have also defeated those guidelines de facto, if not always de jure, in industrialized countries. It is easy to imagine a treatment hierarchy developing. Thus, some Andean countries could end up discriminating among purely national, Andean, other-LA, other-LDC, and several other types of investments from industrialized countries. Because discrimination can arise in the formal and informal handling of the many incentive schemes that LA governments have to achieve regional, export, and other goals, discussions regarding LA FDI can lead to a reexamination of the effectiveness and rationality of many of these rules, and not just from the viewpoint of encouraging socially beneficial intra-LA FDI. One may hope that as many LA countries become both home and host countries for FDI, the people charged with overseeing the flows will enrich and deepen their knowledge of both costs and benefits of that process.

Joint ventures involving public LA enterprises, even when highly desirable on economic grounds, could be hampered by obstacles more powerful than those facing private joint ventures. The armed forces are influential in many public enterprises, and they may fancy that national security is threatened by joint ventures. (Try to imagine, for example, Argentina and Brazil merging their atomic-energy research organizations, or Bolivia, Chile, and Peru joining an Andean steel corporation.)

In other cases, the nonmilitary bureaucracies running other national public enterprises may be more interested in maintaining existing profitable links with extraregional TNCs, which may or may not be socially profitable, than in exploring new links and forming a common front with other LA public enterprises.

Some Major Proposals to Foster Joint Ventures

Initiatives toward greater Latin American economic and political integration have been the major motivation behind general proposals for accelerating the creation of joint ventures among two or more LA countries. In a sense this coupling of commercial integration with cross or joint investments is a variation on the theme played by the North Atlantic community since the Second World War. However, in Latin America, or the LDCs more generally, joint ventures are viewed not only as complements to commercial integration (or trade liberalization), but sometimes also as substitutes for full trade liberalization within a given area.

As early as 1966, I. M. D. Little published a paper on "Regional International Companies as an Approach to Economic Integration."[24] He argued that even when full integration is not possible for whatever reason, but when one or more industries can be reasonably established on a regional basis, a limited, industrial community could still be made beneficial to all parties. The European Coal and Steel Community (ECSC) is a clear precedent. In the Little proposal earnings would be fully paid out, the company would be entirely tax free, and it could buy its inputs in any market. Presumably only projects where unit costs were below c.i.f. (cost insurance freight) prices would be undertaken. Little noticed that it might be easier to negotiate a package deal involving several industries. He also warned that the top management of these companies could degenerate into a "Tower of Babel." Foreign aid could help trigger the creation of these companies in LDCs.

The Central American Common Market (CACM) devised its "Regime of Industries of Integration" to go along with complete trade liberalization within that area, but only two firms were set up under that regime (as of 1973).[25] During its hapless

life, the Latin American Free Trade Area (LAFTA) has made
equally unsuccessful moves toward the creation of joint LA
ventures. Aware of these precedents, the Andean group produced its Decision 46 in December 1971 establishing a uniform
regime for Andean MNCs.[26]

This decision means that Andean countries agree to compro-
mise between treating all investors from other Andean countries as plain nationals and treating them as "real" foreigners.
Each country gives Andean MNCs treatment as favorable as
that granted the most-favored-nation companies, which, of
course, is a more favorable treatment than that given to FDI under the Andean Decision 24, particularly regarding taxes, credits, public purchases, profit remittances, and areas where a
company is permitted to operate. An Andean MNC could be set
up by two or more Andean countries, could have public or private capital, and could have up to 40 percent of its capital from
non-Andean sources. But the chartering of such a MNC would
be limited to projects designed for Andean interest by the
group's authorities. The expectation has been that such MNCs
would be closely linked to (and would facilitate the adoption
of) the sectoral plans for industrial development or the major
import-substitution efforts at the Andean level in areas such as
metalworking, chemicals, automobiles, fertilizers, petrochemicals, and electronics. Andean MNCs in these areas would substitute, at least partly, for extraregional TNCs that would
otherwise take advantage of the newly expanded and protected
markets. These plans call for a parceling out of the new industrial activities among member countries, each "chosen instrument" having a monopoly limited in time and in extent by the
level of the common external tariff. The new MNCs could be
clustered around these projects, in such a way as to minimize
their social cost and/or to provide an equitable fashion for
sharing costs and benefits. One can speculate regarding the
optimum clustering or size of the MNCs as well as the se-
quence in which the projects should be undertaken.[27] These
MNCs are expected to help the least developed Andean countries, Bolivia and Ecuador, in taking advantage of special tariff
concessions granted by the larger Andean countries and in the
speedy construction of plants assigned to them under the in-

dustrial sectoral agreements. One may also note that under Decision 46 a Brazilian and a U.S. investor would be treated equally. Argentine firms, on the other hand, have shown a keen interest in the Andean proposals and have sought a special relationship with the new Andean projects.

To the dismay of Andean enthusiasts Peru has failed to ratify Decision 46 (as of January 1976). Peruvian reservations are said to include fear of capital flight and a weakening of Peruvian company laws requiring workers' participation in management. The Peruvian position brings out two key dilemmas in LA integration efforts that also influence attitudes toward LA FDI: conflict between the recognition of the importance of a dynamic LA private, entrepreneurial group and doubts about such a group among technocrats of social-democratic and leftist leanings; and conflict between emerging Andean and/or LA conciousness and interests and more old-fashioned but strong national interests and idiosyncrasies.

Early in 1976 the Andean Junta proposed the creation of a Multinational Telephone Enterprise that would produce public telephone exchanges beginning in 1980.[28] It remains to be seen whether all of the Andean countries will approve that proposal and how many more such proposals will follow.

Disappointments with LAFTA and the alleged failure of purely commercial liberalization measures for intraregional trade have motivated the search for other mechanisms to carry out LA integration.[29] Joint LA ventures are viewed by some as having the potential to forge stronger intra-LA links than fickle trade flows could. Those ventures may also bring together countries that now belong to different integration efforts (Caribbean, Central American, LAFTA, and Andean).

This line of thinking has been taken up by the new Latin American Economic System (SELA) formed in 1975 not without at least a normal amount of disagreement among its members. Mexico and Venezuela were key leaders in the formation of SELA. A major goal is the promotion of LA MNCs, involving any number of LA countries and in any area of economic activity. The idea is that countries interested in a project would set up a working group to explore its feasibility; the participating countries, as a token of their seriousness, would finance each group. Pragmatism and flexibility are stressed, at least according to some major SELA leaders. So far, the SELA approach seems more similar to that of Little's paper than to the Andean Decision 46.

A navigation company has already been launched under the SELA umbrella, involving Colombia, Costa Rica, Jamaica, Mexico, Nicaragua, Panama, and Venezuela. Cuba's presence in the company is, of course, the most remarkable. Empresa Naviera Multinacional del Caribe (NAMUCAR) is, so far, a purely public-sector initiative. The project was conceived as an alternative to established shipping lines in the Caribbean, but its first steps have been quite modest partly because of fears of the company's being dominated by Mexico.[30] Mexico and Jamaica, and possibly Venezuela, plan joint ventures that will include at least bauxite and alumina-producing plants in Jamaica, and a metallic-aluminum plant in Mexico. While each host country will own 5l percent of the plants located within its boundaries, the countries have agreed in principle that profits from all operations will be pooled and distributed according to the overall investment shares. Links between these activities and NAMUCAR, as well as joint international marketing of part of the output, are foreseen.[31] Jamaica is also reported to be planning construction of a petroleum refinery in cooperation with Pemex to be supplied with Mexican and Venezuelan oil.[32]

Venezuela, Colombia, and Central America have set up another MNC, Suaves Centrales, for the marketing of Central American coffee. Essentially, Venezuelan money is being used to finance coffee stocks so that coffee sales can be timed to the maximum advantage of producers. Venezuelan oil revenues have also been used to set up a trust fund in the Interamerican Bank with the right to engage in equity-capital operations, and it is expected to promote LA MNCs, particularly in fields previously shunned by international lending agencies.

The several state development banks that exist in Latin America, the Mexican Nacional Financiera S.A. (NAFIN) and the Brazilian Banco Nacional do Desenvolvimento (BNDE) as well as the Inter American Development Bank, the Andean Development Corporation, and other such regional financial institutions are expected to play catalytic roles in the promotion of LA

MNCs. Several other proposals exist that may or may not be picked up by SELA. They are all meant to increase cooperation among LA countries, and possibly lead to the formation of LA MNCs. Again it needs to be stressed that not all desirable forms of cooperation will or should lead to the creation of formal new organizations.

The apparently impressive combined buying power of the national state enterprises of Latin America, particularly for machinery and equipment and technological services, suggests possible areas of cooperation, ranging from the creation of LA MNCs to produce goods and services locally to the creation of others to act as purchasing agents for the whole group. There may be an aggregation illusion here. The totals for machinery purchases are likely to hide great heterogeneity in the types of commodities purchased. It may be better first to expand the existing contact and ad hoc contracts between, say, LA state oil or steel enterprises before setting up complicated schemes. The same reasoning applies to joint research and development efforts. It would be splendid if Argentina and Brazil were to combine their atomic energy commissions in one organization open to other LA countries, but it is likely that the more modest, joint Andean research-and-development efforts in such areas as tropical woods, nutrition, and copper technology will yield tangible fruit more quickly. A region that still has a great deal of poverty should not embark on an adventure like the Concorde.

Joint marketing of traditional and new LA exports represents a possible area of expansion for LA organizations, since the region has historically fretted under foreign middlemen reaping marketing quasi-rents. This seems a logical area for cooperation, even though many who see no contradiction between the existence of United Fruit, Exxon, Hershey, and Reynolds Aluminum and the free play of supply and demand in world markets will shout Cartel! and even though, in many cases, the final outcome of such a change could bring the world closer to the competitive solutions outlined in textbooks. National LA firms in the area of natural resources, even if banded together, are unlikely to achieve the degree of backward and forward integration that gave (and still gives) classical TNCs their exorbitant market power.

Joint state enterprises in the Plate River basin give grounds for hoping that other border areas in Latin America, where natural resources (already discovered or only suspected) add to frontier tensions, can be developed peacefully by joint ventures of the countries concerned. A suitable blurring of purely national sovereignties along, say, the Chilean-Bolivean-Peruvian borders and along those between Colombia and Venezuela or Venezuela and Guyana could have important economic and political payoffs. An all-LA enterprise to build a new canal across Central America may become highly desirable if the U.S. Senate hinders the revision of the unequal treaty now governing the one across Panama.

Associations like SELA between Latin America and other LDCs have also been discussed. Mexico and Tanzania, for example, plan joint ventures in sisal processing. Venezuelan projects with other OPEC members will naturally cement that alliance. Argentina and Libya, Brazil and Kuwait, are also coupled in several plans and schemes. Spain, after forty years of solitude, may also play a more dynamic role in Latin America.

Some Concluding Remarks

The largest and richest LA countries have moved or are quickly moving into Southern European ranges of per capita income and have developed important industrial bases. This fact, plus regional and cultural propinquity, has led their private and public entrepreneurs to search in neighboring countries for markets, raw materials, and deals of all kinds. Sometimes exports are the outcome, or licensing agreements, but joint enterprises or other forms of FDI may result. This expansion is also taking some LA firms outside the region. The FDI may involve little more than buying warehouses and service agencies, or it can generate substantial production abroad. Past LA experience and objective conditions discouraging hubris help to balance these joint enterprises and investments somewhat better between home and host interests than has been the case with traditional FDI from industrialized countries. The lack of a co-operative home-country Marine Corps (or Intelligence Agency) is no guarantee that investors will prove flexible and sensitive to host-country conditions, but it appears to help make them, if not less interested in profits, somewhat less pushy.[33] It remains to be seen how important outward flows of LA FDI will become and how large and widespread international LA firms will get. Upper limits on their expansion could cast some light on the role played by noneconomic advantages in the past expansion of TNCs from hegemonic powers.

It has proved difficult to generalize as to the likely social cost-benefit results of either spontaneous LA private FDI or the several proposals for LA MNCs discussed in this paper. This difficulty is in line with the ambiguities surrounding the topic of foreign investment, where departures from case-by-case evaluation are always risky, given the complexies of industrial organization. Even less can be said about the future distribution of benefits and costs of such enterprises within each participating country.

Besides a lack of clear a priori economic guidelines, further questions are raised by powerful political preconceptions and crosscurrents within Latin America. Some of the different ways of viewing LA MNCs, for example, were reflected in the 1975 INTAL conference in Buenos Aires. Particularly representative were the remarks of a Mexican participant who argued for LA MNCs in large, state-sponsored projects, and ridiculed the prospects of LA joint ventures to produce "combs and shampoos," and a Brazilian participant who warned against converting LA MNCs into "mutual-aid organizations" so hampered by restrictions even before they were operating that they could never become efficient enterprises.

Two nightmares are particularly revealing. The first, which may be called the "Dependencia" nightmare, views uncontrolled neocapitalistic expansion of LA firms, even when led by local and public entrepreneurs, as either a front or a first step toward the consolidation of control in the LA economy by TNCs from outside the region. Examples of Fiat-Argentina expanding into Bolivia and Venezuela or reports of Volkswagen do Brasil moving around within and outside Latin America are, in this view, typical of the process.[34] Even successful purely LA joint ventures are doomed to be taken over or manipulated by extraregional TNCs in the "Dependencia" view because the export connection of much spontaneous LA FDI is also viewed with suspicion.

The second nightmare may be called "Statist-Protectionist." The fear is that, partly as a reaction against the earlier scenario, LA MNCs will be created under close public-sector tutelage with their freedom of action severely curtailed and will pursue import-substitution goals such as the creation of capital-intensive fertilizer plants, the social desirability of which is very doubtful. To make matters worse, the trade diversion that might be stimulated could divert purchases not from outside Latin America but from relatively efficient LA producers. The new organizations may not always, on balance, integrate more than they disintegrate. Associations like SELA could weaken Andean solidarity, for example, while Andean MNCs could weaken links between Andean and non-Andean LA countries.

We have seen bits of evidence to feed both the "Dependencia" and the "Statist-Protectionist" nightmares. Coupled with a priori skepticism, they may prevent investors from becoming starry-eyed over the welcome sound of "LA MNCs." Thorny issues hide behind this label. For many years public officials worried about how to control inflowing FDI, confident of their ability to control local firms. As the latter become international, their flexibility and mobility increases, and their ability to react to public policy is enhanced for better or worse. The issue of accountability, of key importance in all discussions about TNCs, will remain—even if LA MNCs are set up only under carefully specified conditions, as the experience of LA national state enterprises shows. One can also speculate that in many cases LA MNCs will be inferior alternatives to a full-fledged Latin American common market.

But let me finish on a positive note. On both economic and political grounds one can conclude that LA MNCs and LA FDI can be a positive force in the region's development, if encouraged in a selective and rational fashion. Neither prohibition nor across-the-board encouragement of inflowing FDI have proven desirable policies for Latin America, and the same will prove true for outflows of FDI. The largest countries can use the outflows as ways of exporting machinery and expertise and decreasing uncertainty about access to raw materials and markets. Smaller countries can find the new FDI useful in their search for cheaper technology that is more suited to their local conditions while they diversify their sources of capital and expertise. Small and large LA countries can use the new organizations to drive better bargains vis-à-vis the outside world, both buying and selling. And small and large LA countries can together devise new forms of joint ventures that, drawing on their historical experience, can reduce asymmetries and the risks of confrontation and uncompensated nationalizations, thus promoting both investment and an equitable sharing of gains between host and home countries.

Notes

1. A meeting, probably the first of its kind in Latin America, on the "Promotion of Joint Latin American Investments and Enterprises" was held in Buenos Aires on November 21 and 22 of 1975. It was sponsored by the Institute for Latin American Integration (INTAL), located in that city. Most participants were from the LA business world, from LA governments, or from inter-American institutions. "Latin America" should be understood to include European excolonies in the Caribbean that have become independent since the Second World War.

2. Here I follow authors such as Charles P. Kindleberger (*American Business Abroad*, New Haven: Yale University Press, 1969, p. 178) and Osvaldo Sunkel, who apply the label of TNC to enterprises that are owned and controlled primarily by citizens of one country and have investments in several other countries.

3. The United Nations Conference on Trade and Development (UNCTAD) held a meeting in Geneva, during October 1975, on ways to encourage cooperation among developing countries. Joint enterprises figured prominently among the possible ways of cooperation.

4. I owe this information, as well as a good share of other information and ideas in this paper, to the pioneering work of INTAL and particularly to the research of Felix Peña and Eduardo White (see note 7).

5. Bunge y Born achieved considerable unwanted publicity during 1975, when it was said to have paid Argentine guerrillas a ransom of $60 million for the release of two heirs of one of the founding families. It was also said to be involved in the grain-shipping scandal in the United States. See *The New York Times*, 25 June 1975, pp. 11–22.

6. This is the impression given by some entrepreneurs and representatives of private-sector groups present at the November 1975 INTAL seminar, men-

tioned in note 1. These observers also emphasized how the expansion of LA FDI is accelerating.

7. See Eduardo White and Jaime Campos, "Elementos para una política latinoamericana de empresas conjuntas." The paper was presented at the November 1975 INTAL conference (mimeographed, pp. 7–8). Of forty-five cases of joint LA enterprises examined, 80 percent corresponded to projects located in lesser-developed LA countries, with the participation of firms from more developed LA countries. Not all of these cases involved the private sector. Nearly half of the cases involved countries in the "southern cone" of Latin America (Argentina, Bolivia, Brazil, Chile, Paraguay, and Uruguay).

8. Besides the White-Campos paper, I rely heavily here on the valuable paper by Marcelo Diamand, "Las Empresas Conjuntas Latinoamericanas: Coincidencias y conflictos de Intereses," also presented at the INTAL conference, and on conversations with Jorge Katz.

9. See the very useful paper by Jose Luis Moreno More, "Quince Años de Inversiones Españolas en El Extranjero," *Información Comercial Española* no. 499 (March 1975): 91–107, especially p. 94. Spanish firms, however, appear less willing to share ownership with host-country investors than LA firms, according to this source (also p. 94).

10. Ibid., p. 97. One may also note that some Irish FDI is reported in the United States and the United Kingdom as well as in Nigeria where the Irish "special relationship" is somewhat different from that linking Ireland to the other two countries. *Times* (London), 29 February 1976, p. 54. Yugoslav-owned plants are said to exist in Holland and Sweden producing motorbikes. Less surprising is the presence of Yugoslav construction firms, hiring Yugoslav workers, in the Federal Republic of Germany.

11. See "A World Financial Survey," *The Economist* of London, 14 February 1976, p. 30.

12. See *Business Latin America*, 14 January 1976, p. 15. Financing foreign trade is said to be the main business of the Banco do Brasil in Chile.

13. See *Business Latin America*, 31 December 1975, p. 424. Colombian law severely limits activities of foreign banks, but the law retains special treatment for banks from other Andean countries as long as Colombian capital receives reciprocal treatment.

14. See *Business Latin America*, 28 January 1976, p. 32.

15. See Werner Baer, Isaac Kerstenetzky, and Annibal Villela, "The Changing Role of the State in the Brazilian Economy," *World Development*, vol. 1, no. 11 (November 1973): 23–34. For the Argentine case, see Carlos F. Diaz-Alejandro, "The Argentine State and Economic Growth: A Historical Review," in Gustav Ranis, ed., *Government and Economic Development* (New Haven: Yale University Press, 1971).

16. See *Business Latin America*, 16 July 1975, p. 228. It has been argued that early Brazilian recognition of the Angolan Popular Movement for the Liberation of Angola (MPLA) was related to Petrobras interest in exploiting the Cabinda oil field. See *Business Latin America*, 6 February 1976, p. 47.

17. See *The Economist* of London, 9 August 1975, p. 64.

18. See *Business Latin America*, 5 July 1973, pp. 209–210.

19. See K. J. Arrow, "Vertical Integration and Communication," *The Bell Journal of Economics* (Spring 1975) vol. 6, no. 1, especially pp. 173 and 182.

20. But there is at least one case where this process, alas, culminated in the new enterprise selling out to an extraregional TNC. In other cases the acquisition of, say, a Uruguayan firm by an Argentine one may be motivated by the desire to eliminate a competitor. See *Business Latin America*, 10 October 1973, pp. 322–323.

21. This view is not incompatible with the emphasis given by some development economists to "institution-building" above and beyond improving markets in developing countries. The institution-building may start with efficient public utilities and rural extension services, move to create efficient local steel corporations, and then extend to efficient MNCs or TNCs.

22. For an excellent review and development of this topic, see Eduardo J. White, *Empresas Multinacionales Latinoamericanas; La Perspectiva del Derecho Económico* (México: Fondo de Cultura Económica, 1973).

23. Ibid., p. 142. The translation from the Spanish is mine.

24. In the *Journal of Common Market Studies*, vol. 5, no. 2 (December 1966): 181–186.

25. See White, *Empresas Multinacionales Latinoamericanas*, p. 83.

26. For the description of Decision 46, I rely heavily on Gustavo Fernández Saavedra, "El Regimen Uniforme de la Empresa Multinacional en El Grupo Andino," in *Revista Derecho de la Integración* (Buenos Aires, 1972), pp. 11–33.

27. See Daniel Schydlowsky, "Asignación de Industrias de Integración en el Grupo Andino," *Revista de la Integración*, INTAL no. 8 (May 1971): 1–11.

28. The subregional multinational firm will be formed within six months of the proposal approval, and Chilean, Colombian, Peruvian, and Venezuelan private or state firms will each put up 17.5 percent of the initial capital, and Bolivia and Ecuador will each subscribe to 15 percent of the equity. See *Business Latin America*, 4 February 1976, pp. 36–37. The first Andean MNC could be said to be Compania de Industrias de Acero Cotopaxi (INDACO), a drill bit factory in Ecuador set up by Peruvian and Ecuadorian interests to take advantage of the metalworking sectoral program. See *Business Latin America*, 7 November 1973, p. 359.

29. Many talk in Latin America as if LAFTA had really led to a serious dismantling of barriers to intraregional trade, adding that such a hypothetical liberalization has failed to significantly increase intra-LA trade flows. The basic LAFTA problem, of course, has been that the governments that make up the association never decided seriously to dismantle intra-LA trade barriers. It is thus incorrect to talk about the failure of "purely commercial measures." Even stranger is the tendency of some to downplay the upsurge in intra-

Andean trade, where trade liberalization has been attempted much more seriously than in the rest of the LAFTA.

30. *Latin America Economic Report*, 5 March 1976, p. 37.

31. See Antonio Casas-González, "Joint Ventures among Latin American Countries," mimeographed UNCTAD document TD/B/AC.19/R.2, 22 October 1975, especially Annex I, p. 12.

32. See *Business Latin America*, 17 December 1975, pp. 405–406.

33. It is said that the Argentine government interceded with the Chilean government, under President Salvador Allende, when the latter nationalized private Argentine FDI in Chile. Compensation was requested and obtained. The style and flavor of such negotiations, however, were quite different from those between the United States and Chilean governments.

34. See *The Economist* of London, 9 August 1975, p. 64, for a report that Volkswagen's subsidiary in São Paulo may build a plant in Iraq. The same magazine, in its issue of 13 December 1975, p. 89, also refers to possible investments by that company in Chile. For a report on how Fiat-Argentina participated in the setting up of a tractor plant in Bolivia, see *Business Latin America*, November 1973, pp. 354–355.

7. Financial Factors and the International Expansion of Small-Country Firms

Tamir Agmon
Donald R. Lessard

The purpose of this paper is to establish a framework for assessing the impact of financial factors on the international expansion of firms based in small countries (SCFs). This is a part of the more general question of the impact of financial factors on the international expansion of multinational firms. Since this latter topic has received relatively little attention in the literature, the paper first deals with the general case and then focuses on the SCF. It identifies situations in which financial factors act as constraints on the expansion of the SCF as well as cases where financial factors motivate such expansion. SCFs with two broad types of base countries are considered: those with open and developed capital markets and those with relatively closed and undeveloped capital markets. It concludes with a brief discussion of public policy implications.

The basic premise underlying the analysis is that financial factors are relevant to the multinational expansion of firms only if there are imperfections in financial markets, such as barriers to capital flows or differences in the efficiency of domestic capital markets. If there are no barriers to international capital flows, and if capital markets are uniformly well developed, investors will diversify their portfolio holdings internationally, and required rates of return on securities (projects) will reflect only their contributions to the risk of the fully diversified world portfolio. The required rate of return, reflecting all the terms of financing, will be the same whether it is undertaken by a multinational corporation (MNC), an SCF, or a local firm. Consequently, financial factors will represent neither a motivation for nor an obstacle to international expansion by an SCF.

Financial Motivations for Multinationalism

The pattern of international investment, both in terms of the location of production and the ownership of firms, can be viewed as the outcome of a supply of investment opportunities occurring through time in different countries and of the demand by potential bidders for these opportunities. The successful bidder can be either a domestic firm, defined as a firm located in the country where the investment takes place, or a foreign firm. Assuming complete information about the prospective return of investment opportunities, the successful bidder will be the one to whom the project is worth most. Successful bidders will be those who can generate larger or less risky cash flows over time from a given investment opportunity—the result of imperfections in goods or factor markets excluding financial markets—or can capitalize uncertain future cash flows at relatively lower required rates of return—the result of imperfections in financial markets, or both.

Higher cash flows to one firm compared to cash flows to other bidders may result from lower costs due to the control over intangible factors of production such as special knowledge not available as such in the market, a preferred market position, or other mechanisms that generate monopoly rents. Lower total risks will result from market positions, special knowledge, and many other factors that also lead to higher returns.[1] Direct investment, foreign or local, can be viewed as a way to capitalize on these potential advantages either in the absence of markets in which the source of the advantage can be sold and the capitalized value of rents obtained directly or in the case where the sale of the advantage would destroy its rent-producing character.

Lower required rates of return for a given level of total project risk reflect a similar phenomenon in financial markets. Risky projects are most attractive when investors are able to diversify away the largest proportion of the project's total risk. When there are barriers to portfolio capital flows, MNCs are able to accept lower rates of return on projects than single-country firms because of their ability to diversify investment risks internationally.[2] A closely related financial advantage of the MNC is its ability to engage in arbitrage between financial markets where restrictions on capital flows or direct government intervention distort the cost of debt capital. The MNC also can accept a lower pretax return because of its ability to shift revenues and costs among its various elements and thus reduce its total taxes.

Factors in Project Valuation
Both the nature of the future uncertain cash flows and the discount rates applied to these cash flows are parts of the valuation process that determines a firm's maximum bid.[3] The value of a project from the perspective of a particular firm is the present value of estimated future cash flows discounted at the required rate of return that reflects the project's risk:

$$V = \sum_{t=0}^{\infty} \frac{CF_t}{(1 + \rho_*)^t} \tag{1}$$

where:

V = total project value

CF_t = annual after-tax project cash flow (prior to financing charges and related tax adjustments)

ρ_* = the overall cost of capital reflecting the required rate of return on equity, an opportunity cost, as well as the explicit costs of other sources of funds.

If the cash flows are perpetual and equal in all years, this reduces to:

$$V = \frac{CF_t}{\rho_*} . \tag{2}$$

In general, real imperfections will be reflected in the cash flows while financial market imperfections will be reflected in the discount rate.

In order to be explicit regarding the various financial effects, we introduce a more generalized present value formula where the tax impacts of the financial structure and other financial effects are treated individually rather than in the more familiar manner and where project cash flows are discounted at a single rate that, in turn, reflects the combination of various financial effects.[4] The value of the project can be viewed as the sum of the present value of the project cash flows after taxes but prior to financing costs (discounted at a rate reflecting the business risk of the project), the present value of tax savings as determined by the financial structure, and savings resulting from access to debt financing at bargain rates:

$$V = \sum_{t=0}^{\infty} \frac{C_t}{(1 + \rho)^t} + \sum_{t=0}^{\infty} \frac{\Delta T_t}{(1 + r)^t} + \sum_{t=0}^{\infty} \frac{\Delta I_t}{(1 + r)^t} \qquad (3)$$

where:

V = total project value

C_t = annual after-tax flows of project if all-equity financed (that is, prior to any financing effects)

ρ = discount rate appropriate to entire after-tax cash-flow stream prior to any financing effects

ΔI_t = annual savings (penalties) on interest costs of debt financing relative to "equilibrium" level due to direct subsidies, differential access to repressed markets, or international arbitrage[5]

r = interest rate on debt as approximation to relevant discount rate for relatively certain tax shields and interest savings.

Within this more general framework, differences in project value as a result of financial factors will be captured by differences in ρ,—the discount rate appropriate to the all-equity stream; by differences in ΔT—reflecting tax effects of financing for firms based in different countries; and by differences in ΔI,—reflecting differential abilities of firms to take advantage of financial market distortions. Each of these are examined in turn below.

The Diversification Motive[6]
Modern capital-market theory holds that the required rate of return on a risky security is a function of its systematic risk—the proportion of its risk common to the universe of risky assets available to investors.[7] This function applies to investment projects as well, since claims against the cash flows generated by these projects are sold as securities, although they are general-

ly part of a package of claims on the many different projects represented by a business firm. Thus, ρ in equation (3) can be identified as a function of the project's systematic risk from the perspective of a particular investor.

For any project j, ρ can be approximated as:

$$\rho_j = E(\tilde{R}_j) = r + B_j[E(\tilde{R}_m) - r] \tag{4}$$

where:

$E(R_j)$ = expected value of the percentage return (cash return plus change in project value/project value in previous period) in a one-period framework

r = required return (interest rate) on riskless assets for the same holding period

$E(\tilde{R}_m)$ = the expected return on the market portfolio, that is, the universe of risky assets available to the investor holding the firm's shares

B_j = the systematic risk of project j in the context of the market portfolio, that is, the risk that cannot be diversified away

= σ_{jm}/σ_m^2 = covariance $_{jm}$/variance$_m$.

Since the outcomes of different projects are not subject to exactly the same risks—that is, the returns generated by these projects are not perfectly correlated—the risk of a portfolio of projects or securities will be less than the average risk of the individual projects. In a highly developed and integrated capital market, individual investors can diversify their holdings of securities broadly, thereby averaging out much of the risk of individual projects. As a result, the rate of return required on the various projects will reflect only their contribution to the risk of a fully diversified portfolio, which is substantially smaller than their total risk. Furthermore, if investors can diversify their own portfolios readily, firms need not concern themselves with their degree of diversification and can judge a project's expected rate of return in relation to its systematic risk.[8] Diversification at the corporate level will be relevant only when there are costs or barriers to such diversification at the investor level. This undoubtedly is the case for projects in many developing countries as well as for investors from these same countries. However, this also appears to be the case for many large, developed countries.

The Potential for Risk Reduction through International Diversification Evidence for a wide variety of countries shows that the risk of diversified portfolios of securities is substantially below that of individual securities and that most of the benefits of diversification are obtained when from twenty to thirty different securities are incorporated in the portfolio.[9] Figure 7.1 illustrates this relationship for the United States, where with thirty securities the risk of the portfolio, as measured by the standard deviation of single-period returns, falls to roughly 50 percent of the average risk of individual securities.[10]

Evidence for developing countries, in contrast, suggests that diversification within these countries also reduces risk, but to a lesser extent than within large, advanced industrialized countries. This reduction reflects both the greater political and economic instability of developing countries—factors that affect the returns on almost all domestic securities—and their relatively smaller diversity of economic activities. Lessard [15] found, for example, that for Argentina the risk of a broadly diversified portfolio, again measured by its standard deviation, was 81 percent of the risk of an average common stock, for Brazil 69 percent, for Colombia 84 percent, and for Chile 71 percent.

Extensions of this same type of research to portfolios diversified across national boundaries indicate that even greater reductions in risk were possible. Solnik [24, 25] and Lessard [14] found, for example, that the risk of internationally diversified portfolios of securities drops to as little as 30 percent of the risk of individual securities. The reason for this result is that the variations in returns on securities in various economies are, in large part, the result of domestic economic and political events rather than international economic factors.

In the case of developing countries, although diversification provides lesser benefits within each country, the benefits of diversification are even stronger across countries.[11] Typically, local investors are restricted to the domestic capital market and

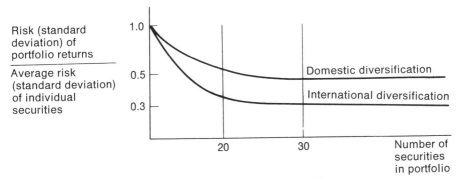

Figure 7.1. The impact of diversification on portfolio risk

foreign investors do not have ready access to local security markets because of official restrictions and/or the undeveloped state of the markets themselves. Thus, a large proportion of the risk of a domestic project undertaken by a local firm is systematic from the perspective of local investors, while a much smaller proportion of the risk of a domestic project undertaken by a MNC is systematic from its shareholders' perspectives. Because of this smaller proportion the MNC's required rate of return for the project will be lower that that of the domestic firm, giving it a competitive advantage.

The diversification advantage, as reflected by ρ, can be substantial. We illustrate this by assuming that the simplest form of the capital asset pricing model—equation (4)—holds. The specific numbers used in the illustration approximate those observed in the United States, $r = 7\%$, and $[E(R_m) - r]/\sigma_m$ (the market price of one unit of risk) $= .5$. For each of six countries we assume a project with a standard deviation of annual returns of 30 percent, which is similar to that of the average common stock in the United States or Europe, with a correlation with the domestic "market portfolio" of securities equal to that for the average share in that country.[12] From these figures, we calculate the systematic risk of the project from the perspective both of a local investor limited to domestic securities and an investor free to diversify holdings internationally.

The resulting estimates, reported in Table 7.1, are striking. The differences in required rates of return from domestic and international perspectives are very large in relation to the rates themselves. This difference is especially true for the smaller, more isolated markets included in the example: Brazil, Colombia, and Spain. Of course, these are only rough estimates, but they suggest that the ability of MNCs to diversify internationally will confer a substantial advantage if individual investors cannot diversify their portfolios along international lines freely.[13]

The Tax Motive
Tax advantages for MNCs can be classed among both real and financial advantages. They derive from the ability of a MNC to reduce taxes relative to the sum that would be paid by its various units, if they were independent firms, by shifting revenues

Table 7.1. Effect of International Diversification on Required Rate of Return

	Brazil	Colombia	France	Germany	Italy	Japan	Spain	U.K.	USA
Average correlation with domestic market portfolio[a]	.69	.84	.68	.67	.66	.52	.63	.61	.55
Required return from domestic perspective (%)[a]	17.4	19.6	17.2	17.1	16.9	14.8	16.5	16.2	15.2
Average correlation with world market portfolio[b]	.14	.17	.21	.31	.16	.15	.04	.25	.44
Required return from world perspective (%)[b]	9.1	9.5	10.2	11.7	9.5	9.2	7.6	10.8	13.6

[a]Sources: See Agmon and Lessard [3].
[b]Correlation with world market portfolio obtained by multiplying the correlation with domestic market portfolio by the correlation of domestic market with the world market portfolio. This implicitly assumes that the only relationship between individual securities and the world market is through their relationships with the domestic market portfolio Figures for Brazil and Colombia are based on subjective estimates of the correlation of the local market portfolio with the world market portfolio of .20. This figure represents an upper limit.

and costs among units to take advantage of differences in tax rates and tax systems in various countries and of methods used to eliminate double-taxation of international activities such as tax credits and deferrals.[14] We include them under the heading of financial factors since much of the revenue or cost and hence tax shifting that can be done by MNCs takes place through the financial structure. For example, costs can be shifted to high tax rate countries by borrowing there to support operations elsewhere through intracompany transfers.[15]

The Arbitrage Motive

The final set of advantages, denoted by ΔI, represent a variety of gains from exploiting financial market imperfections. If interest rates in one market, including adjustments for anticipated exchange rate movements, are out of line with rates elsewhere, firms with access to these markets will benefit. These departures from international equilibrium sometimes will be the result of government subsidized financing for specific activities. More generally they result from a failure of market rates to adjust to an international equilibrium level due to (1) restrictions on the rates themselves—presumably resulting in credit rationing and allocation through nonmarket channels, (2) restrictions on access to domestic markets that shift the domestic equilibrium, and (3) restrictions on international financial transactions including, but not limited to, exchange controls that prevent international forces from acting on the domestic equilibrium.

The MNC, possessing at once the nationality of its home country and the country in which the investment is located, can, in general, compete favorably with domestic firms in obtaining subsidy financing and gaining access to local financial markets. It has a clear advantage in circumventing restrictions on international financial transactions. Furthermore, to the extent that market restrictions result in credit rationing, the generally superior credit standing of the MNC as well as its ability to make side payments to multinational banks and other intermediaries by maintaining business relationships in other countries will allow it to gain disproportionately from these sources.

This argument hinges on the ability of MNCs to exploit capital-market distortions when most other individuals or firms are restricted from doing so. Clearly, such distortions cannot persist without barriers, restrictions, or capital rationing, but MNCs often can circumvent these. For example, international restrictions usually are applied to capital flows and exclude many of the commercial transactions that MNCs can use to shift funds.[16]

Each of the three advantages, the diversification advantage reflected in ρ, the tax advantage reflected in ΔT, and the arbitrage advantage reflected in ΔI, result from the existence of imperfections in financial markets and the ability of the MNC, by internalizing financial transfers, to circumvent these imperfections. Of course, MNCs commonly possess other advantages vis-à-vis local firms resulting from imperfections in the markets for technology and managerial skills, but they also face the disadvantages of operating at a distance without an intimate knowledge of the domestic, political, social, and economic setting. Thus at times the financial advantages of MNCs will be the decisive factors.

Financial Factors and the Small-Country Firm

In this section we concentrate on the effect of financial factors on the ability and motivation of a SCF to invest outside of its base country relative to those of two groups of competitors in the country in which the investment takes place—large-country based MNCs (LCFs) and purely domestic firms.

The fact that the base country is relatively small implies little about the nature of intermarket barriers or domestic financial market imperfections faced by the firm. The small country may be rich or poor, highly developed or underdeveloped, politically stable or volatile. Its economy may be narrowly dependent on a single product or broadly diversified, its capital markets may be relatively open to international transactions or they may be closed, its financial markets and institutions may be sophisticated or unsophisticated. On the one extreme are countries with a minimum of barriers to international financial transactions and sophisticated, highly developed capital markets. At the other extreme are developing countries with virtually absolute foreign-exchange control and very small domestic capital markets. Thus in discussing the impact of financial factors on a firm's ability and motivation to expand internationally, the specific characteristics must be defined explicitly.

In order to simplify the analysis, two situations are considered: a country with open and highly developed capital markets for which Switzerland serves as a prototype and a country with substantial barriers to outward capital flows and a domestic capital market with a formal institutional structure but where many financial transactions, particularly those involving risk capital, take place through conglomerate business groups rather than through public issues of securities. A variety of developing countries, including Argentina, Brazil, Indonesia, and India, are representative of this latter case.[17]

SCF Based in a Country with Open and Developed Capital Markets

At first glance it appears that the financial advantages of multinationalism relative to purely domestic firms are just as great for a SCF based in a small country with open and developed capital markets as for the LCF. The firm's securities will be held in broadly diversified portfolios, since the base-country investors are free to diversify internationally and foreign investors have ready access to the base-country market. In fact, if there are no barriers or costs to international capital flows and if all investors agree on future prospects for various securities, the capital-asset pricing model implies that all investors within the set of integrated markets will hold the market portfolio—that is, a holding of all outstanding securities in the integrated market in proportion to their aggregate market values.[18] Under these circumstances, the ρ that the SCF should apply to a particular project will be the same as that of the LCF whose base country is integrated into the same international financial network. The relevant market portfolio for the SCF will be even broader than that faced by LCFs based in countries with some barriers to international capital flows. This portfolio breadth would give the SCF an advantage.

The SCF, because of its multinational character, will have an advantage over purely domestic firms and could be at either an advantage or disadvantage in terms of tax treatment relative to

LCFs based in various countries. This would be a function of the base-country tax system and, in particular, its treatment of foreign source income. However, there is little reason to expect that these differences are a function of the size of the base country. Similar comments apply to the ability of the firm to exploit financial market distortions. Since the base country is presumed to have an open and highly developed capital market, there should be few opportunities within the home capital market. Also, there is no reason to expect that SCFs generally will have either an advantage or disadvantage relative to LCFs in terms of exploiting distortions in third country capital markets.

The SCF and the National Distribution of Share Ownership There is, however, an important role played by the international diversification of the SCF. It allows a large proportion of the shares of the firm to remain in the control of local investors without forcing them to forego the advantages of international diversification.

If all firms based in the small country were domestic in scope, an efficient international sharing of risk would imply that a vast majority of the shares were owned by foreign investors. For example, the current market values of major world stock markets imply that if Swiss shares were held in globally diversified portfolios, more than 60 percent would be held by U.S. investors and less than 5 percent by local, Swiss investors. Furthermore, local investors holding more than a small fraction of their portfolios in local shares would be bearing unnecessary risk, risk for which they would not be rewarded in terms of expected future return.[19] Internationally diversified SCFs, on the other hand, allow local investors to concentrate their portfolios in local shares and yet be broadly diversified along international lines.

By allowing local investors to concentrate their portfolios in local shares without sacrificing the benefits of international diversification, the SCF serves an important political role and simultaneously reduces its cost of capital. Its political role is that of reducing the opportunity cost, in terms of foregone diversification, of local share ownership. This local share ownership provides legitimate, direct representation within the political framework for the firm's interests. That local ownership is valued by many small countries is evidenced by restrictions on the foreign ownership of shares through percentage limits or the creation of multiple classes of shares.

Furthermore, to the extent that the legal and institutional framework of local capital markets imposes differential costs on foreign investors, the SCF, by allowing local ownership consistent with an efficient international pattern of risk bearing, reduces the required rate of return for business activities undertaken by locally based firms.[20] While this consideration represents a relaxation of the assumption of open capital markets with costless international transfers, it is a realistic one for even the most advanced countries. If this is the case, the SCF will find that foreign investors demand a premium on claims against assets outside their own country even where no formal financial barriers exist. This premium reflects the cost of monitoring distant operations, the risks imposed by having to depend on a foreign legal system to enforce asset holders' rights, and the possibility that the external claims may be subject to a discriminatory taxation and/or exposure to sovereign risk.

In general, the legal and institutional framework of the local financial market affects the way in which foreign investors evaluate the income streams generated through the ownership of residual claims. In calculating the current value of such streams, outsiders are concerned with two basic risk elements in addition to the common economic uncertainty that faces both local and foreign investors. The two elements are the possibility of discriminatory public treatment and the possibility of special advantages gained by local owners who are close enough to influence the firm's affairs.[21] The two elements result in a different valuation of residual claims by local investors and foreign investors. Taxation may affect foreign investors differently from local owners because they are not beneficiaries of the services generated by the tax revenues nor do they have the same political representation. Public measures that have an impact on the profitability of specific firms may also be discriminatory, since foreign-controlled firms may have less political power. If the legal and institutional structure of the base country provides greater protection for shareholder property rights than the foreign investor's home market does, this argument is weakened. If this is the case, however, the SCF based in the country with a legal and institutional structure that is attractive to foreign shareholders will benefit from the lower rate of returns required on its shares; hence their resulting higher value.

SCF Based in a Country with Restricted and Relatively Underdeveloped Capital Markets

Most observers would expect financial factors to act as constraints on the international expansion of firms based in countries that impose restrictions on international capital transfers and whose domestic financial markets are relatively underdeveloped.[22] Ironically, these same factors also may provide incentive for such expansion.

The Nature of Capital Market Imperfections   In contrast to the capital markets faced by large-country based MNCs (LCFs)—the domestic markets in the United States and key European countries and the Eurocurrency markets—capital markets in most developing countries are characterized by barriers to international capital movements and imperfections in the domestic capital markets. Specific barriers and imperfections that exist to varying degrees in different countries include the following:

Formal Barriers to International Transactions:
1. Quantitative restrictions (exchange controls) and direct taxes on international movements of funds
2. Differential taxation of income streams according to nationality of the owner
3. Restrictions by nationality of investor and/or investment on access to domestic capital markets

Informal Barriers to International Transactions:
1. Costs of obtaining information
2. Difficulty of enforcing contracts across national boundaries
3. Transaction costs
4. Traditional investment patterns

Imperfections in Domestic Capital Markets:
1. Ceilings on interest rates

2. Mandatory credit allocations
3. Limited legal and institutional protection for minority share-holders
4. Limited liquidity due to thinness of markets
5. High transactions costs due to small market size and/or monopolistic practices of key financial institutions
6. Difficulty of obtaining information needed to evaluate securities.

Financial Market Imperfections and the Expansion of Developing Country SCFs   The various formal barriers to international capital transfers limit the ability of SCFs to finance overseas operations directly. These same constraints may also reduce the SCFs' ability to borrow outside the base country to finance their international expansion. In the extreme case, if the parent is totally constrained from financial transfers, such financing will be limited to that which can be supported by the overseas projects themselves with no recourse to the parent. This limitation also eliminates the potential financial benefits of multinationalism that depend on being able to shift financing among countries in order to reduce taxes or to exploit financial market imperfections. Of course, if the parent supplies intangible factors of production, which it does not have to price on an arm's-length basis, it will be able to circumvent constraints on the implicit financing transactions that accompany these real transactions. Furthermore, to the extent that SCF direct investment promises returns to domestic factors of production that otherwise would be unobtainable, the base-country government is likely to be more lenient on financial transfers that are part of a SCF expansion. Finally, once the SCF has operations outside of the base country it may be able to transfer funds from these operations to finance new ventures.

The ability of the SCF to circumvent restrictions on capital outflows may, in fact, represent a strong motivation for their international expansion. This will be particularly true in instances where the local political environment is a major element of risk. Under these circumstances international diversification becomes even more attractive, but at the same time barriers are likely to be tightened to stem capital flight.[23] If such conditions persist, the SCF may actually migrate, gradually shifting productive assets to more attractive economies and eventually shifting its economic, if not its legal base.

Imperfections in domestic capital markets will have several effects. Firm size will be limited by the market's inability to aggregate capital. Required rate of return on the firm's equity will reflect the market's less than complete ability to distribute risk among investors. In the extreme case where ownership is not distributed among investors who themselves are diversified, the required rate of return will reflect the firm's total risk rather than its systematic risk in the base-country context—let alone its systematic risk in an international context.

However, some of these effects often are offset by the existence of conglomerate business groups that internalize many capital market functions. Diversification takes place on a group level, although in most cases it is restricted because of limits to the absolute size of the group that must be traded off against the minimum, efficient scale of its individual undertakings. These same groups, the majority of which incorporate financial intermediaries, may actually benefit from distortions in credit markets, and they often have privileged access to low-cost and hence rationed credit. Since their activities typically encompass several economic sectors, they are able to take advantage of concessionary credit allocated to any particular sector and shift the funds internally to other uses.

In summary, it is impossible to generalize regarding the effect of barriers and market imperfections on internationally minded SCFs. Most likely barriers will constrain the SCFs' ability to expand internationally but will also strengthen their motivation to do so. Whether the SCFs' motivation for international expansion is to exploit some real market advantage or whether it is to provide a channel for international diversification—or both—there is a strong incentive to find ways to overcome the constraints imposed by barriers to capital flows. One obvious strategy, which provides the SCF with international diversification but minimized capital requirements, is the joint venture. The joint venture may be with a LCF that has access to international financial markets or with a local firm with access to concessionary financing that would not otherwise be available.

Another related possibility, but one more likely to protect the parent firm's rents if substantial real advantages are involved, is to open the capital structure of the overseas offshoot to incorporate local capital. If this market also is restricted or underdeveloped, the strategy may take the form of an offshore holding company domiciled in a country with open capital markets and a legal and political system that is desirable from the perspective of protecting shareholders and creditor interests. If the SCF is able to transfer valuable real resources to this offshore firm at less than an arm's-length price, it eventually will be able to move capital out of the base country and migrate to this more attractive base.

Public Policy Implications

The discussion, to this point, has focused on the financial constraints to the expansion of SCFs, many of which are the direct result of government policies. Clearly, government encouragement of SCF efforts to surmount these obstacles or changes in government policies to accommodate SCF expansion must rely on demonstrable public benefits from SCF expansion. A detailed discussion of these benefits is outside the scope of this paper, but they result from the increased returns to local factors of production made possible by direct, overseas investment. Further benefits might be the favorable learning impact of foreign operations on the domestic operations of the SCFs. Finally, to the extent to which market imperfections continue to favor MNCs, it seems reasonable for a country to place a value on the participation of local SCFs in industries dominated by LCFs.

Fortunately, certain of the steps required to improve the lot of SCFs appear to us to be beneficial in and of themselves, thereby simplifying the analysis considerably. For example, any scheme of capital restrictions and exchange-rate policies that favors inward, direct investment relative to portfolio investment will impose costs on SCFs relative to LCFs and will also lead to increased domination of the local economy by LCFs.[24]

Similarly, steps that improve the local market for SCF securities presumably also improve the welfare of local investors.

This point becomes obvious when one considers that a primary function of a capital market is to distribute risk efficiently among investors. By allowing local investors to diversify their portfolios more broadly, both by allowing them to invest abroad on a portfolio basis and by allowing the SCF to perform this service for them, such steps serve to increase the value to these investors of risky local ventures.

To the extent that large-scale, local firms holding internationally diversified portfolios of activities develop, they can bid competitively for new, local ventures, thus halting the tendency toward the domination of many industries by foreign based LCFs.

It may be argued that because most of the steps to encourage SCF expansion involve one form or another of capital-market liberalization for developing countries, they will induce capital flight. Furthermore, undoubtedly there will be some occasions where the primary motivation for the SCF itself will be to transfer wealth out of the home country in violation of local restrictions. Neither argument is very convincing, however, when it is recognized that enormous inefficiencies are forced on a capitalist system if local wealth holders are limited to local investment opportunities and local investments are priced only in a domestic context. To the extent that wealthy financial groups, through controlled SCFs and other channels, find ways to evade restrictions, the argument becomes more one of equity for investors whose wealth is not sufficient to justify costly direct-investment mechanisms.

The easiest way to ensure that SCFs are not primarily vehicles for evasion of capital-market restrictions is, of course, to remove the incentives for such activity. This solution may be naive, but there appear to be few arguments that justify the real costs associated with enforcing and evading such restrictions.

Notes

1. It is generally acknowledged that in order to justify foreign investments the multinational corporation must have some advantage relative to local firms in the countries in which it invests that allows it to overcome the costs imposed by cultural and geographical distance not borne by local firms. Most economists have argued that the primary sources of advantages to MNCs relative to local firms arise from imperfections in the market for products and factors of

production, generally excluding capital. Reviews of the theory of foreign investment are provided by Dunning [6], Kindleberger [11], Ragazzi [19], and Stevens [26] (see the bibliography). Ragazzi is one of the few to include capital-market imperfections.

2. The benefits of international diversification are introduced into the literature by Grubel [3]. Ragazzi [19], Rugman [22], and Stevens [26] extend them to FDI. Aliber [5] also presents a financial rationale for FDI but bases it on a preference for the currency of the host-country firm. Since equity returns are not contractually set in monetary terms but depend on business outcomes, this argument is not convincing. However, Aliber's general framework is a useful one and provided much of the inspiration for this paper.

3. For an overview of the relevant literature on corporation finance in the domestic context that serves as the basis for this section, see Pogue and Lall [18]. For a more rigorous discussion of the various elements, see Rubenstein [21], Myers [17], and Jensen [9].

4. This approach is similar to that of Myers [17], who shows that the additive relationship will hold within an integrated, efficient capital market. It will not hold strictly in the more general case where markets in different countries are to some extent segmented by barriers and where there are distortions within particular markets. Nevertheless, it is a useful way to identify the various elements in the process.

5. The "equilibrium" level is not defined in an international setting with barriers and other imperfections. However, the desired figure is one where in the absence of taxes, the market value of the debt claim is identical to the reduction in the market value of the equity claim—that is, the Modigliani-Miller result where total value is unaffected by partitioning the cash flow stream. See Myers [17].

6. This section is abstracted from Agmon and Lessard [3].

7. The capital asset pricing model, which is a key element of modern capital-market theory, was first introduced by Sharpe [23]. Jensen [9] provides an excellent summary of extensions and empirical tests of this model.

8. Myers [16] provides a clear exposition of this rationale. However, it applies only in cases where there are no causal relationships between the risks of the various projects. Niehans (chapter 1 of this collection) stresses diversification where there are causal linkages, for example, a diversified production base in order to protect the value of the firm's distribution network or market franchise. This diversification certainly is a motivation for multinationalism, but of a real rather than a financial nature.

9. See Solnik [24, 25] and Lessard [14].

10. As we shall see, the required return on a diversified portfolio is linearly related to its standard deviation.

11. See Lessard [15].

12. The market portfolio includes all securities outstanding in the market with weights reflecting their respective market values.

13. Agmon and Lessard [4] provide evidence that shareholders recognize the international spread of operations of MNCs. This is but a first step in establishing empirically that financial factors are relevant to FDI.

14. For an excellent review of the literature on taxes and the multinational firm, see Kopits [12].

15. Horst [8] and Robbins and Stobaugh [20], among others, describe how intracompany financial transactions can reduce the firm's overall tax bill.

16. Foreign direct investment often involves transfers of intangible factors of production such as technology or managerial skills. To the extent that these real transfers are not paid for immediately, they are accompanied by financial transfers. Clearly, such inward transfers are not captured by controls over financial flows. Remittances of profits from these transferred resources often will not be restricted and even if they are, the MNC has a number of options for bypassing such restrictions, especially transfer pricing of goods and factors of production.

17. Leff [13] provides a detailed discussion of the financial role of such groups in less developed countries.

18. Solnik [25] extends the capital-asset pricing model to the international case.

19. The capital-asset pricing model implies that investors will hold the market portfolio. The figures cited represent the share of total market value represented by each country's shares.

20. Ragazzi [19] suggests that discrimination against outside investors may be one motivation for direct foreign investment.

21. The latter point, the possibility that insiders will take advantage of outsiders, represents an offset to the benefits of diversification. It has received little attention in the modern theory of finance. Jensen and Meckling [10] provide a provocative introduction to these issues.

22. This view is implicit in the paper by Louis T. Wells, Jr. that appears as Chapter 5 in this volume.

23. Leff [13] points out that capital flight can be viewed as normal investor diversification.

24. See Agmon and Lessard [3].

Bibliography

1. Adler, M., and Dumas, B. J., "The Long-Term Financial Decisions of the Multinational Corporation," in Elton and Gruber, eds., International Capital Markets. Amsterdam: North-Holland, 1975.

2. Agmon, T., "The Relations Among Equity Markets: A Study of Share Price Co-Movements in the U.S., U.K., Germany and Japan," The Journal of Finance (September 1972).

3. Agmon, T., and Lessard, D. R., "International Diversification and the Multi-

national Corporation—Implications for Capital Importing Countries," forthcoming in *Revista Brasileira de Mercados de Capitais*.

4. _____. "Investor Recognition of Corporate International Diversification." Unpublished, M.I.T., May 1976.

5. Aliber, R. Z. "A Theory of Direct Foreign Investment," in C. P. Kindleberger, ed., *The International Corporation*. Cambridge, Mass.: The MIT Press, 1970.

6. Dunning, J. H. "The Determinants of International Production," *Oxford Economic Papers* (January 1973).

7. Grubel, H. G. "Internationally Diversified Portfolios," *The American Economic Review* (December 1968).

8. Horst, T. O. "The Theory of the Firm," in J. H. Dunning, ed., *Economic Analysis and the Multinational Enterprise*. London: Allen and Unwin, 1974.

9. Jensen, M. J. "The Foundations and Current State of Capital Market Theory," in M. J. Jensen, ed., *Studies in the Theory of Capital Markets*. New York: Praeger, 1972.

10. Jensen, M. C., and Meckling, W. H. "Theory of the Firm: Managerial Behavior, Agency Costs, and Ownership Structure." Unpublished, University of Rochester, November 1975.

11. Kindleberger, C. P. *American Business Abroad: Six Lectures on Direct Investment*. New Haven: Yale University Press, 1969.

12. Kopits, G. F. "Taxation and Multinational Firm Behavior: A Critical Survey." Unpublished, IMF, March 1976.

13. Leff, N. H. "Capital Markets in the Less-Developed Countries," in R. I. McKinnon, ed., *Money and Finance in Economic Growth and Development: Essays in Honor of Edward S. Shaw*. New York: Marcel Dekker, 1976.

14. Lessard, D. R. "World, Country and Industry Relationships in Equity Returns: Implications for Risk Reduction through International Diversification," *Financial Analysts Journal* (January/February 1976).

15. _____. "The Structure of Returns and Gains from International Diversification," in Elton and Gruber, eds., *International Capital Markets*. Amsterdam: North-Holland, 1976.

16. Myers, S. C. "Procedures for Capital Budgeting under Uncertainty," *Industrial Management Review* (Spring 1968).

17. _____. "Interactions of Corporate Financing and Investment Decisions—Implications for Capital Budgeting," *Journal of Finance* (March 1974).

18. Pogue, G. A., and Lall, K. "Corporate Finance: An Overview," *Sloan Management Review* (Spring 1974).

19. Ragazzi, G. "Theories of the Determinants of Direct Foreign Investment," *IMF Staff Papers* (July 1973).

20. Robbins, S. M., and Stobaugh, R. B. *Money in the Multinational Enterprise: A Study in Financial Policy*. New York: Basic Books, 1973.

21. Rubenstein, M. E. "A Mean-Variance Synthesis of Corporate Financial Theory," *Journal of Finance* (March 1973).

22. Rugman, A. R. "Motives for Foreign Investment: The Market Imperfections and Risk Diversification Hypothesis," *Journal of World Trade Law* (September/October 1975).

23. Sharpe, W. F. "Capital Asset Prices: A Theory of Capital Market Equilibrium under Conditions of Risk," *Journal of Finance* (September 1964).

24. Solnik, B. H. *European Capital Markets*. Lexington, Mass: Heath Lexington Books, 1973.

25. _____. "Why Not Diversify Internationally?" *Financial Analysts Journal* (July 1974).

26. Stevens, G. V. G. "The Determinants of Investment," in J. H. Dunning, ed., *Economic Analysis and the Multinational Enterprise*. London: Allen and Unwin, 1974.

27. Subrahmanyan, M. G. "On the Optimality of International Capital Market Integration," *Journal of Financial Economics* (Spring 1975).

Index